PLATO'S PHAEDO

PLATO'S PHAEDO

Translated with an Introduction
and Commentary by

R. HACKFORTH, F.B.A.

formerly Emeritus Professor of Ancient Philosophy
in the University of Cambridge

CAMBRIDGE
AT THE UNIVERSITY PRESS
1972

Published by the Syndics of the Cambridge University Press
Bentley House, 200 Euston Road, London NW1 2DB
American Branch: 32 East 57th Street, New York, N.Y. 10022

ISBN: 0 521 08458 X   Clothbound
0 521 09702 9   Paperback

First published 1955
Reprinted 1972

First printed in Great Britain
at the University Printing House, Cambridge

Reprinted in the United States of America

CONTENTS

PREFACE

Study of the *Phaedo* has, for English readers at least, been naturally associated for almost half a century with the name of John Burnet; and if in this book I have mentioned his name more often to disagree with his views than to accept them, this should not conceal the fact that my obligation to him, both on points of linguistic scholarship and of interpretation, is great. Other English scholars upon whose learning and wisdom I have freely drawn are F. M. Cornford, Sir David Ross and A. E. Taylor. Footnotes and commentary acknowledge my remaining debts to published work, so far as I am conscious of them.

English versions of the dialogue are numerous. Among the most recent are that by Dr R. S. Bluck (with introduction and commentary), which did not appear until after this book had gone to press, and that included in the new revised edition of Jowett's *Plato*. I have not consulted this, the preparation of which was unknown to me until my own translation was almost complete; an earlier revision of Jowett, by Sir Richard Livingstone (in *Portrait of Socrates*, 1938), I have consulted now and then; but the only version of which I have made any considerable use is that of Léon Robin in the French Budé series.

My warmest thanks are due to Professor W. K. C. Guthrie, who read the whole of the translation and commentary, and made a number of helpful suggestions; to Mr Walter Hamilton, who did the same for the Introduction; to Professor Dorothy Tarrant for her kindness in checking the proof-sheets; and to Professor D. L. Page and Mr F. H. Sandbach, who helped me on special points. Nor should I omit to mention the vigilant readers of the University Press.

Some critics of my commentary on the *Phaedrus* have deplored the absence of the Greek text; but I think it may be assumed that any of my readers who are interested in the interpretation, as distinct from the translation, of these dialogues, will possess Burnet's text (which I have followed except where noted); moreover the printing of a text would have increased the book's price by more than one-third.

R. H.

CAMBRIDGE
March 1955

LIST OF ABBREVIATIONS

Diels-Kranz or DK = *Die Fragmente der Vorsokratiker, griechisch und deutsch*, von H. Diels: fünfte Auflage herausgegeben von W. Kranz (1934).

E.G.P.[3]   = *Early Greek Philosophy*, by John Burnet (3rd edition, 1920).

P.M.W.   = *Plato, the Man and his Work*, by A. E. Taylor (1926).

P.T.I.   = *Plato's Theory of Ideas*, by Sir W. D. Ross (1951).

Robin   = Platon, *Phédon*: texte établi et traduit par Léon Robin (Collection des Universités de France, 1926).

Archer-Hind   = The *Phaedo* of Plato, edited with Introduction, Notes and Appendices, by R. D. Archer-Hind (1894).

C.Q.   = *Classical Quarterly*.

C.R.   = *Classical Review*.

References to Burnet are, on textual points, to his text of the dialogue in *Scriptorum Classicorum Bibliotheca Oxoniensis* (1905); on other matters, to his edition with introduction and notes (1911).

INTRODUCTION

I.   The purpose of the dialogue and its position in the Platonic writings

That the *Phaedo* is a work of supreme art, perhaps the greatest achievement in Greek prose literature, is something that needs no argument. The serenity of Socrates in the hours before he drank the hemlock, his conviction that the parting of soul from body is not the death of the soul, his unabated zest in argument, the devotion of his intimate friends, the admiration of the gaoler for his prisoner, above all perhaps the moving record of the last few pages, given with inimitable simplicity and restraint of language—all these things contribute to the greatness of a work which for many readers stands, if considered as pure literature, even higher than that other literary masterpiece, the *Symposium*.

Both these dialogues, as also the *Republic*, would be generally admitted to show us Plato at the height of his powers as a writer, and we may assume provisionally that they were all composed in his prime, say between the ages of thirty-five and fifty-five. A closer dating will be suggested in what follows.

But before we come to that, it will be well to ask what is the fundamental purpose of the dialogue. It is not, of course to prove that the human soul is immortal, though much of it is devoted to arguments for that thesis; it is not to pay a tribute of admiration to a beloved friend and master, though that tribute is undoubtedly paid; it is not to expound or propagate a metaphysical doctrine, though the doctrine of Forms (Ideas) bulks large; it is, I would say, to extend and deepen, through the mouth of a consciously Platonised Socrates, the essential teaching of Socrates himself, namely that man's supreme concern is the ' tendance of his soul',[1] or (in more modern language) the furthering of his insight into moral and spiritual values and the application of that insight in all his conduct. That is, for Socrates and Plato alike, the way of philosophy, and only by following that way can man attain real well-being or happiness: only in the philosophic life can the soul's desire be satisfied and the aim of the true self be fulfilled.

I have just spoken of a consciously Platonised Socrates as before us in the *Phaedo*. That there is Platonisation, that we are not given simply

[1] *Apology* 30B. Cf. *Gorgias* 503A.

a picture of the historical Socrates, has nowadays come to be generally recognised.[1] Broadly speaking, what Plato has done is not so much to idealise his master, as even Burnet, who insists on the importance of our dialogue as 'an historical document', is ready to admit; rather has he transformed the Socrates who knew nothing save his own ignorance by crediting him with a firm metaphysical basis for his moral doctrine and an unhesitating belief in the soul's immortality, coupled with a disdain or even hostility towards the 'flesh', which goes far beyond anything recorded or implied in the *Apology* or indeed any other Platonic work which can be regarded as earlier than the present dialogue. This second feature of Plato's Socrates is mainly due, it would seem, to the influence of Orphism and Pythagoreanism. So far as religious and ethical doctrine is concerned Orphics and Pythagoreans are practically indistinguishable: both taught that the body, instead of being a man's self, as it was for Homer,[2] is no more than the tomb or temporary prison of that self, namely of a divine soul which passes through an indefinite number of lives in human or animal bodies, having fallen from its original state of blessedness, to which, however, after due purification from its bodily taint it may hope one day to return; both stress accordingly the need for such purification, and indeed tend to regard it as the whole content of morality: though it should be added that whereas Orphism conceives it in terms of ritual observances and abstinence from meat,[3] the Pythagoreans add to this

[1] Field, *Socrates and Plato* (1913) and *Plato and his Contemporaries* (1930); Robin in *Rev. des Études Grecques* XXIX (1916) and *Phédon* (Budé, 1926); Ross, *Metaphysics of Aristotle* (1924), pp. xxiii–li; Cornford in *Camb. Anc. Hist.* VI (1927), pp. 303 ff.

[2] *Iliad* I, 4; XXIII, 65. The conception of the ψυχή as the self or personality of a man is post-Homeric, but seems to be independent of and perhaps older than Pythagoreanism; it is to be found in such 'secular' poets of the seventh to sixth centuries as Semonides and Anacreon. But as Prof. Dodds observes (*The Greeks and the Irrational*, p. 139): 'In fifth-century Attic writers, as in their Ionian predecessors, the "self" which is denoted by the word ψυχή is normally the emotional rather than the rational self', and it is not conceived as alien to the body. What confronts us in Pythagoreanism—the self as a soul of divine origin, opposed to the body in which it is temporarily lodged, and capable of existing apart therefrom—has been traced by recent scholars, such as Meuli and Dodds, to the contact of seventh- and sixth-century Greeks with the shamanistic culture of northern Europe and Asia: see Dodds, *op. cit.* chapter v, *The Greek Shamans and the Origin of Puritanism*.

[3] When Orphic teachers spoke of punishment for the 'unholy and wicked' (τοὺς ἀνοσίους καὶ ἀδίκους, *Rep.* 363 D), it seems that they drew no conscious distinction between transgression of ritual ordinances and sin: correspondingly the holy and righteous were the punctilious observers of taboos; see Guthrie,

the idea that the soul may be purified by science or philosophy, more particularly by study of the divine order of the universe—the macrocosm whose order may be reproduced in the microcosm of the human soul.[1]

The necessity of purification is very strongly emphasised in the earlier part of our dialogue; but the flight from the body and all its works, together with a contempt for all that empirical world which is apprehended through the senses, is saved from being a purely negative and ascetic attitude to life by its association with another doctrine which, while owing much to Heraclitus and Parmenides, yet seems to have its principal source in a fusion of Socratic teaching with the scientific (rather than the ethical and religious) side of Pythagoreanism. The doctrine in question is known as the Theory of Forms (εἴδη or ἰδέαι): the constituents of real being are not the transient mutable objects apprehended by our senses, but immaterial Forms, immutable and eternal, the objects of thought or reason, existing independently of any mind, and in some way participated in, or imperfectly imitated by, sensible objects. In apprehending these Forms the soul finds its proper activity and its full satisfaction; but it cannot adequately apprehend them while clogged and hampered by the body; hence the need for renunciation of the body's desires and pleasures, and the justification for what Socrates calls the 'training for death'.

It is in asserting the independent existence, the transcendence or 'separateness' of these Forms that Plato in the *Phaedo* and other dialogues of his middle period goes beyond anything asserted or implied in Socrates's quest for definition of ethical terms; for Socrates there was indeed an objective unity belonging to the plurality of just or temperate acts, or of beautiful things, and it is possible that he used the word εἶδος for these *universalia in rebus*; but the testimony of Aristotle that

---

Orpheus and Greek Religion, p. 201: 'The question whether his (*sc.* the Orphic's) prohibitions had a moral side to them would have had no meaning for him. But that he had to *perform* certain moral actions, to do good in the Christian sense of the words, we cannot believe.'

[1] The idea that φιλοσοφία is κάθαρσις, echoed at *Phaedo* 67 A–B, 69 C, is nowhere explicitly mentioned as Pythagorean in ancient sources, but it is a highly probable inference of modern scholarship (Zeller, Döring, Adam, Cornford, etc.) that the Pythagoreans linked their religion and their pursuit of science in this way. On the correspondence of macrocosm and microcosm see especially Cornford in *C.Q.* XVI (1922), pp. 142f., and compare Plato's adaptation at *Timaeus* 90 D.

he did not assign independent existence to them, whereas Plato did, is decisive.[1]

That Socrates 'gave the impulse'[2] to this theory is duly recorded by Aristotle, and is indeed obvious; but Aristotle also regards Plato's metaphysics as closely akin to that of the Pythagoreans, even in its earlier form, before Plato had come to identify the Forms with numbers.[3] Now in the *Phaedo* the Form selected to bring out the imperfection of sensible objects is 'the Equal', a mathematical entity; and in the earlier *Meno* it is a mathematical truth which is elicited from Meno's slave by Socrates's questions. Plato's attention, we may infer, had been drawn to the fixity of mathematical objects and mathematical truths as against the impermanence of sensibles and of propositions about them; and he concluded that it must have been objects like those of mathematics that Socrates was unconsciously seeking in his attempts to define ethical terms. Since mathematics was at this date the special province of Pythagorean study, it is reasonable to ascribe Plato's interest in it, and the inference just mentioned, to acquaintance with Pythagoreans. Cicero tells us[4] that during his first visit to South Italy and Sicily, at about the age of forty, he became intimate with the famous Pythagorean statesman and mathematician Archytas; but it is easier, on chronological grounds, to believe that this journey was undertaken to further an interest already conceived than that it awoke it. Already in the *Gorgias*, a dialogue certainly earlier than the *Phaedo*, the mention of two doctrines, that of the body as the tomb of the soul (σῶμα σῆμα)[5] and that of the universe as an ordered whole (κόσμος) in which proportion, or 'geometrical equality', is a 'mighty power amongst gods and men',[6] reveals Plato's attraction to Pythagorean religious and cosmological tenets before his journey to Magna Graecia.

In the introduction to his translation of the *Republic*, F. M. Cornford brings together the *Gorgias* and the account Plato has given in his

---

[1] Aristotle, *Met.* 1078 B 30–2, where οἱ δ' ἐχώρισαν must refer to Plato and his followers (Ross, *Met. of Arist.* I, xxxvf.).

[2] ἐκίνησε (Ar. *Met.* 1086 B 3).

[3] Ar. *Met.* 987 A 30, 1078 B 10, Ross, *op. cit.* I, xlv. Aristotle's account of the relation between Platonic Forms and Pythagorean numbers in *Met.* A 6 bristles with difficulties; but despite the important divergences there noted, one of which is the 'transcendence' of the Forms as against the Pythagorean identification of things with numbers, it seems clear that he regarded their general resemblance as more fundamental. Moreover the word ἀκολουθοῦσα (987 A 30) is more naturally to be understood as implying conscious following of Pythagorean doctrine than mere factual resemblance.

[4] *De Rep.* I, 16.   [5] 493 A.   [6] 508 A.

Seventh Letter[1] of his early political aspirations and disappointments. He argues, convincingly as I think, that 'between the lines' (*sc.* of the *Gorgias*) 'we can read his final answer to the friends who had sought to draw him into politics'. If so, that answer—a refusal—was, as the letter reveals, the outcome of a progressive realisation of the rottenness of political life throughout the Greek world. In place, however, of personal participation in his city's politics Plato determined to found the Academy, designed primarily as a training school for philosophic statesmen. The precise date of its foundation is not known: the account in Diogenes Laertius (III, 20) seems to imply that it was not long after Plato's return from Sicily, but is compatible with an interval of a year or so. I suggest that it is not unreasonable to believe that the *Phaedo* was written during this interval, when Plato was still repelled from active participation in politics, and had not yet thought of a solution of his personal problem in which his political and philosophical interests might be fruitfully combined.

For the *Phaedo* is notably silent regarding political institutions and government; its ethics are wholly individualistic: every man is to be concerned with his own spiritual welfare; and the eloquent description of the true philosopher, unlike that of *Rep.* VI, contains no hint that he may be called upon to be a 'Guardian'. This silence cannot, I think, be wholly accounted for by the circumstances of the dialogue; one would not, of course, expect Plato to have made Socrates discourse in his last hours on the organisation of an ideal State; but the total absence of any social or political reference, taken together with the strongly Pythagorean colouring of the first part of the work, points to a date such as that above suggested, that is 387 or very little later. If this be accepted, the *Phaedo* precedes not only the *Republic*, which is on many grounds to be put later, but also the *Symposium*, which contains (193A) an anachronistic allusion to the splitting-up (διοικισμός) of the territory of Mantinea in 385.[2] This dating is compatible with the results of stylistic studies, which must be considered at this point.

---

[1] 324Bff.
[2] The allusion has been doubted: but Field, *Plato and his Contemporaries*, pp. 72ff., argues convincingly for its acceptance.
  Scholars are divided on the question of the priority of *Phaedo* to *Symp.* I can claim the support of Wilamowitz, and I suspect that Plato may have felt it desirable to compensate for an over-ascetic Socrates by a study of him in a wholly different situation. Cornford, in his admirable essay on the *Symp.* in *The Unwritten Philosophy*, writes: 'Whichever of the two dialogues was finished first—and I

II. Stylometric arguments. The transcendent Forms

The conclusions reached by 1935 through stylometric studies[1] of the dialogues are stated by the most trustworthy and thoroughgoing inquirer in this field, Constantin Ritter, in a paper in *Hermes* of that year (Band 70, p. 1) as follows:

> Amongst students really familiar with the material there exists to-day complete agreement at least to the extent that these writings can be assigned to three periods; that the third of these, marked out by distinct features of Plato's latest style, includes—over and above the *Laws*—*Philebus, Timaeus, Critias, Sophist, Statesman*; that to the middle period belong *Republic* ii–x, *Phaedrus, Theaetetus and Parmenides*; and that the whole number of the remaining dialogues must be regarded as earlier than these.

Whatever attempts to modify these conclusions may have been made since 1935, they do not, so far as I know, affect the *Phaedo*: that is to say, no one now doubts that it is earlier than any of the four works of the middle group. But in the paper from which I have just quoted Ritter argues for a subdivision of the earliest group; that is to say, he makes four groups instead of three, including in the second earliest *Hippias Major, Euthydemus, Menexenus, Cratylus, Lysis, Symposium, Phaedo* and *Republic* i:[2] and in the course of his argument he adduces certain stylistic features which point to an approximation of *Cratylus, Phaedo* and *Symposium* to the third (the old middle) group. And it is interesting to observe that the same position was assigned to these three dialogues by Lutoslawski in his *Origin and Growth of Plato's Logic* (1897),[3] as Ritter certainly knew, though he does not happen to mention the point in his article.

While sharing a widespread scepticism as to some of Lutoslawski's methods, and doubting whether Ritter's new arguments, at least so far as the *Phaedo* is concerned, are very strong, I nevertheless feel that their placing of the three dialogues close together and next before the *Republic* is not only a welcome confirmation of what I have already

---

suspect it was the *Phaedo*—Plato felt the need to hang beside the picture it gave of Socrates another picture as different as possible.... The man of thought was also the man of passion, constantly calling himself a "lover".... The *Symp.* is to explain the significance of Eros to the lover of wisdom.'

[1] For a general account of these see Field, *op. cit.* pp. 66 ff.

[2] Whether or no *Rep.* i was originally a separate dialogue does not matter for our present inquiry.

[3] p. 189: 'The middle group' (viz. *Rep.* ii–x, *Phaedrus, Theaet., Parm.*) 'is preceded by a first Platonic group, *Cratylus, Symposium, Phaedo*.'

suggested in the foregoing pages, but also finds confirmation itself in a further important common feature of these works: namely that just these three, and no others in the first two of Ritter's four groups, recognise the χωριστὸν εἶδος, in other words treat the Form as having an existence apart from the particulars which fall under it or partake of it.

That this is true of the *Symposium* account (in Diotima's speech) of the ascent from particular beautiful things to Beauty itself is a fact too familiar to need elaboration.[1] In the *Cratylus* (389 A–C) we are told that a carpenter who wants to make a new shuttle looks not to the one he has broken but to 'that Form to which he looked when he made the shuttle just broken': and that Form 'we shall very properly call the Shuttle itself' (αὐτὸ ὃ ἔστιν κερκίς). Surely Plato could hardly have used plainer language to indicate that he conceives the Form as existing apart from its particulars, and indeed before any of its particulars. Sir David Ross, however, doubts this: 'Perhaps on reflexion we ought to admit that, though his language may be interpreted as implying the existence of the Form before it is embodied, that is not a necessary interpretation. When he says that the carpenter looks to the Form, he may not think of the Form as pre-existing any more than, when we say we aim at some end, we think of that end as existing already.'[2] This suggestion seems to me incompatible with the expression αὐτὸ ὃ ἔστιν κερκίς, incompatible too with Ross's own undoubtedly correct protest against the conceptualist version of the Ideal Theory on p. 15: it amounts to saying that 'the Shuttle itself' is a νόημα ἐν ψυχαῖς, a notion summarily dismissed at *Parmenides* 132.

It might be thought, and indeed it has been maintained, that one dialogue which is commonly held to be amongst the earliest, namely the *Euthyphro*, asserts the transcendence of the Form. The passage in question is 6D–E:

μέμνησαι οὖν ὅτι οὐ τοῦτό σοι διεκελευόμην, ἕν τι ἢ δύο με διδάξαι τῶν πολλῶν ὁσίων, ἀλλ᾽ ἐκεῖνο αὐτὸ τὸ εἶδος ᾧ πάντα τὰ ὅσια ὅσιά ἐστιν; ἔφησθα γάρ που μιᾷ ἰδέᾳ τά τε ἀνόσια ἀνόσια εἶναι καὶ τὰ ὅσια ὅσια...ταύτην τοίνυν με αὐτὴν δίδαξον τὴν ἰδέαν τίς ποτέ ἐστιν, ἵνα εἰς ἐκείνην ἀποβλέπων καὶ χρώμενος αὐτῇ παραδείγματι, ὃ μὲν ἂν

---

[1] Ross, *Plato's Theory of Ideas*, p. 21, doubts the philosophical seriousness of this passage, reminding us that these are not the words of Plato nor of Socrates, but of Diotima the prophetess. But surely D.'s whole teaching is endorsed by Socrates, with the result that what she says is as much the 'words of Plato' as anything that Socrates himself says. [2] *PTI*, p. 19.

τοιοῦτον ᾖ ὧν ἄν ᾖ σὺ ᾖ ἄλλος τις πράττῃ φῶ ὅσιον εἶναι, ὃ δ' ἂν μὴ τοιοῦτον, μὴ φῶ.

It is of course true that παράδειγμα came to be used of the transcendent Forms (*Timaeus* 28 A, C; Arist. *Met.* 991 A), and the words εἰς ἐκείνην (τὴν ἰδέαν) ἀποβλέπων inevitably suggest both the shuttle-maker looking to αὐτὸ ὃ ἔστιν κερκίς and the Demiurge of the visible universe looking to his ideal model, the νοητὸν ζῷον (*Timaeus* 30 C ff.). But an earlier passage (5 D) implies nothing more than an immanent ἰδέα—a common character found in a number of objects—and it is hardly likely that Plato would introduce the notion of a χωριστὸν εἶδος in this casual and ambiguous fashion, using words which Socrates's interlocutor allows to pass without any surprise or questioning.[1] Moreover the word παράδειγμα need not in itself imply this: it need mean no more than a standard of reference provided by one person or thing in virtue of which another can be compared thereto; thus at *Rep.* 409 A Socrates remarks that decent people are easily deceived by the wicked because they have no patterns of experience within themselves resembling those of evil men (εὐεξαπάτητοι ὑπὸ τῶν ἀδίκων ἅτε οὐκ ἔχοντες ἐν ἑαυτοῖς παραδείγματα ὁμοιοπαθῆ τοῖς πονηροῖς, where the last words mean, as Adam says, ὁμοιοπαθῆ τοῖς τῶν πονηρῶν παραδείγμασιν). It may be added that another dialogue certainly earlier than the *Phaedo* contains a passage (*Meno* 72 C) in which it is said that the numerous different virtues all have a single form (εἶδος) to which it is proper that anyone should look if asked to disclose what virtue really is: ἕν γέ τι εἶδος ταὐτὸν ἅπασαι ἔχουσιν δι' ὃ εἰσὶν ἀρεταί, εἰς ὃ καλῶς που ἔχει ἀποβλέψαντα τὸν ἀποκρινόμενον τῷ ἐρωτήσαντι δηλῶσαι ὃ τυγχάνει οὖσα ἀρετή. Here, despite ἀποβλέψαντα, the conception is clearly not that of an αὐτὸ ὃ ἔστιν ἀρετή *outside* the plurality of ἀρεταί.

Since then no dialogue earlier than the *Republic*[2] can be adduced for the doctrine of transcendent Forms except *Cratylus*, *Symposium* and *Phaedo*, we may reaffirm with some confidence that our dialogue comes near in chronological order to the *Republic*; but the *Symposium*

[1] Cf. G. M. A. Grube, *Plato's Thought*, p. 9, and Wilamowitz, *Platon* II, p. 80. Against the view taken in the text see Burnet on *Euthyphro* 5 D 3.
[2] The *Rep.* is nowadays commonly admitted to be earlier than the *Phaedrus*. As to the other dialogues of the old 'middle group', the *Theaet.* (183 E) probably refers back to the *Parm.*, but there is legitimate doubt whether these two works are earlier or later than *Phaedrus*. This does not affect the position of *Rep.* as the earliest in the group.

may come, as I think it does, between them. It is difficult to place the *Cratylus* precisely: but that is not a matter which greatly affects our interpretation of the *Phaedo*.

III.   *The nature of the soul*

If further confirmation be needed of the priority of the *Phaedo* to the *Republic*, it may be found in their different conceptions of the soul. In the former the incomposite nature of the soul is asserted in emphatic terms, and made a point of likeness to the eternal Forms, likeness which provides at least a presumption that it is immortal; in the latter (Book IV) we have a long and carefully elaborated argument for three parts or 'kinds' (εἴδη) of soul, the right relation of which to each other, each fulfilling its prescribed function, constitutes the four 'cardinal' virtues. What we should call moral conflict is, for the *Phaedo*, a conflict between the soul, conceived as wholly good and rational, and the irrational passions and desires of the body; whereas for the *Republic* it is faction or disharmony within the soul itself. The Homeric line 'Then did he smite his breast and chide his heart'[1] is quoted in the *Phaedo* as supporting Socrates's contention that the soul, so far from being an attunement or adjustment of the bodily constituents, is at times the opponent of the body's fears and desires; but the same line is quoted in the *Republic* (441 B) as witnessing to the control of the irrational elements in the soul—the 'spirited' and 'appetitive' parts— by the rational.

It is unnecessary here to examine the difficulties connected with the doctrine of the tripartite soul, a doctrine reaffirmed in the *Phaedrus* and *Timaeus*; what is important for a commentator on the *Phaedo* to insist upon is that that doctrine cannot be read into this dialogue by maintaining (with Zeller)[2] that the lower parts are left unmentioned because they do not belong to the soul in its true, i.e. its discarnate, nature, or (with Wilamowitz)[3] that Plato wanted to avoid overloading his exposition. On this point Frutiger's words are surely conclusive: 'if Plato, at the time of writing the *Phaedo*, had allowed that the soul is composed of three parts, of which only one is immortal, he would

---

[1] *Odyssey* XX, 17.
[2] *Phil. d. Gr.* II, 1, p. 844. Archer-Hind modifies Zeller's view by calling the spirited and appetitive elements 'modes of the soul's activity': this is plainly not the representation of *Rep.* IV: cf. Frutiger, *Mythes de Platon*, p. 76 n. 2.
[3] *Platon* I, p. 341.

certainly not have given the last the generic name ψυχή, nor have passed over the others in complete silence.'[1] Moreover the elaborate exposition of *Rep.* IV has all the appearance of new doctrine.

The reason for Plato's assumption that the soul is incomposite is that its objects of knowledge are the Forms; these are themselves without parts, in the *Phaedo*, as was Parmenides's one Being: and like knows like. A juster analysis of the facts of moral experience led him later to a better psychology.

It must not be supposed that by calling the soul incomposite Plato means that its only activity is cognition in the strictest sense of the word. The truth is that the apprehension of the Forms is in part cognition, in part enjoyment of a possession and satisfaction of a desire; in recognising this complex of activities, if it may be so called, which is nevertheless one and the same activity, the conception of Eros elaborated in the *Symposium* is already in Plato's mind. Though less definitely emphasised than there, we find it at 66 E where true philosophers are ἐρασταὶ φρονήσεως, and again at 67 E (οὖ διὰ βίου ἦρων τυχεῖν—ἦρων δὲ φρονήσεως): it is implicit in the conception of the soul's kinship with its objects (79 D), and again at 84 A, where truth is the object of its contemplation and its sustaining food (τὸ ἀληθὲς . . . θεωμένη . . . ὑπ' ἐκείνου τρεφομένη).

The goal of all Eros is union of the lover with the beloved, and that of religious and philosophic Eros is the *unio mystica*. Mysticism is in the *Phaedo* something rather felt than expounded: the word θεᾶσθαι in the passage just quoted, and its earlier occurrence at 66 E (αὐτῇ τῇ ψυχῇ θεατέον αὐτὰ τὰ πράγματα), bring it momentarily to the surface; but there is no passage in our dialogue quite like *Republic* 490 B, where the philosopher 'draws nigh unto, and is united with, that which truly is'.[2]

IV. The characters

The dialogue is reported to Echecrates and a few others by Phaedo of Elis, of whom nothing is known from other sources save what we are told in a brief account by Diogenes Laertius (II, 105) and a few lines of Aulus Gellius (II, 18). He was taken prisoner of war by the Athenians and sold into slavery, but ransomed at the instance of

---

[1] *Op. cit.* p. 77.

[2] πλησιάσας καὶ μιγεὶς τῷ ὄντι ὄντως. To gain the full effect of these words the whole paragraph 490 A 8–B 7 should be read. The best study of mysticism in Plato is Festugière's *Contemplation et vie contemplative selon Platon*.

Socrates by the Cebes of our dialogue, or alternatively by Alcibiades or Crito; thereafter he 'pursued philosophy' says Diogenes 'as became a free man'. He founded a school which seems to have had close affinity with the Megarian, the headship of which passed to the better-known Menedemus of Eretria. The satirist Timon[1] couples him in a disparaging comment with the Megarian Euclides, another philosopher mentioned in our list of those present in the prison.

Why Plato chose Phaedo as reporter we can only guess: my own guess is that it was he who in fact told Plato on his sick-bed the story of Socrates's last hours, thus supplying the factual framework of the philosophical discussion. That the framework is factual in substance—not of course in every detail—there is no reason to doubt. But since he obviously could not have Plato himself to report to in the dialogue, he reports to Echecrates. The choice of this Pythagorean from Phlius may be due, as Archer-Hind suggests, to Plato's feeling that a member of that school would naturally be interested in the theory of Forms, of which so much is heard in the dialogue; but of course there is much else besides metaphysical theory with which a Pythagorean would be in sympathy. Plainly a non-Athenian was wanted in any case, for to an Athenian most of the factual record could not plausibly be presented as news. Echecrates, we learn in the first sentences, was out of touch with events in Athens, and this may well have been a fact.

Of Simmias and Cebes, the Thebans, who are the chief interlocutors of Socrates, we know little beyond what is said of them or by them in the dialogue. The notices in Diogenes Laertius (II, 124 and 125) are merely lists of dialogues attributed to them. In the *Crito* (45 B) they are reported to have come to Athens after Socrates's trial with a sum of money to be used to procure his escape from prison. Cebes is mentioned as still living in the Thirteenth Platonic Letter,[2] addressed to Dionysius II and written, if genuine, about 365: 'The name of Cebes is familiar to you; for he is represented in the Socratic dialogues as speaking to Socrates along with Simmias in the discussion about the soul, and is a friend and well-wisher of us all.' One is led to speculate, assuming the letter to be genuine, whether the writing of the *Phaedo* may have been suggested by this friend of Plato who had been, like himself, an intimate of the master. Simmias appears as a speaker in Plutarch's dialogue *De genio Socratis*, where he says (578 F) that he was

---

[1] *Apud* Diog. Laert. II, 107.   [2] 363 A.

a fellow-student of philosophy with Plato at Memphis—an interesting remark and conceivably true.

Of the others present something will be said in the commentary on our first section: it remains now to supplement what has been said in Section I of the figure of Socrates himself.

The picture of Socrates is of course adapted to the occasion, a gathering of intimates who, though deeply sorrowing for their imminent loss, are yet sufficiently imbued with his own spirit to engage with vigour in, or at least to listen with interest to, the philosophical argument. Hence there is none of that deflating of a conceited interlocutor such as we meet in *Euthyphro*, *Gorgias* and *Meno*, no reducing of a respondent to bewildered helplessness and confession of defeat. The argument is perhaps more than anywhere one between men who genuinely like and respect each other.[1] Outside the passages in which the arguments for immortality are presented, Socrates's most noticeable features are serenity and confidence—the confidence of faith or hope indeed, but hope fortified by intellectual conviction. Consistent with this is an occasional indulgence in banter, as when he speaks of the refutation of Simmias's theory as a propitiation of the tuneful lady Harmonia of Thebes, to be followed by dealing with her husband Cadmus, standing for Cebes (95 A): or the more serious banter in reply to Cebes's question as to the manner of his burial: 'Bury me as you like, if you can catch me' (115 C). Noteworthy too is his concern for the spiritual welfare of those he is leaving behind: 'Look after yourselves' is his reply when asked what they can do for him (115 B): this means of course that what he wants of them is that they should follow the way of philosophy which he has so eloquently described in the early pages of the dialogue; and indeed this is what in the *Apology* he has spoken of as what he would have all men do: though no doubt the conception of ψυχῆς ἐπιμελεῖσθαι there (30 B) has been deepened, even transformed, by what I shall make bold to call the Platonic doctrine that life is a 'training for death'.

In part the master's personality is conveyed to us through the words of others: even as in the *Symposium* Alcibiades utters his wholly sincere but somewhat exuberant hymn of praise, so in the *Phaedo* we have the narrator's encomium at 89 A, and his quietly impressive last words, ἀνδρός...τῶν τότε ὧν ἐπειράθημεν ἀρίστου καὶ ἄλλως φρονιμωτάτου καὶ δικαιοτάτου: and a little earlier the gaoler's description of him as

[1] See Phaedo's outburst of admiration at 89 A.

γενναιότατον καὶ πρᾳότατον καὶ ἄριστον ἄνδρα τῶν πώποτε δεῦρο ἀφικομένων (116c). But indeed, if the whole dialogue has, as I have suggested, for its main purpose the furtherance of the master's teaching, is not this itself the highest testimony that a great philosopher, conscious of his debt to a predecessor, could possibly give?

We have still to ask whether the Pythagorean or Orphic colouring of the portrait, which is especially prominent in the early pages, is faithful to the historical Socrates. That Socrates was acquainted with the eschatological tenets of Orphism and Pythagoreanism is *a priori* likely, and is confirmed by the reference to 'what is said' (τὰ λεγόμενα) on the matter of the life after death in the *Apology* (40C, 41C);[1] moreover this passage clearly implies a sympathy with these λεγόμενα, a hope that they may be true; yet the attitude both here and in an earlier passage (29A) is, as Cornford says,[2] definitely agnostic: Socrates will not profess knowledge where he is conscious of his own ignorance.

[1] I agree with Burnet that τὰ λεγόμενα does not mean 'what is commonly believed', but refers to mystery-doctrine (though perhaps not specifically or exclusively Orphic). In this connexion it may be remarked that Xenophon shows himself acquainted with arguments for the soul's immortality, some of which clearly echo arguments in the *Phaedo*. These are put into the mouth of the dying Cyrus (*Cyrop.* VIII, 7, 17ff.). But if, as seems probable, Xenophon is borrowing directly from the *Phaedo*, that of course does not prove that he regarded the arguments as having been used by Socrates.

Burnet (Introd. pp. lif.) points to a number of passages in the *Memorabilia* which seem to imply Xenophon's acquaintance with the *Phaedo*, and in which things are said about the soul which 'go far beyond the popular use of the word ψυχή'. Doubtless that is true: but that any of them assert or imply a definite belief in immortality cannot, I think, be maintained. The passage on which Burnet lays most stress is *Mem.* IV, 3, 14. Here Socrates has been arguing that though the gods are invisible, yet their operations are manifest to all: even their ministers, such as thunderbolts and winds, are invisible: and he continues: ἀλλὰ μὴν καὶ ἀνθρώπου γε ψυχή, ἡ εἴπερ τι καὶ ἄλλο τῶν ἀνθρωπίνων τοῦ θείου μετέχει, ὅτι μὲν βασιλεύει ἐν ἡμῖν φανερόν, ὁρᾶται δὲ οὐδ' αὐτή.

Here the mention of the soul's rule is regarded by Burnet as derived from *Phaedo* 79E–80A. That seems to me by no means certain—for one thing it may be noticed that whereas Plato's words are ἄρχειν, δεσπόζειν and ἡγεμονεύειν Xenophon's is βασιλεύειν. But even if we allow it to be so, the fact that Xenophon has the *Phaedo* in mind cannot prove that what he makes Socrates say 'implies the mystic doctrine' in the sense of implying either Socrates's adherence to that doctrine or Xenophon's belief in his adherence. Even if Socrates were reported as affirming outright that the soul τοῦ θείου μετέχει, I doubt whether this would be equivalent to calling it θεία and therefore ἀθάνατος: but in fact all that he is made to say is that *if* anything in man partakes of the divine it is his soul. This cautiously expressed statement seems to me to imply nothing beyond the open-minded agnosticism of the final speech in the *Apology*.

[2] *Camb. Anc. Hist.* VI, p. 308: 'If Socrates had professed any definite belief in immortality, no motive could have induced Plato to convey a false impression in the *Apology*, especially if the address to the court after the sentence cannot

That being so, he can hardly have held that attitude to life expressed in the *Phaedo* account of the 'true philosophers'. For only to one convinced that the soul is divine and immortal, not to one who hopes that it may be, will the doctrine of purification, the flight from the body, the contempt for the senses, seem acceptable. As with the metaphysical doctrine of Forms, so in this matter the truth seems to be that the silence of the early dialogues is significant; until the *Gorgias* Socrates's ethical attitude is not determined by any views or speculations about a future life, and the natural inference is that such views begin to be attributed to him when, and because, they are beginning to influence Plato. The injunction to 'look after the soul', and the conviction that the 'goods of the soul' are vastly more important than those of the body, are of course immensely enriched in significance and appeal when set in the context which the *Phaedo* gives them: that is just another way of saying that Plato here is deepening the Socratic teaching; yet what Socrates preached as the duty of man does, from another point of view, actually gain by being what has been called a *Diesseitsevangelium*: the detachment of moral duty from belief in any rewards or punishments hereafter has a grandeur of its own. The sufficient supports for Socrates's lifework were the sense of a divine mission[1]— of co-operation, we may perhaps say, with a righteous power that governs the universe—and the conviction that whether or no there be any life after death, the souls of the righteous are in the hand of God.[2]

V.   The arguments for the immortality of the soul

Important as Plato clearly conceives it that the human soul should be proved to be immortal, no careful reader of the dialogue can believe that such proof is its main purpose. The need for it arises from the feeling of Socrates's friends that his serenity and confidence in the face

have been actually made.' My own feeling is that if Socrates did make any such address, he would certainly then have professed the belief in question unambiguously, if he had held it.

[1] *Apol.* 28 E, 33 C.

[2] *Apol.* 41 D οὐκ ἔστιν ἀνδρὶ ἀγαθῷ κακὸν οὐδὲν οὔτε ӡῶντι οὔτε τελευτήσαντι, οὐδὲ ἀμελεῖται ὑπὸ θεῶν τὰ τούτου πράγματα. In discussing the presentation of Socrates I have deliberately refrained from attempting any deductions from Aristophanes's *Clouds*, *Birds* and *Frogs* or from fragments of other comic poets in which he is mentioned. To separate reasonable caricature from sheer misrepresentation in the *Clouds* seems to me a hopeless task; and the other passages yield nothing credible beyond the undisputed fact that Socrates was something of an ascetic who talked much about the ψυχή.

of death, and the religious faith on which he bases it, ought to be justified rationally. More explicitly, they feel—and Plato means his readers to feel—that that whole conception of the philosophic life which Socrates calls a μελέτη θανάτου, resting as it does on the assumption that the soul survives the death of the body, cannot be maintained in the face of criticism and doubt unless that assumption be justified.

It might perhaps be sufficient to prove something short of immortality, namely that the soul survives death for a time; and plainly it is not necessary, for this immediate purpose, to show that our souls existed before we were born. The fact is, however, that the character of the arguments advanced is such as to bring the wider question before the minds of those participating in the dialogue: thus the argument from ἀνάμνησις, that is to say the argument that our minds can recollect knowledge possessed before birth but lost at birth, although it cannot prove survival, yet is so closely bound up with Plato's metaphysical doctrine that it receives special emphasis, being reaffirmed twice (87A by Cebes, 92A by both Cebes and Simmias) after its original acceptance; and the first argument, that 'living' and 'dead' are opposites which must conform to the universal principle of reciprocal generation of opposite from opposite, is quite as much an argument for pre-existence from all time as for survival for all time. The final argument, which follows upon Socrates's philosophical autobiography, and which is by far the longest and probably the one to which Plato attached the greatest importance, the argument which may briefly be designated as that resting on the logical connexion of Soul and Life, bears as much upon the *a priori* as upon the *a posteriori* existence of the soul.

Yet nowhere in the *Phaedo* is the soul plainly declared to be without a beginning, ἀγένητος, as it is in the *Phaedrus* proof of immortality (245 D). ἀνάμνησις has proved, and can prove, no more than that the soul exists *for some time* previous to its incarnation; and the predominant emphasis in the dialogue taken as a whole is—naturally enough, in view of the greater interest we all have in our fate after death than in our existence before birth—upon the soul's survival.

Two questions arise at this point: (*a*) how many arguments for immortality are advanced, and what is more important, (*b*) is the final argument to be taken as superseding all the earlier ones, and alone completely cogent in Plato's judgement?

(*a*) It is, I think, obvious that the answer to this is either three or four, according as we regard the γένεσις ἐξ ἐναντίων or ἀνταπόδοσις argument (70C–72D) as independent of the ἀνάμνησις argument, or refuse with Bonitz and Archer-Hind to do so. It seems clear to me that this argument is, at the time of its discussion, and in particular at its conclusion in 72D, regarded by Socrates and his two friends as proving both pre-existence and survival; and in fact if it does prove either it proves both. On the other hand it is recalled at 77C, where Socrates says that it ought to be put together with the ἀνάμνησις argument, if both pre-existence and survival are to be accepted as proved. The nature of this σύνθεσις of arguments is not simple, and I must refer to my commentary on Section VIII for my interpretation of it; but this much may be said now, that the probable reason, or main reason, for ἀνταπόδοσις now being treated rather as a *subsidium* to ἀνάμνησις than as cogent *per se* is that in it the soul was not conceived in the way that ἀνάμνησις conceives it, namely as a thinking substance possessing δύναμιν καὶ φρόνησιν (to use the language of 70B) but only as an entity capable of possessing the attributes 'living' and 'dead'. It is the conscious, cognitive, rational ψυχή that comes to the fore after 72D, and it is ψυχή as so conceived that has thenceforth to be shown to be immortal. That being so, it is not surprising that the ἀνταπόδοσις proof is silently dropped;[1] and that when Cebes complains at 86E ff. of the inadequacy of the preceding argument, it is plainly not ἀντα- πόδοσις that is in his mind—nor of course ἀνάμνησις, which he still accepts as cogent—but the argument of 78B–80B, that namely which rests on the incomposite nature of the soul and its likeness to the Forms.

This being so, I conclude that there is no simple and straightforward answer to the question of three arguments or four; but the question was worth discussing in view of the light which my attempted answer throws upon the structure of the dialogue.

(*b*) This question, though of greater importance, can be answered more briefly and definitely. Of the ἀνταπόδοσις argument I have already said all that is here necessary; as to the next, ἀνάμνησις, the reassertions of it which I have noted at 87A and 92A seem a plain indication that it is not intended to be superseded by anything later in the dialogue; hence the third (or second)—the likeness of souls to Forms—alone

---

[1] The principle of γένεσις ἐξ ἐναντίων is no doubt recalled at 103A–B, but only as a general principle, not in respect of its application to 'living' and 'dead'. The example there given is not ζῶν—τεθνηκός but μεῖζον—ἔλαττον.

comes into question. Now, seeing that the weighty criticism of Cebes
is directed against it and it alone, and that the answer to that criticism
does not take the form of justifying the argument in question, but
involves a wholly new approach; and seeing further that Socrates's
own words at 80B claim for it no more than a proof that the soul is
'indestructible or nearly so', we shall surely be right in holding that
it is superseded. Superseded, that is to say, in respect of what it
attempted to prove: but not superseded in respect of its content; by
which I mean that we cannot simply wipe it out as otiose and valueless.
The dialogue is indeed the richer for it, inasmuch as it clarifies Plato's
present conception of the soul, and exalts its nature and capacity by
showing its 'kinship' with the Forms, and moreover leads on by
a natural transition to Socrates's most impressive account of the contrast
between the after-life of the purified and the unpurified soul (80C–84B).
It is not irrelevant, though I hope it is for most people superfluous,
to remark that the value of our dialogue is not confined to its dialectical
arguments, whether or no they stand or fall in the judgement either
of the author or of his readers.

VI.   *Arguments for immortality in other dialogues*

In the *Meno* an argument for immortality, to be later recalled and
improved in the *Phaedo*, is based on the doctrine of Recollection
(ἀνάμνησις). Baffled in his attempt to furnish a satisfactory definition
of Virtue, Meno has confronted Socrates at 80D with a 'contentious
point' (ἐριστικὸς λόγος): how can one search for a thing of which one
has no knowledge? And even if one could, and actually found it, how
could one know that what one had found was what one was searching
for? The reply is that all learning is recollection of knowledge possessed
by our souls before birth, and this is established by an experiment
conducted by Socrates with Meno's slave, which results in eliciting
from him the solution of a mathematical problem, the duplication of
the square. Socrates goes on to infer, by an argument which will not
survive logical scrutiny, not merely the soul's possession of knowledge
for a certain time before its incarnation, but its eternal possession
thereof in the past and the future; thus ἀνάμνησις, which in the *Phaedo*
is recognised as incapable of proving survival, is here taken as proof
of absolute immortality (86B οὐκοῦν εἰ ἀεὶ ἡ ἀλήθεια ἡμῖν τῶν ὄντων
ἐστὶν ἐν τῇ ψυχῇ, ἀθάνατος ἂν ἡ ψυχὴ εἴη). Nevertheless, a note of

doubt is sounded immediately thereafter; so far as the argument has demonstrated the possibility, and the duty, of searching for knowledge, Socrates will zealously uphold it: but τὰ ἄλλα οὐκ ἂν πάνυ ὑπὲρ τοῦ λόγου διισχυρισαίμην. τὰ ἄλλα is no doubt vague; but it is most natural to refer it to the inference of immortality, which is in fact only incidental to the main thesis that Socrates is here concerned to establish.

In the *Symposium* the series of discourses on Love (ἔρως) is concluded by Socrates's report of what he had learnt about the nature of Love from Diotima, the wise woman of Mantinea. As her teaching is fully endorsed by Socrates himself (212 B), ταῦτα δή. . .ἔφη μὲν Διοτίμα, πέπεισμαι δ' ἐγώ), we may safely take it to express Plato's own position at the time of writing. It may be summarised as follows:

Love is the desire for immortality or self-perpetuation, which mortal creatures, unlike the gods who abide for ever changeless, can only achieve by procreation. This may be either physical procreation, by which a man lives on in his offspring, or spiritual, whether in its more ordinary forms, to be seen in the abiding work of poets, artists and legislators, or in the sublimer form to be seen in that begetting of true virtue by the philosopher through his mystical union with Beauty itself. To him who has thus 'begotten true virtue and nurtured it it is granted that he should become dear to the gods and—if any man may be so—immortal' (τεκόντι δὲ ἀρετὴν ἀληθῆ καὶ θρεψαμένῳ ὑπάρχει θεοφιλεῖ γενέσθαι, καὶ εἴπερ τῷ ἄλλῳ ἀνθρώπων ἀθανάτῳ καὶ ἐκείνῳ, 212 A).

It seems clear that throughout Diotima's discourse, even in these her concluding sentences, it is a vicarious survival, not an immortality of the personal self, the individual soul, that is proclaimed. It has been urged (e.g. by Bury) that the immortality of the sentence just quoted is rather a *qualitative* conception than one involving temporal duration: the mystical union in which a man 'sees Beauty by that whereby it may be seen' (ὁρῶντι ᾧ ὁρατὸν τὸ καλόν), the union, that is, of νοῦς with its proper object, is the attainment of divinity: such a man is as a god, ἀθάνατος. This may be a legitimate interpretation, though the persistence of the notion of spiritual begetting seems to me to tell against it. But in any case it is only in the exceptional case of the philosophic lover that this question arises; for all others, that is to say for the great mass of mankind including the poets, the artists and the statesmen, immortality can only mean survival in and through their physical or spiritual progeny.

This is plainly something different from the doctrine of the *Phaedo*: is it actually inconsistent with that doctrine? Now it is true that, as A. E. Taylor remarks, 'Man, according to the *Phaedo*, is strictly mortal; what is immortal is not the man, but the "divine" element in him, his ψυχή. There is not a word in the *Symposium* to suggest that the ψυχή is perishable.'[1] On the other hand there is, unfortunately, not a word to suggest that the ψυχή of the individual—unless it be the ψυχή of the philosopher-mystic—is imperishable. We are of course told by scholars naturally reluctant to find divergence between the two dialogues that we must not argue from silence, that Plato is not bound to give us his whole doctrine everywhere, that it is unfair to isolate the *Symposium* from the *Phaedo*, *Republic* and *Phaedrus*, that it is Diotima speaking, not Socrates. For myself, I cannot resist the conclusion that, for whatever reason (possibly, as I have suggested elsewhere,[2] a dissatisfaction with the proof offered in the *Phaedo*), Plato has deliberately avoided asserting a belief in individual immortality. If he had wished his readers to supplement Diotima's assertions by their memories of the *Phaedo*, he might, one would have thought, have given a clearer indication of his wish than the alleged hint (to my mind not even a hint) in the words (208 B) ἀθάνατον δὲ ἄλλῃ.[3]

The *Republic* offers a proof of the soul's immortality in its last Book (x). The question of rewards for justice (or righteousness) has been deliberately excluded until its intrinsic superiority to injustice has

---

[1] *P.M.W.*, p. 228.

[2] *C.R.* (1950), pp. 43–5; and see Mr J. V. Luce's counter-arguments in *C.R.* (1952), pp. 135–7. Prof. Cherniss, in a note in *C.R.* (1953), p. 131, refers to *Laws* 721B–C as 'by itself proving the invalidity' of my inference. I cannot agree that it does so. The speaker is urging the duty of marriage on the ground that this is nature's way of securing for mankind a 'participation in immortality', i.e. of self-perpetuation: and the language certainly resembles that of *Symp.* 208A–B. But the passage is without prejudice to the doctrine of the soul's immortality asserted in Book XII and implied in Book X; for the soul's immortality is simply not within its purview, being irrelevant to the speaker's insistence on the duty of marriage. In the *Symp.* the case is very different: Diotima's purview extends beyond ordinary marriage and physical procreation to the procreation of spiritual progeny; and it is because of her predominant concern with ψυχή, above all with its highest activity—the knowledge of and union with Beauty itself—that we expect, and miss, an assertion of that immortality of soul which in the *Phaedo* is bound up with its apprehension of the Forms.

[3] If ἀδύνατον were the right reading (which I do not believe), even this supposed hint would disappear.

been established; but now that that has been done, Socrates feels free
to speak on this topic. This present life on earth is too short to offer
adequate rewards: we must look beyond it. 'Do you not realise',
he asks Glaucon, 'that our souls are immortal and never perish?'
(608D): and on Glaucon's expressing surprise at this assertion he
maintains that it can be easily defended (οὐδὲν γὰρ χαλεπόν). It seems
plain that since writing the *Phaedo* Plato has conceived a fresh argument which he deems simple, straightforward and cogent; the proofs
of the *Phaedo* (if, as is generally believed, it is they that are alluded
to as 'the other arguments' at 611B) are not indeed superseded, but
supplemented by this new proof.

Nothing, Socrates maintains, can be destroyed except by its own
peculiar evil, its σύμφυτον κακόν: for example, grain is destroyed by
mildew, iron by rust, the body by disease. Now the soul's peculiar
evil is vice or wickedness: but this, though it makes the soul bad
(μοχθηρόν), does not destroy it; on the contrary, experience shows that
it increases a man's vitality and energy. The disease that kills the body
cannot kill the soul because, even if the soul's peculiar evil could
destroy it, bodily disease does not introduce that evil.

Modern commentators have not failed to remark on the weakness
of this argument, and indeed it is not easy to defend it. The notion of
a single σύμφυτον κακόν for the soul rests merely on analogies, and
doubtful analogies at that: since grain can obviously be destroyed
otherwise than by mildew, and the human body otherwise than by
disease. Moreover, granting that the soul has one σύμφυτον κακόν,
and one only, it is not necessarily ἀδικία: that is its κακόν *qua* seat of
moral conduct, not *qua* principle of life. Again, as Adam remarks
(on 609D), 'our experience of the effect of injustice on a human soul is
limited to a single life; and why should not one soul wear out many
bodies and perish at last through its own vice?' If Cebes had been
present, might he not have put this question?

A little later (611B) the difficulty is brought up of attributing immortality to a composite entity, as the soul has been held to be in
Book IV: but the solution offered is a debatable matter, into which it is
impossible here to go. Socrates suggests that the true nature of the
soul is to be seen by 'looking at its love of wisdom', but he does not
say outright that that nature is 'of a single form' (μονοειδής). Perhaps
he is deliberately non-committal: for in the *Phaedrus* the discarnate,
as well as the embodied soul, is declared to be tripartite.

The *Phaedrus* (245 c ff.) has an argument for immortality based on the conception of soul as that which moves itself. A self-mover never intermits its own motion 'inasmuch as it cannot abandon its own nature': μόνον δὴ τὸ αὐτὸ κινοῦν, ἅτε οὐκ ἀπολεῖπον ἑαυτό, οὔποτε λήγει κινούμενον. It is the source of motion in all things that are not self-moved, but is itself without source or beginning, ἀγένητος: it is also indestructible (ἀδιάφθορος), for its destruction would involve the utter annihilation of the universe and all that comes to be therein, with no possibility of a restoration—an inconceivable notion (compare *Phaedo* 72 B).

As is the case with almost all Plato's arguments on this matter, this argument is treated as involving *individual* immortality. On the connexion between it and the final proof of the *Phaedo* I may refer to my commentary on the *Phaedrus*, p. 68.

The dialogue proceeds to describe the tripartite soul in mythical terms.

The *Timaeus* contains no argument for human immortality, but distinguishes between an immortal part of the soul, created by the Divine Craftsman himself, and two mortal parts created by those celestial gods whom he has already made (41 c–d). The myth assigns separate parts of the body to these three parts: the immortal as lodged in the head, the higher mortal part in the heart, the lower in the belly (69 d–70 e).

In the tenth Book of the *Laws*, which contains Plato's 'natural theology', soul is conceived, conformably to the *Phaedrus*, as the self-moved source of all motion, and the supreme government of the universe is assigned to an intelligent and beneficent 'best soul'. The indestructibility of soul is not explicitly asserted, but the conclusions of the *Phaedrus* argument are clearly implied, and reincarnation of human souls in a series of bodies (though not transmigration into animal bodies) is declared to be determined in accordance with moral desert. A clear statement in the twelfth Book (959 a–b) may be taken as Plato's last word, and is worth quoting in full, particularly as it recalls much that has been said in the *Phaedo*:

As in other matters it is right to trust the lawgiver, so too we must believe him when he asserts that the soul is wholly superior to the body, and that in actual life what makes each of us to be what he is is nothing else than the soul, while the body is a semblance which attends on each of us, it being well said that the bodily corpses are images of the dead, but that which is the real self of each of us, and which we term the immortal soul, departs to the presence of other gods, there (as the ancestral law declares) to render its account,—a prospect to be faced with courage by the good, but with uttermost dread by the evil. But to him who is dead no great help can be given; it was when he was alive that all his relatives should have helped him, so that when living his life might have been as just and holy as possible, and when dead he might be free during the life which follows this life from the penalty for wickedness and sin. (Bury's translation)

TRANSLATION & COMMENTARY

The scene is at Phlius, a town in the Peloponnese, the home of Echecrates who, meeting Phaedo, asks for news about the last days of Socrates. Phaedo explains why a considerable interval occurred between his trial and his death, and goes on to describe the scene in the prison at Athens on the final day, giving the names of those present.

Echecrates. Were you there yourself, Phaedo, with Socrates on the 57 day when he drank the poison in the prison, or did you hear the story from someone else?

Phaedo. I was there, Echecrates.

Ech. Then what was it that Socrates had to say before he died? And how did he meet his end? I should much like to hear; for nowadays hardly anyone from Phlius goes to stay in Athens, and it is a long time since any visitor from Athens has reached us who could give any B reliable report, beyond the mere fact that he died by poisoning: no one could tell anything more than that.

Phaedo. Haven't you even heard how the trial went? 58

Ech. Yes, some one told us about that; and we were surprised to find that his death came such a long time[1] afterwards. What was really the reason, Phaedo?

Phaedo. It was a matter of chance, Echecrates: it so happened that on the day before the trial they had crowned the stern of the ship which the Athenians sent to Delos.

Ech. Oh, what ship is that?

Phaedo. According to the Athenian story, it is the ship in which Theseus once upon a time went off to Crete with the famous 'seven pairs',[2] whose lives he saved as well as his own. Now the Athenians B had made a vow, it is said, to Apollo that if they were saved Athens would dispatch a sacred mission to Delos every year; and ever since that time down to the present day they have sent it year by year in honour of the god. And in the period following the initiation of these

---

[1] Thirty days, according to Xenophon, *Mem.* IV, viii, 2.

[2] The seven boys and seven girls whose lives were exacted every nine years as the Athenian tribute to Minos. Theseus slew the Minotaur, and saved himself and the other victims. See Bacchylides XVI and Plutarch, *Theseus*, c. 19.

proceedings custom ordains that the city shall be pure of bloodshed, and that no public execution shall take place until the ship has got back from its voyage to Delos. And sometimes, when the wind happens to c be against them, this takes a considerable time. The period in question starts as soon as the priest of Apollo has crowned the ship's stern; and as I was saying, that happened to occur on the day before the trial, which explains the long interval which Socrates spent in prison between his trial and his death.

Ech. I see; but when it came to his actual death, Phaedo—what was said, what was done, which of his close friends were present? Or did the authorities forbid that anyone should be with him, so that he died with no one at his side?

D   *Phaedo.* No, no: some friends were there, quite a number indeed.

Ech. Well, please do your best to give us[1] a reliable report, unless you chance to be busy.

Phaedo. No, I am not busy, so I will try to tell you the whole story. For indeed it is always a great delight to me to recall Socrates, whether by speaking of him myself or by hearing others do so.

Ech. And I assure you, Phaedo, that your audience feel just as you do. So see if you can give us a full and detailed account of the whole matter.

E   *Phaedo.* Very well.[2] When I came on the scene, I was curiously affected: on the one hand I didn't feel the pity that one usually feels at a dear friend's deathbed, because in behaviour and speech he struck me as so happy, Echecrates. What a fearless, noble ending it was! It made me realise that even as he passed to another world he had heaven's blessing; with him, if with any man, all would be well there too.[3] That 59 is why I had hardly any feeling of pity such as might naturally be expected at a scene of mourning; nor on the other hand did I feel pleasure in the prospect of one of our regular philosophical discussions, as in fact it was. No: it was quite an extraordinary feeling that came upon me, a strange sort of blend of pleasure and pain, when I realised that he was to die forthwith. All of us, indeed, were affected much as I was, laughing at one moment, weeping at the next. This was notably

---

[1] The plural pronouns in 58 D 2 and 4, as well as τοὺς ἀκουσομένους in D 7, show that Echecrates is accompanied by one or more friends.

[2] καὶ μήν is 'inceptive-responsive': Denniston, *Greek Particles*, p. 355.

[3] Compare the declaration of his faith by the Socrates of the *Apology* (41 D), ὅτι οὐκ ἔστιν ἀνδρὶ ἀγαθῷ κακὸν οὐδὲν οὔτε ζῶντι οὔτε τελευτήσαντι, οὐδὲ ἀμελεῖται ὑπὸ θεῶν τὰ τούτου πράγματα.

true of one of our number, Apollodorus; I expect you know about him and the way he behaves.   B

Ech. Of course.

Phaedo. Well, his was an extreme case; but I myself was agitated, and so were the rest of us.

Ech. Who actually were there, Phaedo?

Phaedo. The Athenians included Apollodorus, of whom I was speaking, Critobulus and his father,[1] Hermogenes, Epigenes, Aeschines, Antisthenes, Ctesippus of Paeane, Menexenus, and others. Plato, I believe, was sick.[2]

Ech. And were there foreigners present?

Phaedo. Yes: Simmias of Thebes and Cebes and Phaedondes; and c the Megarians, Euclides and Terpsion.

Ech. What about Aristippus and Cleombrotus?

Phaedo. No, they were said to be in Aegina.

Ech. Was there anyone else?

Phaedo. I think those were about all there were.

Ech. Well now, what do you say they talked about?

The choice of Phlius, a small town in north-east Peloponnese, as the scene of the introductory dialogue is natural enough; it was one of the centres of Pythagoreanism in mainland Greece, as we may infer from the fact that three out of the four persons described by Diogenes Laertius (VIII, 46) as 'the last of the Pythagoreans', and as known to Aristoxenus (a pupil of Aristotle), belonged to it; they include Echecrates himself; moreover it was to a tyrant of Phlius that Pythagoras himself, according to Heraclides of Pontus (*ap.* Cicero, *Tusc.* v, 3), told the famous story of the 'three lives'. Thus by taking us to Phlius, and by making Phaedo give his report to the Phliasian Echecrates, Plato suggests at the outset a connexion between Socrates, as he is to be portrayed in the main dialogue, and the religious side of Pythagoreanism, a connexion which will become plain as we proceed.

Quite natural, too, as his interlocutor is not an Athenian, is Phaedo's full explanation of the interval between Socrates's trial and death. But it serves also to connect Socrates at the outset with Apollo, the god in whose service (διὰ τὴν τοῦ θεοῦ λατρείαν, *Apol.* 23 c) his life

---

[1] This is Crito who, according to the dialogue named after him, had entreated Socrates to escape from prison.

[2] This must be accepted as a fact. Phaedo's οἶμαι, like his ἐλέγοντο in c 4, is perfectly natural; neither word is intended to raise doubts about the reasons for the absence of the friends mentioned.

had been spent. A little later on (61 A–B) Socrates will himself emphasise this connexion: he will account for his composition of a hymn to Apollo by the fact that his month in prison was the month of Apollo's festival: and at 85 B he will describe himself as consecrated to that same god.

I have suggested (Introd. p. 13) that it is reasonable to assume that Plato had been told by Phaedo himself of the events, as distinct from the philosophical conversation, of Socrates's last hours; and I do not doubt that his striking account of the feelings of those present, as well as his list of their names, reproduces what Phaedo had reported, though no doubt some touches may be due to the accounts of others here mentioned, such as the Megarian, Euclides, with whom Plato is said to have taken refuge after Socrates's death (Diog. Laert. III, 6, on the authority of Hermodorus).

Only two of those named as present, Simmias and Cebes, take any part in the philosophical discussion. If the *Phaedo* were the historical report which some recent scholars have supposed it to be, it would be surprising, as Robin remarks, that this should be so; in particular the silence of Antisthenes and Euclides, both names of some note in the history of philosophy, would be remarkable. Robin may be right in suggesting[1] that 'literary convention debarred Plato from attributing to his contemporaries views which at the dramatic date they had not in fact held, or which they no longer held at the date of composition'; but I think we need not look for any more recondite explanation than that Plato, as often,[2] is content to give Socrates not more than two interlocutors: in the *Republic*, for example, the considerable company mentioned at 328A all fade out after Book I except for Glaucon and Adimantus.

Of the others present the most important are Euclides, the founder of the Megarian school and Antisthenes, the reputed founder of the Cynic; Aeschines, of whose Socratic dialogues considerable fragments are extant; Crito and Menexenus, who give their names to Platonic dialogues; and Apollodorus, the narrator of the *Symposium*. The last-named appears at 117D, unable to restrain his emotion; he is said at *Symp.* 173D to have been nicknamed μαλακός or μανικός ('soft' or 'fanatical'): Burnet is probably right in accepting the former as the correct reading.

Cleombrotus and Aristippus are evidently persons who might have been expected to be present. As to the former, an epigram (XXIV) of Callimachus[3] tells of a person of this name who committed suicide after reading the *Phaedo*. It is not certain that the two are the same,

---

[1] *Phédon*, Introd. p. xiii.
[2] Not of course always: the *Protagoras* and *Symposium* are notable exceptions.
[3] The epigram is discussed by Wilamowitz, *Platon* II, p. 57.

but if they are, the natural inference is that drawn by Nonnus and quoted in Stallbaum's note on the present passage, namely that his reading of the dialogue had convinced him that death is better than life; nevertheless he must have forgotten the passage (61 c ff.) in which suicide is forbidden.

More interesting, perhaps, is the mention of Aristippus. Diogenes Laertius has a fairly long life of him (II, 65 ff.) well stocked with anecdotes, and making him out to have been the founder of the hedonist sect of 'Minor Socratics' known as the Cyrenaic; but probably this is mistaken, the real founder being a grandson of the same name.[1] From the long conversation between Socrates and Aristippus in Xenophon *Mem.* II, 1, an exhortation to practise moderation in indulging the appetites, Diogenes infers that Xenophon was on ill terms with him; and he adds that Plato 'abused' him (ἐκάκισεν) in the dialogue *On the Soul*. The last point is amplified in Diogenes's life of Plato (III, 36): 'Plato was also on bad terms with Aristippus: at all events in the dialogue *On the Soul* he disparages him by saying that he was not present at the death of Socrates, but was close at hand in Aegina.' The inference is plainly unwarranted; there is no abuse or disparagement. Plutarch (*Life of Dion*, c. 19) tells us that Aristippus was present at the court of Dionysius II when Plato paid his second visit in 361 B.C., but he does not suggest any ill-will between the two men, nor do Plato's own letters mention Aristippus. There is nothing to make us doubt that he was a faithful admirer of Socrates, who but for an accident would have been present at the last scene.

[1] See Ritter and Preller, *Hist. Phil. Gr.* § 264; Field, *Plato and his Contemporaries*, p. 160.

II

59 C–62 C   SOCRATES AS POET.   THE WICKEDNESS OF SUICIDE

Continuing his narrative, Phaedo tells how he had come with the others very early in the morning, and found Socrates released from his fetters. His wife Xanthippe was with him, but her distress moved Socrates to ask that she should be taken away.

The loss of his chains now prompts Socrates to some reflexions about pleasure and pain, in the course of which he happens to mention Aesop, the author of the celebrated fables; this reminds Cebes that he had been asked by Evenus, a sophist and poet, about certain poems, including versifications of Aesop, which, as was rumoured, Socrates had been composing during his imprisonment. Socrates replies that he has done this in obedience to a command laid upon him in a dream. He sends greetings to Evenus, together with advice to follow him as soon as possible; yet not by way of suicide, for that is wicked. Cebes is puzzled about this, and Socrates proceeds to justify his position by reference to religious doctrine.

59 C   *Phaedo.* I will try to tell you everything from the beginning. You
   D   must know that for some days before the end I and the others had been
in the habit of visiting Socrates; we used to meet in the morning at the
court-house in which the trial took place, as it was near the prison.
Each day we used to wait chatting with each other until the prison was
opened, which was not until well on in the morning. As soon as it was,
we would go in to Socrates and usually spend all day with him. Well
now, on this particular day we had assembled earlier than usual; for
   E   when we left the prison the evening before, we learnt that the ship was
back from Delos. So we passed the word to be at the usual place as
early as possible next day. When we arrived, the porter who habitually
answered our knock told us to wait and not come in until he gave us
the word; 'for', said he, 'the authorities are taking Socrates's fetters
off, and arranging for his death this very day.' However, we hadn't
long to wait before he came back and bade us enter. On entering we
   60   found Socrates just freed from his chains, and Xanthippe, whom you
know, sitting beside him and holding his baby son. Xanthippe on seeing
us cried out, and said the sort of thing that women always say—
'Socrates, this is the last time your dear friends will speak to you and

you to them.' Upon which Socrates glanced towards Crito and said, 'Crito, someone had better take her home.' So she was taken off by some of Crito's attendants, sobbing and lamenting.[1]

Then Socrates, sitting up on his bed, began to bend his leg and rub B it with his hand, and as he did so remarked, 'What a queer thing this pleasure, as they call it,[2] seems to be, my friends! How remarkable is its relation to what we regard as its opposite, pain! Think of it: they won't both come to us at the same time, but if we run after one of them and grasp it, we are practically compelled to grasp the other too; they are like two creatures attached to a single head. I fancy that if Aesop C had thought of it, he would have composed a fable telling how God wanted to put an end to their hostility, but found that he could not, and so fastened their heads together, with the result that anybody who is visited by one of them finds the other following it up afterwards. That is just what seems to be happening in my own case: the discomfort of my leg due to the fetter appears to have departed, and the pleasure following close upon it to have arrived.'

Here Cebes interrupted:[3] 'I am grateful, Socrates, truly I am, for your reminding me of something. Do you know, I have had several people asking me about those poems that you have composed, putting into verse[4] stories by Aesop and composing the hymn to Apollo; only D the other day Evenus[5] wanted to know what induced you, after coming

---

[1] Diog. Laert. II, 36f. makes Xanthippe a shrew, and Xenophon (*Mem.* II, ii, 7) makes her eldest son, Lamprocles, complain of her bad temper. There is nothing in our dialogue, nor elsewhere in Plato, to support this. Socrates's treatment of her here may best be interpreted, with Burnet, as the sensible and considerate treatment of a woman distraught with grief. She will reappear towards the end (116B).

[2] The words τοῦτο ὃ καλοῦσιν οἱ ἄνθρωποι ἡδύ are perhaps intended to suggest that many so-called pleasures are unreal (ψευδεῖς) or 'impure' (οὐ καθαραί), in particular the mere cessation of pain, which is the pleasure now felt by Socrates. Cf. *Rep.* 584C μὴ ἄρα πειθώμεθα καθαρὰν ἡδονὴν εἶναι τὴν λύπης ἀπαλλαγὴν μηδὲ λύπην τὴν ἡδονῆς. *Phil.* 43D οὐκοῦν οὐκ ἂν εἴη τὸ μὴ λυπεῖσθαί ποτε ταὐτὸν τῷ χαίρειν.

[3] Burnet denies that ὑπολαμβάνειν can mean 'interrupt'; but that seems to be the meaning required here, and L. and S. give two instances which appear certain.

[4] ἐντείνειν can mean either 'versify' or 'set to music'. Burnet argues that it must have the latter meaning here, since no προοίμιον could have been in prose. But can we imagine anyone, even Socrates, setting Aesop's fables to music? In any case they were presumably in prose (this is not excluded by the word μύθους at 61B6, and is almost certainly implied by λόγους at 60D1), and would therefore need to be versified before being so set. The προοίμιον I take to be Socrates's original composition (for ἐντείνειν thus used cf. *Hipparchus* 228D); this is borne out by the use of ποιεῖν later on, πρῶτον μὲν εἰς τὸν θεὸν ἐποίησα, 61B.

[5] A native of Paros, a sophist or teacher of 'goodness', and elegiac poet. Fragments of his poems are extant. He was in Athens at the time of the trial, and in the *Apology* (20Aff.) Socrates speaks of his abilities with light irony.

here, to compose these works, when you had never produced any composition before. So if you would like me to have an answer for Evenus when he repeats his question, as I am sure he will, do tell me what to say.'

'Well, Cebes,' rejoined Socrates, 'tell him the truth: it wasn't with any wish to compete with him or his work that I wrote these composi-
E tions—I knew that would not be easy; no, I was trying to get at the meaning of certain dreams which I had had, and discharging a sacred obligation, thinking that perhaps it was this sort of music they were bidding me compose. I must tell you what the dreams were like. Often in the course of my life the same dream-figure has visited[1] me, differing in its visible form but always saying the same words, 'Socrates, be diligent and make music.' In the past I had supposed that it was urging and encouraging me to go on with what I was doing, just as people
61 urge on runners to run; I was to "make music" in the sense in which I was already doing so: the highest music was philosophy, and philo-sophy was my business. But now that my trial was over, and the festival of Apollo prevented my being put to death, it occurred to me that possibly the injunction of the dream might be to compose music in the commonly accepted sense,[2] and that I ought to obey by so doing; it was safer, I felt, not to depart until I had fulfilled my sacred obligation
B by composing what the dream enjoined. Hence my first work was in honour of the god whose feast was being kept; and after that, feeling that one who means to be a real maker of music should concern himself with fancy rather than fact, and that I myself had no gift for that sort of thing, I made my poems out of the first readily available material, some-thing that I knew by heart, namely Aesop's fables. So there, Cebes, is your reply to Evenus; say good-bye to him for me and tell him that, if
C he is wise, he should make all haste to follow me who am, it seems, to take my leave to-day on my country's orders.'

'What a strange piece of advice', said Simmias, 'for Evenus! From what I know of him (and I have come across him frequently) there is very little likelihood of his obeying you, if he can help it.'

'Why not,' said Socrates, 'isn't he a philosopher?'[3]

---

[1] For φοιτᾶν of the dream-figure cf. (with E. R. Dodds) Aesch. *P.V.* 657, Eur. *Alc.* 355, Hdt. VII, 16B.

[2] Viz. of writing poetry.

[3] Evenus would no doubt have called himself by profession a σοφιστής, like Protagoras. But he would not have disclaimed being φιλόσοφος, for a man can hardly profess to teach σοφία without being 'fond' of it. But there is no reason

'Yes, I believe so', replied Simmias.

'Well then, he will be as ready to comply as anyone else who has a proper attitude to philosophy. Yet probably he will not lay violent hands upon himself; for we are told that that is wicked.'[1]

As he said this, Socrates let his legs down to the ground, and for the D rest of the conversation remained seated.

A question then came from Cebes: 'How do you make that out, Socrates, that it is wicked to do violence to oneself, and yet that a philosopher will be ready to follow in the steps of the dying?'

'What, Cebes? Haven't you and Simmias been told about such matters in your studies with Philolaus?'[2]

'Nothing definite,[3] Socrates.'

'Well, of course I myself can only say what I have been told about it; however, I have no objection to repeating that; indeed I suppose it is highly suitable, now that I am on the point of passing to another place, E that I should examine our ideas about it, and let fancy dwell upon our habitation yonder. What else should one do until the sun goes down?'

'Why is it then, Socrates, that they call it wicked to kill oneself? For to go back to the question you asked me just now, I did hear from Philolaus, when he was living amongst us, and indeed from other people earlier, that we ought not to do that; but from no one have I ever heard anything definite on the subject.'

'Well, we must do our best about it', he replied; 'maybe you will 62 hear something yet. But I daresay it will strike you as surprising if in this matter, and this matter alone, we have something that holds good invariably, if (that is to say), as an exception to the general rule in

to suppose that σοφία and φιλοσοφία meant for him what they meant for the Socrates of our dialogue and for the Pythagoreans on whose doctrines Socrates will build; rather would they denote a humanistic culture designed to promote success in public life, as they did for Protagoras and later for Isocrates. A philosopher of that type will not be likely, as Simmias observes, to make all haste to follow Socrates.

[1] The use of φασί without subject perhaps implies that others besides Orphics and Pythagoreans, the 'official' exponents of this doctrine, had accepted it. Cf. 61 E ἤδη...καὶ Φιλολάου ἤκουσα...ἤδη δὲ καὶ ἄλλων τινῶν.

[2] A Pythagorean philosopher of some importance who had settled at Thebes after the expulsion of the sect from South Italy about the middle of the fifth century. Fairly considerable fragments of his work are printed in Diels-Kranz, *Vors.* I, pp. 406ff.: but it is doubtful whether any are authentic.

[3] It would be unsafe to deduce from this οὐδὲν σαφές (cf. 61 E 8) anything as to Philolaus's religious views. I take it to be no more than a device to allow Socrates to explain the point, much as Simmias's defective memory of the ἀνάμνησις doctrine (73 A) allows him to expound that.

human affairs, we never find that at some times and for some men death is better than life; so you think it surprising, I daresay, that it should be sinful for those for whom death *is* better to do themselves a good service, and that they should have to wait for someone else to do it for them.'[1]

At this Cebes laughed quietly, and falling into his own dialect exclaimed 'Guid sakes, yes!'

B 'Put like that,' rejoined Socrates, 'it might certainly seem unreasonable; still, perhaps there is a reason for it. There is of course the reason given in mystery doctrine, that we men are in a sort of prison,[2] and no one ought to attempt his release or run away from it; that seems to me an impressive saying, and not easy to get to the bottom of,[3] but this much at least, I think, Cebes, is well said, that there are gods who look after us, and that we men are amongst the possessions of the gods. Do you not agree?'

'I do', said Cebes.

C 'Then wouldn't you yourself be angry if one of the creatures you possessed were to put an end to itself without your signifying that it was your wish for it to die? And if there were any punishment you could inflict, would you not inflict it?'

'Certainly.'

'Well, perhaps that shows that it isn't unreasonable that a man ought not to put an end to himself until God brings constraint upon him, as he does now upon me.'[4]

In the earlier part of this section we are still probably in the realm of historical fact; I have little doubt that Socrates did have this dream, that he did obey it in the way that he says he did, and that Evenus did want to know the reason for his poetical activity. For why should

[1] On this difficult passage see Additional Notes, p. 191.

[2] Burnet's informative note on B3 shows that the balance of the evidence is against taking ἔν τινι φρουρᾷ as 'on a sort of guard-duty'; and the meaning 'prison' is strongly confirmed by 81E and 82E below.

[3] Plato, as often, expresses some diffidence about the religious beliefs and traditions of which he makes use; cf. *Meno* 86B, *Tim.* 40D. Yet in the sequel (81E, 82E, 83D) he seems fully to accept the symbol of the prison.

[4] It is implied that Socrates's drinking of the hemlock was a self-inflicted death, despite the compulsion. The same view can be seen (as is pointed out by Hirzel in *Archiv für Religionswissenschaft* XI (1908), p. 244) in Lysias XII, 17 and 96, where the Thirty Tyrants are represented as compelling people to suicide in the same way. It was presumably the normal view at the time. Hirzel also compares *Laws* 873 C ὃς ἂν ἑαυτὸν κτείνῃ, τὴν τῆς εἱμαρμένης βίᾳ ἀποστερῶν μοῖραν, μήτε πόλεως ταξάσης δίκῃ μήτε κ.τ.λ.

Plato have invented this strange dream—stranger, surely, than the other dream of Socrates, in the *Crito*—with its twofold interpretation? And if the poems were in fact composed, what more natural than that Evenus, himself a poet, and one who had been the target of Socrates's irony at his trial, should be curious about them?

The subject of dreams in the ancient Greek world has recently been discussed by Prof. E. R. Dodds,[1] who calls special attention to the type called by Macrobius χρηματισμός and by Chalcidius (the fifth-century A.D commentator on the *Timaeus*) 'admonitio'. This type, says Macrobius, occurs 'when in sleep the dreamer's parent, or some other respected or impressive personage, perhaps a priest or even a god, reveals without symbolism what will or will not happen, or should or should not be done'.[2]

The present dream plainly belongs to this type, though whether the visitant was taken to be divine or human we are not told; that in the *Crito* was 'a fair woman clothed in white', but she had no command to lay upon Socrates, whereas this figure has, and it seems more likely to have been a god in view of Socrates's words at *Apology* 33 C: 'It has been enjoined upon me by God that I should do this, both through oracles and dreams and all other means employed by divine providence for giving its injunctions.'

The words spoken by the dream-figure were ὦ Σώκρατες, μουσικὴν ποίει καὶ ἐργάζου. It is unfortunate that their true meaning cannot be given in English save by an intolerably clumsy periphrasis; μουσική must inevitably be translated by 'music'; in Greek it sometimes of course has that meaning, but it is often used to cover anything over which one of the Muses presided, so gaining the associations of 'humanism' or 'culture'. What it meant in the mouth of the dream-figure it is not for us to guess; but I believe that Socrates's later interpretation—'music in the commonly accepted sense'—refers to this wider meaning, and that throughout this section there is no reference to music in the English sense of the word;[3] in short, Socrates decided that he was bidden to write poems, and proceeded accordingly.

But what of his earlier interpretation? Why should he have thought that it was enjoined upon him to continue in his 'philosophical' activity? In other words, why and in what sense did he believe that 'the highest music is philosophy'? Conformably to what has just been said I do not think there is any allusion to the well attested Pythagorean[4] practice of κάθαρσις—purification of the soul—by means of music

[1] *The Greeks and the Irrational,* ch. IV.
[2] I have quoted Dodds's translation, *op. cit.* p. 107.
[3] Of course those who take ἐντείνας (60 D) to mean 'setting to music' will disagree.
[4] But not exclusively Pythagorean: it was probably a very ancient idea: see Dodds, *op. cit.* p. 154.

(generally, it seems, the music of the aulos, which Plato, if not Socrates, highly disapproves of;[1] such music would be the last kind that they would identify with philosophy). The words can be understood more simply and naturally: μουσική is in essence the culture or tendance of the soul or spirit, the ψυχῆς ἐπιμέλεια or θεραπεία (cf. *Apol.* 30B), and 'philosophy' for Socrates meant just that. In fact, the interpretation which he put upon this dream, until in the last days he substituted a different one, is precisely that which he conceived as his divine mission according to the *Apology*: 'God laid upon me, so I thought and believed, the duty of living a life of philosophy, examining both myself and others' (τοῦ θεοῦ τάττοντος, ὡς ἐγὼ ᾠήθην καὶ ὑπέλαβον, φιλοσοφοῦντά με δεῖν ζῆν καὶ ἐξετάζοντα ἐμαυτὸν καὶ τοὺς ἄλλους, 28E).[2]

'Say good-bye to Evenus for me': a natural message: but one may doubt whether the rest of the message was actually given. In any case it serves neatly to introduce the paradoxical doctrine that death is for the philosopher a consummation devoutly to be wished, and to suggest, through Simmias's comment, that the real philosopher is not such an one as Evenus.

In defending the prohibition of suicide as reasonable, Socrates first appeals to a doctrine which from another dialogue (*Cratylus* 400C) we know to have belonged to the sect called Orphic, to the effect that 'we are in a sort of prison'; that is to say, the gods have imprisoned our souls in our bodies until (as the *Cratylus* passage puts it) 'they have paid the penalty that they owe'. This probably implies the injunction not to attempt to escape, though there appears to be no other passage where this is recorded as an Orphic injunction. A Peripatetic writer of the early third century B.C., however, Clearchus, is quoted[3] as ascribing it to a Pythagorean source, and we shall probably be safe in regarding the whole religious doctrine referred to at 62B as both Orphic and Pythagorean.[4] The closely allied doctrine of the body as the *tomb* of the soul (σῶμα σῆμα) appears from the *Cratylus* passage and from *Gorgias* 493A to have been Pythagorean rather than Orphic.

---

[1] *Rep.* 399D.

[2] It may be noted that, agreeably to the notion of philosophy as the highest music, the *Phaedrus* (259D) makes Calliope, the eldest of the Muses, and her next sister Urania the patrons of philosophers.

[3] Athenaeus IV, 157C=DK, I, p. 414.

[4] It seems probable that the early Pythagoreans took over many of their religious beliefs from Orphism; certainly many are common to Orphism and Pythagoreanism, and where there was borrowing it was probably the Pythagoreans who borrowed. See Ziegler's article *Orphische Dichtung* in Pauly-Wissowa, *RE* XVIII, 2 and Dodds, *op. cit.* p. 149.

III

To Cebes and Simmias it seems strange that a philosopher, or indeed any man of intelligence, should be well content to die; for death must mean parting from the gods who have been his kindly masters throughout life. Socrates replies with a declaration of faith that after death he will still be under divine protection; death is not the end: there is a future, and a better one for the good than for the evil.

Called upon to explain and justify his faith, Socrates begins by declaring that the whole life of a true philosopher is a training for death—a doctrine at which, as Simmias remarks, the vulgar will gibe, but only because they do not understand it. They indeed may be ignored; but Socrates must explain it to his friends.

'I think that is probably right', said Cebes. 'But to go back to your 62C point, that a philosopher will be ready and willing to die, that strikes me as astonishing, Socrates, if there is good ground for saying, as we did D just now, that there is a god who looks after us, and that we are his possessions. That men of high intelligence should not complain at having to leave a service in which theirs were the best of all masters, the gods, is not reasonable; they can hardly suppose that they will look after themselves better than their former masters did. No: only an unintelligent person could possibly have the idea that he ought to escape from his owner, not stopping to think that a good owner is not one to run away E from, but to stay with if one possibly can: hence he will only run away because he doesn't stop to think, whereas any man of sense would desire always to be with one better than himself. Yet that seems to point to the opposite of what we were saying just now, Socrates: it behoves the intelligent to complain of dying, and the unintelligent to rejoice.'

On hearing this Socrates seemed to me to be delighted with Cebes's insistence; glancing at us he remarked, 'Cebes is for ever hunting up 63 arguments, you know: he is not exactly inclined to believe promptly everything he is told.' At this Simmias put in a word: 'But in point of fact I think, myself, there is something in what Cebes says this time: for why should men who are truly wise want to run away from masters better than themselves? Why should they lightly get rid of them?'

Moreover I fancy that Cebes is pointing his argument at yourself, for taking so lightly your separation from us and from the gods whom you yourself acknowledge as your good rulers.'

B 'A just remark', he replied. 'I think what you both mean is that I ought to defend myself on this charge as I would in a court of law.'

'Exactly', said Simmias.

'Come then, let me attempt a more convincing defence before you than I made before the court. If I did not believe, Simmias and Cebes, that I shall find myself in the presence of other gods both wise and good, and moreover of men better than those that still live on earth, then I should be wrong not to complain of death. But as it is, rest assured

C that I expect to join the company of good men, though that indeed I will not affirm with full certainty; but that I shall come to be with gods that are the best of masters, yes: you may rest assured that, if there is one thing that I will affirm in such a matter, it is that. And for that reason I am the less disposed to complain, but am of good hope that there is a future for those that have died, and, as indeed we have long been told, a far better future for the good than for the evil.'

'What then, Socrates?' said Simmias. 'Do you propose to keep these ideas to yourself, or will you let us share in them before you leave us?

D I really think this is a blessing in which we have a right to share: and moreover if you can persuade us of what you say, that defence you spoke of will be achieved.'

'Well, I will try. But first let us see what it is that Crito here has for some time, I fancy, been wanting to say.'

'Simply this, Socrates,' said Crito, 'that the officer who is to administer the poison has for some time been telling me that I ought to warn you to have as little conversation as possible; his point is that one gets heated by talking too much, and we mustn't let anything heating inter-

E fere with the draught; if anything of that sort happens, it is sometimes necessary to take a second or even a third dose.'

'Never mind about him', rejoined Socrates; 'just let him make his own arrangements for administering two, or if need be, three doses.'

'I was pretty sure you would say that', said Crito; 'only the man has been bothering me for some while.'

'Let him be.[1] But to you, my judges, I wish now to give my grounds

---

[1] The little interlude of 63 D–E may well be factual, but in any case it serves to show that Socrates was not to be deterred by considerations of convenience from pursuing an argument.

for thinking that a man who has truly spent his life in philosophy has good reason to be confident when he is about to die, and to be of good 64 hope that when life is over he will secure very great blessings. Now therefore, Simmias and Cebes, I will endeavour to explain how that can be so. It is probable that people in general do not realise that all those who betake themselves to philosophy in the right way are engaged[1] in one thing only, namely training themselves for dying and being dead. Now if that is true, it would surely be absurd to devote the energy of a lifetime to that one end, and then, when it had come, to complain of that for which they had all the time been so energetically training.'

Simmias laughed at this: 'Upon my word, Socrates,' he said, 'you make me laugh, though I wasn't feeling much disposed to mirth B a moment ago. I fancy that most people, hearing what you have just said, would think—and my own countrymen would emphatically agree—that it hit off the philosophers very aptly: it is a fact, they would say, that such folk want to die,[2] and we are well aware that they deserve it.'

'Yes, and they would say that with truth, Simmias, except for the last point: for the multitude are not well aware in what sense the true philosopher wants to die, and in what sense he deserves to die, and what manner of death. Then let us not bother about the multitude, but C talk it over amongst ourselves.'

Socrates begins his 'defence' against a new charge, of ungrounded confidence in face of death, before a jury of good friends, with a declaration of faith so strong that he can use the strong word διισχυρίζεσθαι of it. He is certain that after death he will 'find himself in the presence of other gods both wise and good'. This is of course far from an assertion that the soul is immortal, in the sense of not belonging to a temporal order at all, or even that it will survive

---

[1] I leave αὐτοί in A 5 untranslated, as I think it is inserted simply to underline the contrast with τοὺς ἄλλους. Burnet, however, takes it to mean 'of their own accord', and that may be right.

[2] I do not understand why Burnet says 'this is not the meaning required here' and renders θανατῶσι by 'are moribund'. Surely θανατῶσι echoes the προθυμεῖσθαι μηδὲν ἄλλο ἢ τοῦτο (sc. ἀποθνῄσκειν τε καὶ τεθνάναι) of 64 A 7. The same meaning is found in the pseudo-Platonic *Axiochus* (366 C) and in the comic poet Alexis, *frag.* 211 (Kock). But I agree with Burnet's explanation of the Thebans' attitude: 'we have here a reflexion of the impression made by the Pythagorean refugees on the *bons vivants* of Thebes. The φιλόσοφοι would not appreciate Copaic eels and ducks.'

throughout all time. But it does at least mean that the possibility of death bringing no more than a 'dreamless sleep'—one of the alternatives suggested in the *Apology* (40C)—is rejected; εὐελπίς εἰμι εἶναί τι τοῖς τετελευτηκόσι: the dead 'have a future' as he here says with intentional vagueness. He is also confident that it will be a better future for the righteous than for the wicked.

These beliefs will gain in definiteness as we proceed; but it is well to realise now that for the Platonic Socrates, and for Plato himself, the *manner* of the soul's discarnate existence is always a matter of faith, not of knowledge, and one for the most part dealt with in myth. At bottom Socrates's faith is in the moral order of the universe, which demands that a good life on earth should have some reward hereafter; but he, or Plato, is to some extent influenced by the teaching of the Eleusinian mysteries, which promised bliss to the initiated, and even more by Orphic teaching, which held out a hope of the soul's restoration to its original purity and divinity; but most of all, in this dialogue at least, by the Pythagorean demand for moral and intellectual purification of the soul as a substitute for ritual cleansings, initiations and observance of taboos; all these sources or influences may be implied in the words 'as indeed we have long been told' (63c).

One puzzling passage here is that in which Socrates expresses doubt as to his dwelling hereafter in the company of good men (63 B–C). In the *Apology* (41 A–C) he had spoken of this possibility in a tone approaching levity, though with an undercurrent of seriousness: how good it would be to meet in the after-life with other victims of unjust condemnation, and especially to find famous heroes of old time on whom he might practise his art of critical examination! Whether these words do or do not represent what was said at the trial, there is nothing in the *Phaedo* to suggest that one who has died continues in the same activities as before; and I think it probable that Socrates's doubt here is not whether he will still be able to practise his ἐξέτασις, nor yet whether his soul will dwell with the souls of others departed, but rather whether those whose company he will join will be better than those he knew on earth. It is clear from a later passage (69D) that he conceived that his own life had been that of a true philosopher; he would therefore hope that hereafter he would be in the company of philosophers, a company certainly 'better' than that of men who had not practised the μελέτη θανάτου: but of course he would not confidently affirm this.

This interpretation assumes that the emphasis in 63 B 4 is on ἀμείνους τῶν ἐνθάδε rather than on ἀνθρώπους, and in C I on ἀγαθούς rather than on ἄνδρας: also that ἀμείνους τῶν ἐνθάδε means 'better than the common run of men in this world'. Others, however, may prefer to rest content with Archer-Hind's comment: 'Socrates does not feel sure enough as to the exact condition of souls after death to make any positive statement about their association with one another.'

After the little interlude with Crito, Socrates announces (63 E) in careful language the account (λόγος) which he proposes to give to his new judges of his confidence in the hour of death. The giving of this account is to occupy almost the whole remainder of the dialogue; it will obviously involve a vindication of his belief in the soul's continued existence.

IV

64 C–67 B THE PHILOSOPHER'S DETACHMENT
FROM THE BODY

At death soul and body are separated, but the philosopher will anticipate this separation so far as may be during his life. Setting no value upon bodily adornments and physical pleasures, he will seek to attain intelligence (φρόνησις); in this, body is a hindrance, for the activity is that of the soul by itself; 'the just itself', 'the beautiful itself' and other like objects are not to be apprehended by any of our senses.

The section ends with an impassioned declaration of faith put into the mouth of an imaginary philosopher, in which the opposition of body and soul is given heightened expression: the soul must be purified from the body's infection. Such purification can only be fully achieved at death; but the life of the true philosopher will be a preparation for and an approximation to it.

64 C 'Do we believe there is such a thing as death?'

'Undoubtedly', replied Simmias.

'And by death do we not mean simply the departure of soul from body? Being dead consists, does it not, in the body having been parted from the soul and come to be by itself, and in the soul having been parted from the body, and being by itself. Can death possibly be anything other than that?'

'No, it can only be that.'[1]

'Well now, turn your mind to this, and perhaps you will find you
D share my view. I think we shall make some progress in our inquiry if

---

[1] The definition of death as the parting of soul and body has already occurred at *Gorg.* 524 B, and doubtless represents the normal contemporary view. It was retained by Democritus (DK 68 A 106), by the Stoics (Chrysippus apud *Sto. Vet. Frag.* II, 790), and by the Epicureans (Lucr. III, 838 f.). It is true that Cicero (*Tusc. Disp.* I, 9, 18) says 'sunt qui discessum animi a corpore putent esse mortem: sunt qui nullum censeant fieri discessum, sed una animum et corpus occidere, animumque in corpore extingui'; but the context suggests that this rests, at least so far as fifth- to fourth-century views are concerned, on a misinterpretation of Empedocles's words αἷμα γὰρ ἀνθρώποις περικάρδιόν ἐστι νόημα. It must, however, be added that Simmias's assent to the definition is hardly to be reconciled with his belief (85 E ff.) that the soul is an 'attunement' of the bodily constituents.

The definition does not, of course, prejudge the question of the soul's survival; all that Socrates here wants is an admission that we can properly think and speak of soul 'apart' from body; whether soul continues to exist when thus apart is the question at issue.

we start like this: Do you regard it as befitting a philosopher to devote himself to the so-called pleasures of, let us say, food and drink?'

'No indeed, Socrates', Simmias replied.

'What about the pleasures of sex?'

'Certainly not.'

'And what about all the other ministrations to bodily needs? Does that type of man set a high value on them, do you think? The possession of elegant clothes and shoes, for example, and other such bodily adornments: does he value them, or does he despise anything beyond the absolutely necessary minimum of such things?' E

'The true philosopher, I should say, despises them.'

'In general terms, then, would you say that such a man's concern is not for the body, but, so far as he can detach himself from the body, is directed towards the soul?'

'Yes, I should.'

'Is it not then primarily in such things as we have mentioned that the philosopher manifests his effort to release his soul from association 65 with his body to a degree that surpasses that of the rest of mankind?'

'Evidently.'

'And may we not add, Simmias, that in the eyes of the multitude the life of one who finds no pleasure in such things, and has no part or lot in them, is not worth living? One who pays no regard to the pleasures which come by way of the body has, they would say, one foot in the grave.'

'Yes indeed, you are perfectly right.'

'And now as regards the actual[1] attainment of intelligence: if we bring in the body as the soul's partner in our quest, is it a hindrance or B not? To illustrate what I mean, is there any truth conveyed to mankind by seeing and hearing: or are not even[2] the poets always harping on the

---

[1] αὐτήν, because the attainment of φρόνησις or σοφία is the direct concern of the φιλόσοφος, as his name implies.

[2] 'Even' the poets, because in Plato's view poets are not given to discerning the truth. What poets Plato has in mind here we cannot tell. Olympiodorus's suggestions (see Burnet's note) do not seem to me helpful; I agree with Burnet that a reference to Parmenides or Empedocles is unlikely; Epicharmus's line νοῦς ὁρῇ καὶ νοῦς ἀκούει· τἆλλα κωφὰ καὶ τυφλά (DK 23 B 2) is not near enough to what Socrates says, and this objection applies even more strongly to Homer, Iliad v, 127-8. It seems to me likely, despite the generalising words οἱ ποιηταὶ ἀεὶ θρυλοῦσιν, that Plato is thinking of some particular line or lines in which the two senses of seeing and hearing (and no others) are mentioned, and which probably contained the word ἀκριβής (e.g. κλύομεν ἀκριβὲς οὐδὲν οὐδὲ λεύσσομεν). That something like this had often been said by poets we may well believe, when we remember how much Greek poetry is lost.

theme that we neither hear nor see anything accurately? Yet if these two bodily senses are not accurate nor reliable, it is hardly likely that the rest are, since they are presumably inferior to these, as I expect you will agree.'

'Certainly they are.'

'Then when does the soul attain truth? For it is plain that when accompanied by the body in its attempts to inquire into things it is utterly deceived thereby.'

c 'True.'

'If then any part of reality is ever revealed to it, must it not be when it reasons?'[1]

'Yes.'

'Furthermore reasoning is, I suppose, at its best when none of those senses intrudes to trouble the soul, neither hearing nor sight nor pain nor pleasure;[2] when it is, so far as may be, alone by itself, taking leave of the body, and having as little communion and contact as possible therewith while it reaches out after reality.'

'That is so.'

D 'Then here again[3] the philosopher's soul utterly despises his body and flees from it, seeking to be alone by itself.'

'Clearly so.'

'And now a further question, Simmias. We maintain, do we not, that there is such a thing as "the just itself"?'

'Yes indeed, we certainly do.'

'And a "beautiful itself" and a "good itself"?'

'Of course.'

'Well, have you ever seen anything of that sort with your eyes?'

'Of course not.'

'Then have you apprehended them with some other bodily sense? I mean the *being* of things in general, greatness, health, strength, or whatever else it may be: in short I mean the *reality* of this or that; is

---

[1] Burnet renders ἐν τῷ λογίζεσθαι by 'in mathematical reasoning', remarking that the primary sense of the verb is 'calculate'. But in 65 E–66 A it seems clear that no distinction is intended between διάνοια (διανοεῖσθαι) and λογισμός, and in 66 B 4 μετὰ τοῦ λόγου echoes the μετὰ τοῦ λογισμοῦ of A 1. I therefore take λογίζεσθαι to have here, as often elsewhere, the sense of reasoning in general.

[2] Pleasure and pain are not, of course, acts of sensation co-ordinate with hearing and seeing; but bodily pleasures and pains (i.e. strictly speaking, those which come *through* the body, διὰ τοῦ σώματος, 65 A 7) are consequent upon such acts.

[3] As before, in the matter of bodily pleasures (64 D ff.).

the full truth of them beheld through our bodies, or is it the fact that E those of us that have trained ourselves to think most fully and precisely of the object in question, in and by itself, will come closest to knowing that object?'

'Yes, certainly.'

'Then the clearest knowledge will surely be attained by one who approaches the object so far as possible by thought, and thought alone, not permitting sight or any other sense to intrude upon his thinking, not dragging in any sense as accompaniment to reason: one who sets 66 himself to track down each constituent of reality purely and simply as it is by means of thought pure and simple: one who gets rid, so far as possible, of eyes and ears and, broadly speaking, of the body altogether, knowing that when the body is the soul's partner it confuses the soul and prevents it from coming to possess truth and intelligence. Is it not such a man, Simmias, that will grasp that which really is?'

'What you say, Socrates,' replied Simmias, 'is profoundly true.'

'On all these grounds then, must not genuine philosophers find B themselves holding the sort of belief which will lead them to say, one to another, something like this: "It would seem that we are guided as it were along a track to our goal by the fact that,[1] so long as we have the body accompanying our reason in its inquiries,[2] so long as our souls are befouled by this evil admixture, we shall assuredly never fully possess that which we desire, to wit truth. For by reason of the nurture which it must have, the body makes countless demands upon us, and furthermore any sickness that may befall it hampers our pursuit of true C being. Then too it fills us with desires and longings and fears and imaginations of all sorts, and such quantities of trash, that, as the common saying puts it, we really never have a moment to think about anything because of the body. Why, what else is it that causes war and faction and fighting but the body and its desires? It is always to acquire riches that men go to war, and the necessity of acquiring them is due to

---

[1] Both Archer-Hind and Burnet take ὅτι to mean 'because': I prefer to take it as introducing the substantival clause which is the grammatical subject of κινδυνεύει.

[2] I accept Schleiermacher's transposition of μετὰ τοῦ λόγου ἐν τῇ σκέψει to follow ἔχωμεν in the next line. Burnet thinks it 'more likely that they are a marginal note on ἔχωμεν which has got into the wrong place', but ἔχωμεν seems to me to need some such supplement. I prefer the transposition to Prof. Verdenius's suggestion (*Mnemosyne* (1933), p. 92) of taking μετὰ τοῦ λόγου as = καὶ τὸν λόγον, though it is true that, as he says, Plato often represents the λόγος as a companion of the personages of his dialogues.

D the servile attention that we pay to the body. And so, for all these reasons, we have no leisure for philosophy; but the worst trouble of all is that, if we do get a respite from the body's demands, and embark on some investigation, it obtrudes itself at every point of our inquiries, confusing, disturbing and alarming us, and so preventing us from discerning truth.

E "However, this fact is manifest to us: if we are to have clear knowledge of anything, we must get rid of the body, and let the soul by itself behold objects by themselves. And one day, we may suppose, that intelligence which we desire and whose lovers we claim to be will be ours: not while we yet live, as our argument shows, but when we have died. For if we cannot come clearly to know anything when united to the body, there are two alternatives: either the attainment of knowledge is altogether impossible for us, or it can be ours after death; for then, 67 and only then, will our souls be by themselves, apart from our bodies. While we are alive we shall, it would seem, come nearest to knowledge if we have as little as possible to do with the body, if we limit our association therewith to absolute necessities, keeping ourselves pure and free from bodily infection until such time as God himself shall release us. And being thus made pure and rid of the body's follies we B may expect to join the company of the purified, and have direct knowledge of all truth unobscured;[1] for that the impure should apprehend the pure heaven will hardly permit."

'In such a strain I think, Simmias, must all those that love knowledge rightly address each other, and such must be their belief. Do you agree?'

'Unquestionably, Socrates.'

The conception of the mind or soul (ψυχή) and the body as hostile to each other, which runs through this section, goes further than anything said by the Socrates of the *Apology*. He there says 'What I do as I go about amongst you is simply to urge both young and old not to make their bodies nor their possessions their primary and chief concern, but rather to strive for the fullest perfection of their souls' (30 A–B). Xenophon depicts him as something of an ascetic (e.g. in *Mem.* I, vi, 2 ζῆς οὕτως ὡς οὐδ' ἂν εἷς δοῦλος ὑπὸ δεσπότῃ διαιτώμενος· σῖτά τε σιτῇ καὶ ποτὰ πίνεις τὰ φαυλότατα κ.τ.λ. and makes him lay special emphasis on the virtue of ἐγκράτεια, mastery of physical appetite,

[1] I follow Archer-Hind in excising the words τοῦτο δ' ἐστὶν ἴσως τὸ ἀληθές as a gloss on τὸ εἰλικρινές: they are surely intolerable as part of the text.

declaring this to be the foundation of moral goodness (ἀρετῆς κρηπῖδα I, v, 4); Plato makes Alcibiades enlarge upon his endurance or toughness (καρτερία) and disregard of bodily pain and discomfort, as also upon his power to resist sexual temptation. But, outside the *Phaedo*, his general attitude does not seem to be that of an enemy of the 'flesh' and its pleasures; he can on occasion enjoy his wine, and drink with the best; but he is, in the Greek phrase, 'master of himself' (κρείττων αὑτοῦ), one who is not to be *overcome* by pleasure (ἥττων ἡδονῆς).[1]

The aim ascribed to the true philosopher in our present section— the greatest possible detachment of soul from body—is then a Platonic rather than a Socratic doctrine. And it is one which Plato never wholly abandoned, though he never elsewhere proclaims it with quite so much fervour. Yet later dialogues, particularly the *Republic*, modify it considerably; in the first place the *Republic* enjoins a training in 'gymnastic' upon the Guardians (of whom the philosopher-rulers are an *élite*), though rather for the effect which it will have on their souls than for the sake of the body itself; in the second place, the simple contrast between good soul and evil (or at least contemptible and troublesome) body is replaced in *Republic*, *Phaedrus* and *Timaeus* by a recognition that the soul, at least ἐν τῷ ἀνθρωπίνῳ βίῳ (*Rep.* 612A), contains irrational elements; in the *Phaedrus* myth the horse which symbolises the lower of these elements is roundly called evil (253D). Moral conflict occurs within the soul in all dialogues from the *Republic* onwards; it is not a simple conflict between soul and body, though the *Timaeus* (86B–D) recognises that some[2] disorders of the soul arise from bad conditions of the body. In the *Laws* (896E) we hear not merely of an irrational or evil element in the soul, but of actual irrational or maleficent souls; but it may be doubted whether Plato intends this as a serious philosophical doctrine: despite the great importance attached to it by later Platonists, this doctrine occurs nowhere else in the dialogues, and in any case Plato is not there speaking of human souls.

Nor is the human body, particularly in the *Timaeus*, regarded any longer as contemptible; much of that work is devoted to explaining and extolling its functions and purposes; while of the body of the universe, the direct creation of the Demiurge, there is naturally no word of dispraise. Nevertheless there are passages, even in the dialogues which proclaim these modifications of the *Phaedo* antithesis, where the human body continues to be regarded as something which hampers the soul's activity, and even as the source of its disorder and corruption. In *Republic* X (611C) the soul is described as marred (λελωβημένον) by association with the body; at *Timaeus* 43B–C we are given a picture

---

[1] Cf. Xen. *Mem.* IV, v, 11 δοκεῖ μοι, ὦ Σώκρατες, λέγειν ὡς ἀνδρὶ ἥττονι τῶν διὰ τοῦ σώματος ἡδονῶν πάμπαν οὐδεμιᾶς ἀρετῆς προσήκει.

[2] Not all: see Cornford, *ad loc.* (*Plato's Cosmology*, pp. 346ff.).

HPP

of the soul in infancy assailed and disturbed by physical motions which pass into it through the body; while in the myth of the *Politicus* (273 B) it is the bodily element in the universe (τὸ σωματοειδὲς τῆς συγκράσεως) that causes it, in its reverse revolution, to forget the instructions of its creator and father.

At 65 D, where Socrates asks Simmias whether we maintain 'that there is such a thing as the just itself' and receives an emphatically affirmative answer, we have the first mention of the famous Theory of Forms. I call it a mention rather than a statement, since the existence of the Forms is not argued for, but taken as a datum, and it is not their existence that is stressed but the fact that they cannot be apprehended by the bodily senses, but only by the soul itself.

Despite Prof. Grube's careful analysis[1] of the various mentions or uses of the Forms in the *Phaedo*, I cannot agree with his contention that the common view, namely that the theory is represented as familiar to Simmias, and probably to all or most of those present, is wrong.[2] But I do not think the point is of great importance: for if we hold, as almost all present-day scholars hold, that Socrates had no metaphysical doctrine whatever, the sharing of any metaphysical beliefs with his friends must be as fictitious as the ascription to Socrates himself. The reason for this fictitious sharing in the present passage is surely that Plato does not wish to divert his readers' attention from the point of immediate interest, the soul's activity αὐτῆς καθ' αὑτήν: and such diversion would inevitably have resulted if Simmias had asked: 'What on earth do you mean by the just itself, or the beautiful and good themselves?'

The fiction of a shared metaphysical doctrine recurs at one or two points in the sequel, when successive aspects and implications of the Theory of Forms are touched upon by Socrates; thus at 74B, where the transcendent character of the Forms is plainly asserted, Simmias assents even more emphatically than in our present passage, where it is at most implied. Again, Cebes has often heard Socrates assert his theory of Recollection (72E), though Simmias has rather forgotten

---

[1] *Plato's Thought*, Appendix I.

[2] One of his arguments is based on the theory later put forward by Simmias, that the soul is a ἁρμονία: he contends that 'such a conception of the soul could not have been held by anyone who was acquainted with the epistemological implications of the theory of Forms'. But at 77A, when Socrates has fully expounded his theory of ἀνάμνησις, Simmias emphatically proclaims his acceptance of the existence of πάντα τὰ τοιαῦτα...καλόν τε καὶ ἀγαθὸν καὶ τἆλλα πάντα ἃ σὺ νυνδὴ ἔλεγες, and his conviction that the soul's pre-natal existence stands or falls with theirs. Is not this an acceptance of the epistemological implications in question? And yet he can bring forward his ἁρμονία theory afterwards, at 85 E. That Simmias, or at least the Simmias of this dialogue, was a man who could simultaneously hold two beliefs without realising their inconsistency, is plain from 92A.

about it—this latter point being obviously made in order to give Socrates an excuse for expounding it fully. But for the most part such devices are deemed unnecessary: everything is explained and expounded as if it were something fresh to these interlocutors; in short, the fiction of a common doctrine is used by Plato when it is convenient, while at other times it is quietly dropped.

I have said that the transcendent character of the Forms is at most implied in this passage, and it must be added that the terms εἶδος and ἰδέα are not yet used, and will not be used (as Prof. Grube has pointed out) until 103 E. I do not think any great significance need be attached to the latter point, but as to the former it is difficult to decide whether or not the language of 65 D–E necessarily implies that 'the just itself', etc., is an entity existing apart from the just actions which it informs. If we decide that this is not necessarily implied, it will be best to say that we have not as yet come to the actual theory of Forms, of which transcendence (χωρισμός) is an essential feature.[1] But in any case we are more than half-way towards it, and shall very soon find it openly proclaimed. As to the other main part of the theory, namely that sensible objects in some way partake of the Forms (cf. *Parmenides* 130B χωρὶς μὲν εἴδη αὐτὰ ἄττα, χωρὶς δὲ τὰ τούτων αὖ μετέχοντα), this does not come up until 100 D, and the actual words for 'partaking' (μετάσχεσις, μετέχειν, μεταλαμβάνειν) do not occur until 101 C. This I believe to be due not to the necessity of initiating Simmias and Cebes, or the reader, gradually into the full doctrine, but to the fact that not until then is it directly relevant to the argument.

---

[1] As Aristotle tells us: *Met.* 1078 B 30, 1086 B 1 ff.; cf. Ross, *Metaphysics of Aristotle*, I, Introd. p. xxxiv.

V

67B–69E MORAL VIRTUE, GENUINE AND SPURIOUS

Summing up the preceding argument, and applying it to his own case, Socrates reaffirms his confidence in face of death: he is not so foolish as to complain at the approach of that for which his whole life has been a preparation. Many have died by their own hand that they might rejoin their loved ones who have passed away: will not the lover of wisdom be equally ready to pass to another world, that he may behold and enjoy that wisdom which he cannot fully attain in this world?

Socrates proceeds to contrast the philosopher with the 'lover of the body', and to show that the moral virtues as practised by the latter are spurious and self-contradictory. All true virtue involves intelligence (φρόνησις), which is declared to be a purge (καθαρμός) to rid the soul of the body's taint.

67B   'Well then, my friend,' said Socrates, 'if that is true, I may well hope that when I have reached the place whither I am bound I shall attain in full measure, there at last, that for which I have spent the effort of C a lifetime; wherefore it is with good hope that I set out upon the journey now appointed for me, as may any man who deems that his mind[1] is made ready and purified.'

'Yes indeed', said Simmias.

'So purification turns out, does it not, to consist in just what we have been discussing for some time past,[2] in separating so far as may be the soul from the body, and habituating it to assemble and gather itself together from every region of the body,[3] so as to dwell alone and apart, so far as possible, both in this present life and in the life to come, D released from the body's fetters.'

'Certainly.'

---

[1] The use of διάνοια here, rather than ψυχή, brings out the cognitive conception of the soul which predominates in this part of the dialogue.

[2] For the meaning of ὅπερ πάλαι ἐν τῷ λόγῳ λέγεται see J. V. Luce in *C.R.* (June 1951), pp. 66f.

[3] This is perhaps the most materialistic language used by Socrates about the soul in the whole dialogue. Taken literally, it would imply the spatial diffusion of a sort of vital fluid throughout the body; but of course it must not be taken literally, but rather as a vivid metaphor to bring out the completeness of the soul's detachment.

'Then what we call death is a releasing or separation[1] of soul from body?'

'Undoubtedly.'

'Moreover they that strive unceasingly for this release are, so we maintain, none other than those that pursue philosophy aright; indeed this and nothing else is the philosopher's concern, the release and separation of soul from body. It is not so?'

'Plainly it is.'

'Hence, to repeat what I said at the outset, it would be ridiculous that a man should spend his life in a way that brought him as near as possible E to being dead, and then complain of death when it came.'

'Ridiculous indeed.'

'Then it is true, Simmias, that the real philosophers train for dying, and to be dead is for them less terrible than for all other men. Look at it like this: if their continual quarrel with the body, their desire to have the soul by itself, were to result in fear and complaint when that is achieved, how unreasonable it would be! How unreasonable not to be 68 glad to go to a place where they may hope to get what they have longed for all their lives, to wit intelligence, and to be rid of the presence of their old enemy! Why, there have been not a few persons ready and willing to descend into Hades in quest of a lost wife or son or darling, led by the hope of beholding and rejoining their loved ones in another world:[2] shall then he who truly loves not any human object, but intelligence, and has conceived this same lively hope that in that other world, and there alone, he will attain it in full measure, shall he, I say, B complain when death comes? Shall he not rather depart in gladness? We must needs think so, if he is in truth, dear Simmias, a philosopher; for

[1] What at 64 c was called an ἀπαλλαγή, a *parting* of soul from body, has now become a λύσις καὶ χωρισμός. The latter word does not add much to the notion of ἀπαλλαγή, and indeed χωρίς was used at 64 c 6; the operative word is λύσις, *releasing*, which sums up in itself much of what has intervened.

[2] Burnet remarks that in *Symp.* 179 B ff. 'Alcestis, Eurydice and Patroclus are examples of human loves whom men have gone to seek beyond the grave.' But this is quite untrue as regards Alcestis; while as to Eurydice, Orpheus, we are told, was too cowardly to die in order to rejoin her, but contriving to enter Hades alive came empty away; and Achilles, who courted early death by slaying Hector, is not represented as doing this from a desire to *rejoin* Patroclus, but to avenge him. Hence it is unlikely that Plato is thinking of any of these figures. More to the point would be Evadne (Eur. *Suppl.* 985 ff.) or Jocasta (Eur. *Phoen.* 1455 ff.): Evadne is suggested by Olympiodorus. On such suicides see R. Hirzel's paper on *Der Selbstmord* in *Archiv für Religionswissenschaft* XI (1908), especially pp. 78 f.

he will be very sure that only in that other world can he attain to intelligence in purity, and that being so, would it not, I repeat, be utterly unreasonable for such a man to fear death?'

'Yes, to be sure; utterly unreasonable.'

'Then if you see a man about to die complaining, is not that good evidence that he is not really a philosopher, a lover of wisdom, but c what we may call a lover of the body? And probably he will be a lover of riches too, or of honours, or maybe of both.'

'Yes, you are quite right.'

'Tell me then, Simmias: is not what is called courage notably characteristic of the type we have been describing?'

'Assuredly.'

'And what of temperance,[1] I mean the quality which is so named in common parlance, the sober attitude of one who disdains to be excited by his desires? Isn't that also characteristic of these men alone, these who utterly disdain the body and live in the pursuit of wisdom?'

D   'It must be.'

'Yes: and if you will give a moment's thought to the courage and temperance of other people, you will find them astonishing.'

'How so, Socrates?'

'You know, do you not, that all other people count death as a great evil?'

'Yes indeed.'

'And isn't it because they fear some greater evil that those of them who are brave face death firmly, when they do?'

'Yes.'

'Then it is through fear, through being afraid, that anyone who is not a philosopher is brave: yet surely it is illogical that a man should be brave through fear and cowardice?'

E   'It certainly is.'

'Again, doesn't the same thing hold good of such as are of sober conduct,[2] doesn't their temperance spring from a sort of profligacy? Of course people say that is impossible: nevertheless it is a fact that something like that does happen to those who are temperate in the

---

[1] It is commonly acknowledged that σωφροσύνη is an untranslatable word: I think it is best therefore to retain the traditional 'temperance', as Adam does in his edition of the *Rep.* and Cornford in his translation. Nettleship has 'self-control': that is better kept for ἐγκράτεια, but it is true that the two Greek words overlap in meaning.

[2] κόσμιοι is used as a synonym of σώφρονες.

naïve fashion we refer to; they abstain from one sort of pleasure simply because the longing for another sort, and the fear of losing it, are too strong for them to resist. Of course to be mastered by pleasures is what they call profligacy: nevertheless the fact is that they master one kind 69 of pleasure only because they are mastered by another; which amounts to what we said just now, namely that in a sense they have attained temperance as the result of profligacy.'

'So it seems.'

'Yes, my dear good Simmias: for I fancy that that is not the right way to exchange things for virtue, that exchanging of pleasures for pleasures, pains for pains, fears for fears, small ones for great and great ones for small, as though they were coins; no, there is, I suggest, only one right sort of coin for which we ought to exchange all these things, and that is intelligence; and if all our buying and selling[1] is done *for* B intelligence and *with* its aid, then we have real courage, real temperance, real justice; and true virtue in general is that which is accompanied by intelligence, no matter whether pleasures and fears and all the rest of such things be added or subtracted. But to keep these apart from intelligence and merely exchange them for each other results, I fear, in a sort of illusory façade of virtue, veritably fit for slaves, destitute of all sound substance and truth; whereas the true virtue, whether it be of temperance, of justice, or of courage, is in fact a purging of all such C things, intelligence itself being a sort of purge.[2] And it may well be that those[3] persons to whom we owe the institution of mystery-rites are not to be despised, inasmuch as they have in fact long ago hinted at the truth by declaring that all such as arrive in Hades uninitiated into the rites shall lie in mud,[4] while he that comes there purified and initiated shall dwell with the gods. For truly, as their authorities tell us, there are

Many that carry the wand, but Bacchants few are amongst them;

where by 'Bacchants' I understand them to mean simply those who D have pursued philosophy aright; to be numbered amongst whom I have

---

[1] The linguistic objections to ὠνούμενα and πιπρασκόμενα seem sufficiently answered by J. V. Luce in *C.Q.* (Jan.–Apr. 1944), pp. 60f.

[2] On the passage 69 A 6–C 2 see Additional Notes (pp. 191 ff.).

[3] In οὗτοι Burnet finds a 'touch of ironical condescension characteristically Socratic'. I think rather that its force is 'these whom the mention of κάθαρσις and καθαρμός brings to my mind'.

[4] The burying in mud is an Orphic punishment referred to again at *Rep.* 363 D as taught by 'Musaeus and his son'. See Burnet's note here; also Guthrie, *Orpheus and Greek Religion*, pp. 160 and 243.

bent all the effort of a lifetime, leaving nothing undone that was within my power. Whether that effort was well directed and has had any success I shall know for certain, if God will, when I come to the place to which I am going; and I think that will be very soon.

'There then is my defence, Simmias and Cebes, to show that it is not unreasonable for me to leave you and my masters in this world without E misgiving or complaint, inasmuch as I believe that I shall find good masters and friends yonder, just as I have found them here.[1] So now, if you find my defence more convincing than the Athenian court did, I shall be well content.'

The first half of this section is almost wholly resumptive, and calls for no comment. But new matter is introduced at 68 B 8, where Socrates begins to contrast the philosopher with the ordinary man from a moral rather than an intellectual point of view. He begins by suggesting that one who does not face death serenely is a 'lover of the body' (φιλοσώματος), and probably also a lover of riches, or honours, or both (φιλοχρήματος, φιλότιμος).

There is possibly an allusion here to the distinction of three types of men which Heraclides of Pontus[2] ascribed to Pythagoras: as at the festival of Olympia, there are some who come to buy and sell and make profit, some who contend for the prizes and honours, some who contemplate the scene as spectators. Prof. Jaeger, however, has given reasons[3] for doubting the ascription to Pythagoras, and thinks that the classification originated within the Academy; and certainly the distinction of τὸ φιλόσοφον γένος, τὸ φιλόνικον καὶ φιλότιμον, and τὸ φιλοκερδές is found, without any suggestion of Pythagorean origin, in *Republic* IX, 581. However this may be, the tripartition in *Rep.* IX is associated with the doctrine of tripartite soul elaborated in Book IV, whereas in our present passage we have rather a bipartition, corresponding to the ruling antithesis in our dialogue of unitary soul on the one hand and body on the other. The φιλοχρήματος and the φιλότιμος are merely aspects of the φιλοσώματος, and the same man may combine all three characters. It is certain, I think, that there is no implication here, as Burnet supposes, of a tripartite soul; nor indeed is this to be found anywhere in the *Phaedo.*[4]

The contrast between the philosopher and the 'lover of the body'

---

[1] I follow Archer-Hind and Burnet in bracketing the words τοῖς δὲ πολλοῖς ἀπιστίαν παρέχει for the reasons that Burnet gives.

[2] As reported by Cicero, *Tusc.* v, 3, 8. Cf. Iamblichus, *Vit. Pythag.* 58.

[3] *Aristotle* (E.T.), p. 98.

[4] See Frutiger, *Mythes de Platon*, pp. 77f.; G. M. A. Grube, *Plato's Thought*, p. 133; Dodds, *op. cit.* pp. 227f.

is developed by an account of the way in which they respectively exhibit the virtues of courage and temperance. It may surprise us that Socrates should say that the philosopher exhibits *what is called* courage and *what is recognised in common parlance* as temperance; for this might seem to deny him the true virtues in question. But the meaning, as appears shortly, is that these virtues, even as commonly conceived, involve an absence of fear and of lust for pleasure respectively, and only in the philosopher, who despises the body, are such fear and lust not found; their presence in other men involves a contradiction of the very conception of the virtues which they profess to exhibit; they are brave, as Socrates paradoxically puts it, through fear, and 'temperate' through profligacy.

But the mere absence of fear and lust is not enough to constitute true courage and true temperance; it is in fact (though Plato does not put it so) merely the negative aspect of these virtues. The positive aspect, the positive condition or constituent of all moral goodness, is intelligence (φρόνησις). The difficult passage 69 A–C, in which φρόνησις is described as the only coin which will purchase virtue, is followed immediately by a second metaphor (though this is less of a metaphor than the first): φρόνησις, and the moral virtues themselves as well, are a purging of all bodily desires and pleasures and fears. The soul thus purged or purified will (so we may interpret) be possessed by a passion for philosophy, a passion which will rule a man's whole life and conduct; it will provide a new scale of values; the philosopher not only acts rightly but is purged of all desire to act otherwise, because he knows 'justice itself, and beauty itself, and goodness itself': he knows with certainty—or at least with such certainty as can be attained in this present life—what is right and why it is right.

So Socrates, who all his life long has practised philosophy as thus conceived, ends his 'defence', his second *Apology*.

VI

Cebes now objects that what Socrates has been saying implies the continued existence of our souls and their retention of intelligence after death. This, as Socrates agrees, needs to be proved. We accordingly come to the first argument for immortality, which is briefly that wherever we have a pair of opposites they are generated from each other in a cycle of perpetual recurrence; 'living and dead' are therefore on a par with 'waking and sleeping', or with 'greater and smaller'. Moreover, in all such cases two opposite processes are involved; in the case before us one of these processes, dying, is an obvious occurrence, from which we may infer the occurrence of its opposite, returning to life.

69 E   To this speech of Socrates Cebes replied as follows:

'Most of what you have been saying, Socrates, seems to me excellent,
70 but your view about the soul is one that people find it very hard to accept; they suspect that, when it has left the body, it no longer exists anywhere; on the day when a man dies his soul is destroyed and annihilated; immediately upon its departure, its exit, it is dispersed like breath or smoke,[1] vanishing into thin air, and thereafter not existing anywhere at all. Of course if it could exist somewhere gathered together by itself, and quit of all the troubles which you were enumerating a while ago, then, Socrates, one might confidently cherish
B the hope that what you say is true; but to show that the soul exists when the man has died, and possesses some power and intelligence—well, that, I feel, needs a great deal of persuasive argument.'

'You are right, Cebes,' replied Socrates, 'but what then are we to do? Would you like to talk over[2] this particular point amongst ourselves, and see whether or not the thing is likely?'

---

[1] Homer speaks of the departing soul as 'smoke' (*Il.* XXIII, 100) and later in our dialogue (80 D) the belief that the soul is 'blown to pieces' is referred to as that of 'most people'.

[2] There are of course many passages in Plato where μῦθος is explicitly or implicitly contrasted with λόγος, as fictitious or imaginative discourse with true; but, as Frutiger remarks (*Mythes*, p. 17) there are also many passages where the distinction is not maintained, or the primary meanings are interchanged. The verb διαμυθολογεῖν appears to recur in Plato only at *Apol.* 39 E, where it seems

'At all events,' said Cebes, 'I should like to hear your opinion about it.'

'Well,' said Socrates, 'I don't think that anyone listening to me now, even were he a comic poet, could maintain that I am a vain babbler[1] who c talks about matters that don't concern him. If you agree then, we had better have a discussion; and we may put our question like this: do the souls of men that have departed this life exist in Hades or do they not? Now there is an ancient doctrine[2] that comes into my mind, that souls which have come from this world exist in the other, and conversely souls come and are born[3] into this world from the world of the dead. If that is so, if the living are reborn from those that have died, presumably our souls must exist yonder; for they could hardly be born again if they did not exist; and there you have good evidence for what D we have been saying, if it could be clearly demonstrated as a fact that the living originate from the dead, and only from the dead. But if that is not so, we shall need another argument.'

natural to take it, as well as the verb διαλέγεσθαι used a few lines earlier, as meaning simply to have a talk or discussion. Burnet on 61 E 2, where the simple verb μυθολογεῖν is used, says that 'Socrates regards all definite statements with regard to the next life as μῦθοι i.e. as not λόγοι': but that is surely not true of the actual assertion that there is a next life; indeed Burnet himself adds 'the immortality of the soul is capable of scientific proof; the details of the ἀποδημία are not'. Now it is just scientific proof of immortality that our dialogue purports to give; it would therefore be inappropriate for Socrates to suggest their having a μυθολογία in the sense of an imaginative discourse, though indeed we do get a myth at the end, when the 'proof' has been achieved. I therefore think that here, as in the *Apology*, the word means simply 'discuss'.

[1] Socrates may be thinking, as Olympiodorus suggests, of Eupolis *frag.* 352, μισῶ δὲ καὶ τὸν Σωκράτη, τὸν πτωχὸν ἀδολέσχην κ.τ.λ. In Aristophanes *Clouds* (1480) Strepsiades confesses to an 'insanity of babbling' (ἐμοῦ παρανοήσαντος ἀδολεσχίᾳ) due to Socrates; and the word seems to have been frequently used as a gibe at philosophers.

[2] Plato often appeals to 'ancient doctrine', especially in his latest dialogue, the *Laws*. It is not always Orphic doctrine that is so described, as a glance at the passages quoted in Novotny's note on *Epistle* VII, 355 A will show. But in the present case it probably is; the doctrine of the rebirth of the soul has already been referred to at *Meno* 81 A in language plainly suggestive of Orphism, though it is not there called ancient, as it is here and in *Epistle* VII. There is an apparent illogicality in what follows (C6–D4), inasmuch as the existence of our souls 'yonder' is first stated as part of the premiss (the παλαιὸς λόγος) and then (ἄλλο τι ἤ...ἐκεῖ) as an immediate inference therefrom. But the illogicality is only apparent: for Socrates chooses to disregard the first part of the premiss (ὡς εἰσὶν ἐνθένδε ἀφικόμενοι ἐκεῖ) and to base his inference on the second part only. Probably he does so because Orphic believers would naturally stress this second part, the rebirth of souls, rather than the first (their continued existence between births).

[3] The verb γίγνεσθαι here, as often in the sequel, is used not of an absolute coming-to-be of the soul, but of its 'birth' in the sense of incarnation.

'Just so', said Cebes.

'Well now, if you would grasp my point more readily don't think only of mankind, but of the whole animal and vegetable world, in short of everything that comes into being: and let us put the general question: E isn't it always a case of opposite coming to be from opposite whenever the relation in question exists? Take for example the opposition of beautiful to ugly, or of just to unjust, out of the thousands of similar instances; and then let us ask ourselves whether it is not necessary that, when a thing has an opposite, it can come to be only from that opposite; for instance, when something comes to be bigger it must (I suggest) necessarily pass to the later state of being bigger from the earlier state of being smaller.'

'Yes.'

'And conversely, when it becomes smaller it must pass to being now 71 smaller from being then bigger?'

'That is so.'

'And of course there is the same transition from stronger to weaker, and from slower to faster?'

'Quite so.'

'Again, anything that becomes worse must have been better, anything that becomes more just must have been more unjust?'

'Of course.'

'Are we satisfied then that all coming-to-be means the coming to be of an opposite thing from its opposite?'

'Quite satisfied.'

'To proceed then: is there not a further fact involved, namely that between any and every pair of opposites there are two "becomings" B or processes, from this to that and conversely from that to this: thus between bigger thing and smaller there are increase and decrease, so that we say that this is increasing and that decreasing?'

'Yes.'

'And similarly with separating and combining, cooling and heating, and so on and so forth: we may sometimes have no name for the process, but the actual occurrence must conform to our principle: they all come into being from each other, and there is a process in which each becomes the other.'

'Quite so.'

C 'Well now, is there an opposite to living, corresponding to sleeping as the opposite of being awake?'

'Certainly.'

'And what is it?'

'Being dead.'

Then if these are opposites, they must come to be from each other, and between the two of them there must be two processes.'

'Of course.'

'Now I will tell you one of the pairs that I was mentioning just now, together with its processes; and you must tell me the other one. My pair is sleeping and being awake: the latter comes into being from the former, and the former from the latter: and the processes here are going D to sleep and waking up. Is that satisfactory?'

'Perfectly.'

'Then do you give me a similar account of life and death. You allow that being dead is the opposite of being alive?'

'I do.'

'And that they come into being from each other?'

'Yes.'

'Then what is it that comes to be from that which is alive?'

'What is dead.'

'And from what is dead?'

'I am bound to admit that the answer must be "What is alive".'

'Then, Cebes, living things and living people come into being from dead things and dead people.'

'Evidently.'   E

'Hence our souls do exist in Hades?'

'Apparently.'

'Now of the two processes here involved one is really obvious; for dying is an obvious fact, is it not?'

'Yes, of course.'

'Then what is our next step? Shall we not supply the opposite process to balance dying? Is Nature to be lame on one side, or must we needs supply her with an opposite process to this one?'

'Certainly we must.'

'And what is it?'

'Coming to life again.'

'Well then, if there is such a thing as coming to life again, the process from dead to living must be that.'

'Quite so.'

'Hence we have another ground[1] for agreeing that the living come into being from the dead no less surely than the dead from the living. And we felt, I believe, that if this were so we should have a satisfactory indication that the souls of the dead must exist somewhere, and thence be reborn.'

'Yes, Socrates: I think that what we have agreed necessarily leads to that conclusion.'

'And here's another point, Cebes, which will show, I think, that we are not at fault in our agreement. If this circular process[2] of one B opposite coming into being to balance the other were not always going on, if instead of that there were only a one-way process in a straight line, with no bending back, no turning in the other direction, you will realise that ultimately all things would arrive at the same state, would undergo the same experience, and the coming into being of things would be at an end.'[3]

'How do you mean?'

'My point is easy enough to understand. Suppose we had the process of going to sleep, but no balancing process of waking up again from sleep, you will realise that the ultimate state of things would make the C story of Endymion pointless: he would turn out to be a nobody, since his experience of sleeping would be the universal experience. Again, if everything were to be combined and nothing separated, we should soon have that condition of "all things together" which Anaxagoras describes.[4] And similarly, my dear Cebes, if everything endowed with life were to die, and having died were to remain in the state of death and not come to life again, is it not beyond dispute that ultimately there would be a universal absence of life, a universal death? Even supposing D that the living had some other origin than the dead,[5] yet if they were to

---

[1] ὁμολογεῖται. . .καὶ ταύτῃ must mean that the recognition of 'coming to life again' as a necessary process, logically inferred, confirms the result already established by the general principle of opposite replacing opposite.

[2] To call this process 'circular' is perfectly natural, but Plato probably has in mind the Orphic κύκλος γενέσεως, the 'cycle' of births in the body, from which the human soul seeks ultimately to escape. It may be remarked that the present argument leaves room for transmigration of the human soul into animal bodies.

[3] It seems better to put (with Robin) a full stop rather than a question-mark after παύσαιτο γιγνόμενα.

[4] Anaxagoras used these words to describe the initial state of things, before an orderly universe was created by Mind (νοῦς). This action of Mind is referred to later (97c).

[5] This is the meaning required, but I do not see how it can be got from ἐκ τῶν ἄλλων, and therefore propose τινῶν for τῶν. With the following words τὰ δὲ ζῶντα θνῇσκοι we should understand καὶ μένοι ἐν τούτῳ τῷ σχήματι, though indeed this addition is logically implied in the μέν clause.

die what escape could there possibly be from the whole stock of things being exhausted and dying out?'

'None whatever that I can see, Socrates. I think what you say is perfectly true.'

'Yes, Cebes, I feel quite certain that it is so: in agreeing on this particular point we are not deceiving ourselves. These are real facts: coming to life again, coming-to-be of the living from the dead, existence of the souls of those that have died.'[1]   E

Perhaps the first point that strikes us in this section is the open-mindedness of Cebes. It is true that he speaks at the outset not of his own scepticism, but of that of people in general; but plainly his attitude is not that of an orthodox Pythagorean: he needs to be convinced of the soul's continued existence 'itself by itself' as much as anyone else. His role, like that of Simmias, is that of the sympathetic sceptic, ready to listen to Socratic arguments, but not too ready to accept them.

Next we should note that the sceptical attitude here is one which goes further than the familiar Homeric picture of the 'gibbering' soul in Hades, in which is no 'wit' (φρένες); Cebes suggests that it may just vanish into thin air and 'not exist at all anywhere'. It is true that Homer in one passage (*Iliad* XXIII, 100) uses the word 'smoke' (καπνός) in this reference, and Plato may be thinking of that passage: but the comparison of the departing soul to smoke clearly does not for Homer imply total annihilation. If we may believe what Socrates says later on (80D 10), such annihilation was accepted by most people at the end of the fourth century.

At 70C we come to the first argument for the soul's immortality, generally known (from a word used at 71E 8 and 72A 12) as the ἀνταπόδοσις argument. It begins with a mention of an 'ancient doctrine', but this παλαιὸς λόγος is naturally not treated as authoritative; on the contrary it states in its own terms just what has to be proved, namely that there is a cyclic recurrence in which the dead come from the living and the living from the dead. In order to establish this Plato represents 'living' and 'dead' as instances of a general principle according to which opposites are generated from their opposites. This principle had been asserted by Heraclitus, who regarded it as establishing the *unity* or *identity* of opposites; Socrates does not contend for the unity of 'living' and 'dead', nor indeed of any of his pairs of opposites, but the occurrence in Heraclitus *frag.* 88 (DK) of 'waking and sleeping' alongside of 'living and dead', as also of the words τάδε γὰρ μετα-πεσόντα ἐκεῖνά ἐστι κἀκεῖνα πάλιν μεταπεσόντα ταῦτα, makes it prac-

---

[1]   As most editors have seen, the words καὶ ταῖς μέν...κάκιον are out of place, and must be a gloss taken from 63C6.

tically certain that Plato has Heraclitus in mind, although the instances of relative pairs like 'greater and smaller' (which incidentally weaken the argument, since they are not genuine opposites) are doubtless his own addition.

At the end of 71 A Socrates proceeds to argue that there must be two opposite *processes* (γενέσεις) in which opposites are generated from opposites; and Plato evidently thinks that the recognition of these in the opposition of 'living' and 'dead' will strengthen his argument. Briefly, his point is that as one of the processes (dying) is a matter of actual experience, and therefore placed beyond doubt, the other (return to life) must be equally undoubted.

It does not seem to me that the passage 71 A 12–72 A 8 really adds anything to the logical strength of the argument; the appeal to experience and the inference therefrom are no doubt ingenious in their very simplicity; but an opponent might retort that the fact that returning to life is *not* obvious throws doubt on the ranging of the opposites 'life' and 'death' along with the other pairs.

In the last part of the section it is argued that on no other hypothesis could the continuance of life be accounted for: without the reverse process, from death to life, everything would, sooner or later, be permanently dead. This argument can only have force on the assumption that there can be no *new* life, properly so called, but only a periodical resumption of former life. But that is of course something which Plato holds to be proved by, or to be an instance of, the general principle of ἀνταπόδοσις. There is, indeed, a momentary glance at the possibility of new life in the words 'even supposing that the living had some other origin than the dead' (72 D); and if Plato had in mind an *unlimited* stock from which new lives could originate, the logical necessity for the cyclic process would disappear; but evidently the hypothetical source is conceived as finite and exhaustible.

It is important to observe that only on the strength of this last argument—the argument, namely, that on any other hypothesis all life would be permanently extinguished—is Socrates able to assert that the two-way pair of processes, or (as he now calls it) the cyclic process, is never-ending. Hitherto the principle of opposites generated from opposites has only justified him in inferring that a soul which at any given time comes to be 'born' (incarnated) has previously existed 'in Hades': he has not inferred, and could not properly have inferred, that a soul now existing 'in Hades' will necessarily be reincarnated, any more than he could infer that, because what is now greater was previously smaller, it will necessarily become smaller again. It is no accident that the word 'always' has not been applied to ἀνταπόδοσις until 72 A 12.

Lastly, it is evident both from the words εἰσὶν ἄρα αἱ ψυχαὶ ἡμῶν ἐν Ἅιδου (71 Ε) and from what is said later (77 C) that Plato intends the argument to prove *personal* immortality, an eternal existence of individual souls eternally retaining their identity. In fact, however (and this is true of all his arguments for immortality, with the doubtful exception of the argument from Recollection, soon to follow), it cannot be held to do so; that souls persist through the cycle as individual souls is simply assumed: it is not a necessary part or corollary of the principle that 'living' comes from 'dead', or that the process of dying is balanced by the process of coming to life.[1]

[1] Cf. my commentary on the *Phaedrus*, pp. 64f. and Wilamowitz, *Platon* I, p. 331: 'Er hält den Analogieschluss für zwingend, dass dem Sterben ein Wiedergeborenwerden entsprechen muss, nicht bloss die Verwendung des freigewordenen geistigen Stoffes zu einer neuen Verbindung, einer neuen Geburt. Wie kann hier plötzlich die persönliche, unteilbare Seele eintreten?'
    The same criticism, expressed in different terms, is found in Strato, *frag.* 122 3' (g), Wehrli; see p. 195 below.

VII

72E–77A   A COMPLEMENTARY ARGUMENT.
THE THEORY OF RECOLLECTION

At this point Cebes recalls Socrates's doctrine of Recollection (ἀνάμνησις) as providing a further proof of the soul's existence before birth. As Simmias has no clear memory of this, Socrates proceeds to expound it fully. The content of our sense-perceptions resembles the Forms, but does so only defectively, and our recognition of this defectiveness implies a pre-natal knowledge of the Forms; thus two 'equal' logs are only approximately equal, and remind *us of the Form of equality. All so-called learning is really recollection or reminder of this sort. After an argument to rebut the alternative suggestion of innate knowledge, it is emphasised that the doctrine of Forms is interlocked with that of the soul's existence before its incarnation: in other words, they stand or fall together; and Simmias, declaring himself a convinced believer in the Forms, consequently accepts the other doctrine with equal conviction.*

72 E   To this Cebes rejoined: 'There is also another theory which, if true, points the same way, Socrates: the one that you are constantly asserting, namely that learning is really just recollection, from which it follows presumably that what we now call to mind we have learnt at some
73   previous time; which would not be possible unless our souls existed somewhere before being born in this human frame. Hence we seem to have another indication that the soul is something immortal.'

Simmias now intervened to ask: 'But how is that proved, Cebes? Please remind me, as I can't quite remember at the moment.'[1]

'First,'[2] replied Cebes, 'by the excellent argument that when people are asked questions they can produce the right answers to anything of their own accord, provided that the questioning is done properly.[3] Of course they wouldn't be able to do so unless they had knowledge and

---

[1] Simmias's defective memory is doubtless no more than a device to make it more natural for Socrates to expound and defend a theory which, if it had in fact been his own, would presumably have been quite familiar to his present audience.

[2] I accept Bury's πρῶτον for ἑνί (*C.R.* xx, p. 13).

[3] καλῶς may possibly hint that the questions put to the slave in the *Meno* are often 'leading' questions, but I am inclined to think that it means no more than 'skilfully'. We can hardly doubt that, if not here, at all events in the reference to 'diagrams' in B1 there is an allusion to the experiment in the *Meno*.

correct views within them. Secondly, if you confront people with anything in the nature of a diagram,[1] you have the plainest proof of the B point in question.'

'And if that doesn't convince you, Simmias,' said Socrates, 'I will suggest another consideration to which you may perhaps agree. You are evidently sceptical about the possibility of what is called learning being recollection.'[2]

'Not sceptical', said Simmias: 'what I need is just what we are talking about, namely to recollect. In point of fact, thanks to Cebes's setting out of the arguments I do already almost remember, and am almost convinced; all the same, I should like now to hear how you yourself have set them out.'

'I will tell you. We agree, I take it, that to be reminded of something c implies having at some previous time known it?'

'Certainly.'

'And can we further agree that recollection may take the form of acquiring knowledge in a particular way, I mean like this:[3] a man who has seen or heard or by some other sense perceived something may come to know something other than that, may think of something else besides that, something that is the object of a different knowledge.[4] When this happens are we not justified in saying that he recollects or is reminded[5] of the new object that he has thought of?'   D

'How do you mean?'

[1] Literally 'diagrams or something else of that sort'. At *Rep.* 510D Socrates speaks of ὁρώμενα εἴδη, the 'visible shapes' which the geometer uses as aids to his thinking. That these may be either diagrams or models of geometrical figures is clear from their description as ἃ πλάττουσί τε καὶ γράφουσιν *ibid*. In our passage the 'something else' is therefore probably a model.

[2] I prefer a full-stop rather than a question-mark here.

[3] I keep Burnet's punctuation, but to preserve the rhetorical question would be unnatural in English.

[4] Burnet thinks that the words ἕτερον...οὗ μὴ ἡ αὐτὴ ἐπιστήμη ἀλλ' ἄλλη allude to the principle that opposites are known together (τῶν ἐναντίων μία ἐπιστήμη): a man who knows 'dark' necessarily knows 'light', but that is not the kind of reminder that Socrates has in mind. In view, however, of the instance in D3 ἄλλη που ἐπιστήμη ἀνθρώπου καὶ λύρας I think he more probably means that the perception of, for example, a man may remind us of things that we know about him but do not perceive: the perceived characters and those of which they remind us would all alike be included in our total knowledge of the man, and therefore objects of the same knowledge. This kind of reminder Socrates rules out as irrelevant.

[5] By my double translation of ἀνεμνήσθη I mean to convey that in expounding his theory Socrates uses ἀνάμνησις and its verb to cover both recollection and reminder. It seemed best to use 'recollection' down to this point, where the second meaning begins to emerge more definitely.

'To give an example, the knowledge of a man is different from that of a lyre.'

'Of course.'

'Well, you know how a lover feels when he sees a lyre or a cloak or some other object commonly used by his beloved: he apprehends the lyre, but he also conceives in his mind the form of the boy to whom it belongs; and that is reminder. Similarly one who sees Simmias is often reminded of Cebes, and we could think of any number of similar cases.'

'Yes indeed, any number', agreed Simmias emphatically.

E   'Reminder then may take that form: but it is most apt to occur in connexion with things that we have forgotten owing to the lapse of time and our not having thought about them. Isn't that so?'

'Yes, certainly.'

'Another point: is it possible to see the picture of a horse or a lyre and be reminded of their owner: or again to see a picture of Simmias and be reminded of Cebes?'

'Certainly.'

'Or alternatively to see a picture of Simmias and be reminded of Simmias?'

74   'Yes, that is possible.'

'And from all this it follows, doesn't it, that we may be reminded of things either by something like them or by something unlike them?'[1]

'It does.'

'Moreover, when it is by something like the other thing, are we not certain to find ourselves doing something else besides, namely asking ourselves whether the similarity between the object and the thing it reminds us of is defective or not?'

'Certainly we shall.'

'Well now, see if you agree with my next point. We maintain, do we not, that there is such a thing as equality, not the equality of one log to another, or one stone to another, but something beyond all these cases, something different, equality itself. May we maintain that that exists, or may we not?'

B   'Most asuredly we may', answered Simmias: 'not a doubt of it.'

'And have we knowledge of it, in and by itself?'[2]

---

[1] The reason for making this point is that a particular is obviously 'like' a Form, and yet may be said to be unlike it because they belong to different orders of existence. See 74c11 ff. where this point is dismissed as unimportant.

[2] If we analyse this sentence grammatically (though a Greek reader would not pause to do so) we should probably take αὐτό as doing double duty, first as

'Certainly we have.'

'Then where do we get that knowledge from? Mustn't it be from the objects we mentioned just now,[1] the equal logs or stones or whatever they were that we saw? Didn't they lead us to conceive of that other something? You do regard it as something other than those things, don't you? Look at it like this: two stones or two logs equal in length sometimes seem equal to one man, but not to another, though they haven't changed.'

'Yes certainly.'

'But now, what about equals themselves?[2] Have they ever appeared C to you to be unequal, or equality to be inequality?'

'Never, Socrates.'

'Then those equal objects[3] are not the same as the equal itself.'

'Far from it, I should say.'

'And yet it is from those equal objects, different as they are from this equal, that you have conceived and acquired knowledge of the latter?'

'That is perfectly true.'

'This latter being either like those others or unlike?'

'Just so.'

'However, that point is immaterial; but so long as the sight of one thing leads you to conceive another, whether like it or unlike, a case D of reminder must have occurred.'

---

anticipatory accusative (as in οἶδά σε ὅστις εἶ) and secondly as the subject of ἔστιν. There is no difficulty, save for grammarians, in a pronoun being simultaneously nominative and accusative.

[1] Socrates, as will soon appear, does not mean that knowledge of the Forms *originally* came to us through sense-perception of their imperfect copies, but only that we recover through sense-perception a knowledge belonging to us before we were born.

[2] The words αὐτὰ τὰ ἴσα do not of course imply that there is more than one Form of equality, but that, since 'equal' implies at least two terms, there must be objects, other than sensibles, in which that Form is perfectly exemplified. These can only be mathematical objects, for example, two triangles or (as Burnet suggests) the angles at the base of an isosceles triangle. It is, however, very unlikely that Plato had as yet formulated the doctrine that all mathematical objects are intermediate between Forms and sensibles, for which see Aristotle, *Met.* 987B 14 and Ross *ad loc.*

[3] ταῦτα τὰ ἴσα (unlike αὐτὰ τὰ ἴσα above) of course refers to the (so-called) equal logs, stones, etc. If we take account of a later passage (102C) in which tallness and shortness are treated not as *relations* between two persons, but as *properties* which one has 'towards' the other, we may infer that *each* of the logs is thought of as exhibiting in itself an approximate equality towards the other, and *each* as 'striving' (75A) to be like 'the equal'. On the treatment of relative terms in Plato and Aristotle see Cornford, *Plato's Theory of Knowledge*, pp. 282 ff.

'Yes, to be sure.'

'And to continue: in the instance of those equal logs and other equal objects that we mentioned just now, is it our experience that they appear equal to the same degree as the equal itself? Is there some deficiency in respect of the likeness of the former to the latter, or is there none?'

'Yes, a considerable deficiency.'

'Then when someone sees a certain object and says to himself "The thing I am looking at wants to be like something else, but can resemble
E that other thing only defectively, as an inferior copy", may we agree that what he is saying necessarily implies a previous knowledge of that which he finds the object seen to resemble thus defectively?'

'That is necessarily implied.'

'Well then, is our own experience of the equal objects and the equal itself that just described, or is it not?'

'Undoubtedly it is.'

'So it necessarily follows that we knew the equal at a time previous
75 to that first sight of equal objects which led us to conceive all these as striving to be like *the* equal, but defectively succeeding.'

'That is so.'

'And we agree moreover on a further point, that the conception referred to has arisen only, and could have arisen only, from seeing or touching, or some other form of sense-perception: what I am saying applies to them all alike.'

'And alike they are, Socrates, in respect of the point that our argument seeks to establish.'

'But the fact is that these very sense-perceptions must lead us to
B conceive that all those objects of perception are striving for that which *is* equal, but defectively attaining it. Is that right?'

'Yes.'

'Hence before we ever began to see or hear or otherwise perceive things we must, it seems, have possessed knowledge of the equal itself, if we were going to refer the equal things of our sense-perceptions to that standard, conceiving that[1] all such objects are doing their best to resemble it, yet are in fact inferior to it.'

'That must follow from what we said before, Socrates.'

---

[1] Perhaps the simplest way of explaining the syntax of the ὅτι clause is to say that ἐκεῖσε ἀνοίσειν is felt as equivalent to ἐκεῖσε ἀναφέροντες ἐννοήσειν. Cf. ἐνενοήσαμεν ὅτι ὀρέγεται above (75 A 1).

'Well, we have been seeing and hearing things, and employing our other senses from the very moment we were born, have we not?'

'Certainly.'

'And before doing so we must, so we maintain, have possessed c knowledge of the equal?'

'Yes.'

'Then it seems that we must have possessed it before we were born.'

'It does.'

'Then if we were born with this knowledge,[1] having acquired it before birth, must we not have had knowledge, both before birth and immediately afterwards, not only of the equal, the greater and the smaller,[2] but of all things of that sort? For our argument applies not merely to the equal, but with the same force to the beautiful itself, the good itself, the just, the holy, in fact, as I have just said, to everything D upon which we affix our seal and mark as being "the thing itself",[3] when we put our questions and give our answers.[4] Of all these then we must have possessed the knowledge before we were born.'

'That is so.'

'And if we do not each time forget what we have acquired, we must be possessed of knowledge always, we must have it throughout our whole life; for to know means to have acquired knowledge of something and not have lost it. The losing of knowledge is what we mean by forgetting, isn't it, Simmias?'

'Undoubtedly, Socrates.'   E

'But if on the other hand we lost at the moment of birth what we had acquired before birth, but afterwards by directing our senses to the

---

[1] It is important to realise that both the introductory clause of this paragraph οὐκοῦν εἰ μέν...τὰ τοιαῦτα and the second εἰ μέν clause at D7 put forward hypotheses which Socrates does *not* accept; that which he does accept comes at E2 with the εἰ δέ clause.

[2] The use of the comparatives τὸ μεῖζον καὶ τὸ ἔλαττον must not of course be taken to imply that Plato postulated, now or at any stage, Forms of greater-ness and smaller-ness. The language, natural enough in conjunction with τὸ ἴσον, is loose for τὸ μέγα καὶ τὸ σμικρόν, for which Forms see below, 102 C–D.

[3] For a similar generalising formula cf. *Rep.* 507 B κατ' ἰδέαν μίαν ἑκάστου ὡς μιᾶς οὔσης τιθέντες "ὃ ἔστιν" ἕκαστον προσαγορεύομεν. Whether or no the present passage implies that Plato had already come to hold the doctrine of *Rep.* 596 A, that there are Forms corresponding to every group of things we choose to make, and if so whether he already discerned the difficulties inherent in it, are questions which it would take us too far from our purpose to discuss. For a recent discussion see Ross, *Plato's Theory of Ideas*, ch. XI.

[4] I.e. in philosophical dialogue or dialectic.

relevant object recover that old knowledge, then, I take it, what is called learning will consist in recovering a knowledge which belongs to us; and should we not be right in calling this recollection?'

'Certainly.'

76   'The reason being that we found that it was possible for a person who had seen or heard or otherwise perceived an object to go on to conceive another object which he had forgotten, something with which the first object was connected, whether by resemblance or contrast. Hence my two alternatives: either we are all of us born knowing the things in question,[1] and retain the knowledge throughout our life, or else those who are said to learn are simply recollecting, and learning will consist in recollection.'

'I am quite sure you are right, Socrates.'

B   'Then which do you choose, Simmias? Are we born with that knowledge, or do we recollect a knowledge which we once possessed?'

'At the moment, Socrates, I don't know which to choose.'

'Well, here is something about which perhaps you can choose, and give me your view. If a man knows certain things, will he be able to give an account of them,[2] or will he not?'

'Unquestionably he will, Socrates.'

'And do you think that everybody could give an account of those objects we were speaking of just now?'

'I only wish I did', replied Simmias; 'alas, on the contrary I fear that by this time to-morrow there will be no man left alive capable of doing so adequately.'[3] .

C   'So you don't think that everybody knows those objects, Simmias.'

'By no means.'

'Can they then recollect what they once learnt?'

'It must be so.'

---

[1] αὐτά means the ἕτερόν τι of A2, the shift to the plural being easy enough.

[2] To 'give an account' of a Form is to state its resemblances to and differences from other—ultimately all other—Forms. This is the goal of dialectic, and involves, as expounded in *Rep.* VII, knowledge of that Form from which all knowledge and all being are derived, the Form of the Good. This doctrine may well have been inchoate in Plato's mind when he wrote the *Phaedo*, but was probably not yet fully formed.

[3] Burnet comments: 'It seems to me that, if Plato originated the theory, he could not possibly have put this statement into the mouth of Simmias.' But Simmias is speaking within the framework of the whole dialogue, and conformably to its assumptions. Throughout the dialogue Socrates is the exponent of a theory of Forms, and there is nothing unnatural in Simmias's present remark that he is unrivalled at expounding and applying it.

'But when did our souls acquire this knowledge? Evidently not since our birth as human beings.'

'No indeed.'

'Before that, then?'

'Yes.'

'Then, Simmias, our souls did exist before they were within this human form, apart from our bodies and possessed of intelligence.'

'Unless possibly it was at the actual moment of birth that we acquired the knowledge in question, Socrates; there is that moment still left.'

'Yes yes, my friend; but at what moment, may I ask, do we lose it? D We are not born with the knowledge: that we agreed a moment ago: do we then lose it at the very moment that we acquire it, or is there some other moment that you can suggest?'

'No indeed, Socrates; I see now that I was talking nonsense.'

'Then may our position be put like this, Simmias? If those objects exist which are always on our lips, a beautiful and a good and all reality of that sort, and if it is to that that we refer the content of our sense-perceptions, thereby recovering what was ours aforetime, and compare E our percepts thereto, it must follow that as surely as those objects exist so surely do our souls exist before we are born; but if the former do not exist, all our argument will have gone for nothing. Is that our position? Does the existence of our souls before birth stand or fall with the existence of those objects?'

'I am utterly convinced, Socrates,' replied Simmias, 'that it does so stand or fall: our argument is happily reduced to this, that it is equally certain that our souls exist before birth as that the reality of which 77 you now speak exists. I say happily, because there is nothing so plainly true to my mind as that all that sort of thing most assuredly does exist, a beautiful and a good and all those other things that you were speaking of just now. So I think we have had a satisfactory proof.'[1]

Although it is quite true, as Sir David Ross says,[2] that mention of the Forms in our dialogue is always subordinate to the proof of immortality, it is plain that this section sheds important new light on the theory of Forms. Their *existence*, indeed, is still assumed rather than proved; but we are told how we come to know them, and that they are only imperfectly represented in sensible things.

[1] *Sc.* of the pre-natal existence of the soul; not, of course, of the existence of the Forms, which has been a premiss of the proof.

[2] *PTI*, p. 22.

The doctrine of Recollection has already figured in the *Meno* (80 E–86 C); and indeed what Cebes remembers about it at 73 A is pretty clearly Plato's reminder to his readers of what he had there written.[1] But what Socrates himself adds to Cebes's memories goes far beyond the *Meno*: there the connexion with the Forms was only implicit, inasmuch as those objects which the soul knew in its discarnate state could not have been sensibles; but now it becomes explicit, and the conclusion is reached, and stressed, that the pre-existence of our souls and the existence of the Forms stand or fall together.[2]

The description of the *Meno* argument as 'excellent' (κάλλιστος) is partly offset by Socrates's doubt whether Simmias finds it convincing. In the *Meno* itself (86 B) Socrates expresses doubt as to the complete cogency of the experiment with the slave: τὰ μέν γε ἄλλα οὐκ ἂν πάνυ ὑπὲρ τοῦ λόγου διισχυρισαίμην, where, however, the vague τὰ ἄλλα can be variously interpreted. It seems fair to say that Plato, while not repudiating the earlier argument for recollection and immortality, regards that now to be expounded as far superior. I cannot agree[3] with Frutiger (*op. cit.* p. 75) that 'l'exposé du *Ménon* a un caractère mythique indéniable': it is of course introduced as a religious doctrine supported by poets, or perhaps rather as a corollary of such doctrine; but the argument for it is completely rationalist.

It might seem that, in insisting that we come to know the Forms as the result of perceiving the failure of sensibles to be wholly what they purport to be, Plato is going back on what he has said earlier about the philosopher's utter detachment from the body and the world of sense experience. I do not think this is really so. The ideal of detachment leaves room for *necessary* attention to the body, and in bidding us attach little or no value to what the senses tell us Plato does not bid us attempt the impossible task of eradicating our perceptions. Valueless though they may be in themselves, it does not follow that they may not have value in so far as they point beyond themselves; and that is all that the ἀνάμνησις doctrine claims for them. Hence it seems to me misleading to say, as Mr Norman Gulley says in a recent valuable paper,[4] that one of the 'assumptions necessary to justify the role which Plato assigns to the senses' is 'that the senses are to be always trusted'. If we

---

[1] This is obvious in regard at least to the mention of diagrams; it is perhaps less so as regards the 'proper questioning' which in the *Meno* is not a process distinct from the confronting with diagrams, and may be a quite general reference to that Socratic 'midwifery' which is abundantly illustrated in early dialogues, though not explicitly described and named before the *Theaetetus*.

[2] Although the two doctrines are thus interlocked, Plato does not regard ἀνάμνησις as proving the existence of the Forms; his position is rather that the denial of the soul's pre-existence would entail the denial of something of which he is already certain.

[3] As I too hastily did in *Plato's Phaedrus*, p. 91.

[4] *C.Q.* July–Oct. 1954, pp. 194 ff.

are to speak of 'trusting' anything in this matter, it is not the senses but the judgement of deficiency[1] aroused by sense-perception. Nor does Plato, I think, imply that any and every perception gives rise to that judgement; for down to 75 C 10 he is concerned with one Form only, that of Equality, and plainly it is only a very limited range of perceptions that can have any bearing on our recollection of that. Mr Gulley has, however, clearly expressed, and rightly emphasised, one difficulty in Plato's argument. 'The main fault', he writes, 'is clearly that Plato is apparently assuming that the fact that we attain a conceptual level of apprehension automatically affords a recollection of Forms, and thus implicitly assumes also the impossibility of false judgement.'[2] Now this assertion is undoubtedly justified if we take at their face value the words ἐπιστήμη and ἐπίστασθαι in 74B–C; but need we do so? I would suggest that we need not. The *Meno* had made it clear that the 'arousing of true opinions' (85C) is only a first step towards the knowledge of reality, only the prelude to the process of dialectic there called αἰτίας λογισμός (98A). That process is in the next words identified with Recollection, and by this we are surely to understand that Recollection in its fullest sense is a long and gradual process which includes both the prelude to dialectic and dialectic itself. Now in the present passage Plato's main concern is not to give a full account of how we can attain knowledge of the Forms, but to prove the pre-natal existence of a soul which knows them; and for that reason it is forgivable, and indeed natural, that Socrates should speak imprecisely, using words which suggest that the full knowledge of Forms is given at once in or through the judgement of deficiency, but leaving it to us to remember the doctrine of the later pages of the *Meno*, where it was his concern to differentiate opinion and knowledge.

Moreover, the concept of the Equal is one which readily lends itself to such imprecision; it is no doubt Plato's doctrine that knowledge, in the full sense, of the Equal can only be attained through a dialectic which connects that concept with others, such as Triangle, Square and Cube, and which ultimately embraces all Forms under the Form of Good; yet we do in fact suppose ourselves to understand the full meaning of Equality without any such dialectic, and it is fair to say that we do so as soon as we have made that judgement of deficiency of which Plato speaks; and similarly with other mathematical concepts, τὸ μεῖζον καὶ τὸ ἔλαττον καὶ σύμπαντα τὰ τοιαῦτα (75C). But with moral concepts, of which he only comes to speak after the words just quoted, it is a different story: no reasonable person will suppose himself to understand the full meaning of goodness or justice simply because he has observed that this or that so-called good or just action

---

[1] The προσπάθημα, as we may conveniently call it in view of προσπάσχειν 74A 6.   [2] *Loc. cit.* p. 199.

is not perfectly good or just; and it is these moral Forms that Socrates has in mind[1] when at 76B he asserts that we cannot know anything unless we can 'give an account' of it.

If we bear in mind this distinction between mathematical and moral Forms, and allow Socrates that natural looseness of language of which I have spoken, we shall be ready to admit that there is no real inconsistency between the two passages 74B–C and 76B, nor between the *Phaedo* account of Recollection as a whole and the theory of knowledge expounded in the *Meno*.

This argument comes nearer than the previous one to being a proof of individual immortality: it is *my* soul which recollects what *I* knew before birth in the body. Yet in default of recollection of personal experience it is difficult to see how there can be that consciousness of identity preserved through a series of incarnations without which we cannot properly speak of individual immortality. As Cornford says, 'The memory implied in the doctrine of *Anamnesis* is an impersonal memory: its contents are the same in all human beings.'[2]

Cornford finds 'the weak point in the argument in the statement that we make such judgements, implying acquaintance with perfect equality as soon as we begin to use our senses; whereas in truth such judgements are highly reflective and not made by infants'.[3] That is of course true; nevertheless it is perhaps not fatal to Plato's whole argument; it is arguable that in our moral judgements at least we appear to have ideal standards not contributed by experience, and that the reflexion upon, and progressive clarification of such standards largely by *contrast* with our experience might be not unplausibly represented as the recovery of ante-natal knowledge lost at birth.

The length and precision of Socrates's exposition of this doctrine, and the absence of any hint of indebtedness, suggest that it is original to Plato; and that, I believe, is substantially true. In *Meno* 83C–D we cannot be sure whether Socrates represents Recollection as *part* of the religious belief of which he has been speaking or as something which he builds on to it; but in default of any other evidence for Orphic influence on this point the latter alternative may be preferred. As to the Pythagoreans, Prof. Dodds rightly observes[4] that the two authors Diodorus and Iamblichus, who tell us that the school attached importance to memory-training, 'do not connect it with the attempt to recover memory of past lives'; he adds, indeed, that 'it seems a reasonable guess that this was originally its ultimate purpose': this, I confess, seems to me doubtful. On the other hand, some lines of Empedocles,[5]

---

[1] Hence Simmias's fear that when Socrates is dead there will be no one left capable of 'adequately doing this'. Socrates would presumably have no special capacity for giving an account of mathematical Forms.

[2] *Principium Sapientiae*, p. 56. [3] *Ibid.* p. 51.
[4] *Op. cit.* p. 173. [5] *Frag.* 129 DK.

which are commonly believed to refer to Pythagoras, speak of a wise man who 'whenever he strained with all his mind, easily saw every one of the things that are in ten, yea twenty lifetimes of men'. These somewhat obscure words may mean that Pythagoras claimed to remember experiences of his previous incarnations, but even so they do not suggest anything more than empirically accumulated wisdom; and it is a far cry from that to the Platonic doctrine that by 'recollection' we can regain knowledge of a different order from that gained through experience; there is, of course, no suggestion that we can recollect past *experience* at all.

I can see no necessary implication of Recollection as conceived by Plato in the Pythagorean doctrine of reincarnation; and I am inclined to apply to Plato, in this reference, what Prof. Dodds says of Pythagoras, that 'we must surely credit him with some power of creative thinking'.[1]

Did Plato retain the doctrine of Recollection? This is a disputed question, and the arguments are too complex to be considered here: I would refer the reader to Mr Gulley's above-mentioned paper, which contains the most thorough examination of the matter; he has, for one thing, cogently disposed, in my opinion, of the notion that ἀνάμνησις is somehow replaced in later dialogues by διαίρεσις—the divisional process which bulks so large in the *Sophist* and *Statesman*. He is doubtless right in finding it implied in *Republic* 518 B–C, as did Adam in his edition. But nowhere does ἀνάμνησις reappear *eo nomine* except in the *Phaedrus* (249 C); the setting there is mythical, and it is possible that Plato has come to conceive ἀνάμνησις as no more than a mythical description of the process of dialectic, with which he once more, as in *Meno* 98 A, identifies it.

Cornford, holding that 'there is no ground for supposing that Plato ever abandoned the theory of Anamnesis', satisfactorily accounts for its absence from the *Theaetetus*, where we might expect to find it, by pointing out that 'it presupposes that we know the answer to the question here to be raised afresh: what is the nature of knowledge and of its objects?'[2] Prof. Skemp, in his recent commentary on the *Statesman*, suggests that in the 'sensible likenesses' (αἰσθηταὶ ὁμοιότητες) of 285 E 'we have the late form of the earlier doctrine of Recollection'.[3] Certainly Plato is there saying that some sensible objects can help us to the knowledge of the Forms which they resemble; but the essential part of the *Phaedo* doctrine, namely that the judgement of deficiency is only possible on the assumption of our pre-natal knowledge of the Form, is not there to be found; nor of course does Prof. Skemp suggest that it is.

---

[1] I am moved to say this because in the search for origins of Platonic doctrines this possibility sometimes seems to be overlooked.
[2] *Plato's Theory of Knowledge*, p. 28.   [3] P. 76.

VIII

*Simmias, speaking for Cebes as well as himself, suggests that only half of
what is needed has been achieved: the soul exists before birth, but does it also
exist after death? Socrates replies that by combining the argument from
Recollection with that which preceded it we find that this has already been
established. Yet he recognises that his hearers may still not be wholly
convinced; and before the discussion is resumed a short interlude occurs in
which they speak of him as a master-charmer, whose loss may be irreparable.*

77 A   'And what about Cebes?' asked Socrates; 'we must convince him too.'

'He is satisfied, I think,' said Simmias, 'though indeed he is the most
obstinate sceptic in the world. I think he is fully persuaded that our
B souls existed before we were born; but will they still exist after we die?
That I myself don't think we have proved; we are still left with the
ordinary man's misgiving which Cebes voiced a while ago, that when
a man dies his soul is simultaneously dissipated and thus comes to the
end of its existence. May it not be that, deriving its origin and construction from some external source,[1] it exists before entering into
a human body, yet when it quits the body it has entered it too comes
to an end and is destroyed?'

C   'You are right, Simmias', said Cebes. 'We seem to have proved half
of what we want, namely that our souls existed before we were born;
but we have yet to prove that they will equally exist after we die; only
then will our proof be complete.'

'But you have the complete proof already, my friends,' said Socrates,
'if you will combine the present argument with that which we agreed
upon previously, that is to say the principle that everything that lives
comes from what is dead. For if the soul exists before birth, and if its
D entry into life, its being born, must necessarily have one and only one
origin, namely death or the state of being dead, must it not follow,
seeing that it is to be born again, that it still exists after it has died?[2] So

---

[1] Reading ἄλλοθεν with the MSS. and Burnet's edition of 1911, in which he
withdraws his earlier acceptance of Bekker's ἀμόθεν.

[2] From this point the word γίγνεσθαι is frequently used of the soul's entrance
into a body, and ἀποθνῄσκειν of its leaving a body.

your point is indeed proved already. Nevertheless I fancy you and Simmias would like to have further discussion of this point too; you seem to have a childish fear that the wind literally blows a soul to bits E when it quits the body, and scatters it in all directions, more especially if one happens to die when it's blowing a full gale.'

'Then, Socrates,' replied Simmias with a smile, 'see if you can argue us out of our fear. Or rather, not so much us as the child, maybe, within us that is given to such fears. See if you can persuade him to abandon his fear of this bogy called death.'

'Well,' said Socrates, 'you will have to pronounce charms over him every day until you have charmed the bogy away.'

'And where, Socrates,' said Cebes, 'are we going to find an expert at 78 such charms,[1] now that you are leaving us?'

'There is a wide field in Greece, Cebes, which must surely contain experts, and a wide field also in the world outside Greece, the whole of which you ought to explore in quest of your charmer; and you should spare neither money nor trouble, for you couldn't spend your money on a more pressing object. But you should search amongst yourselves too: I daresay you won't easily find anyone better at this task than you are.'

'Very well,' said Cebes, 'we will see to that. But let us now, if it suits you, go back to the point at which we broke off.'[2]   B

'Why, of course it suits me; what do you expect?'

'Excellent.'

The first part of this section indicates the complementary relation of the two arguments so far employed, ἀνταπόδοσις and ἀνάμνησις. It is important to realise that this does not consist simply (as Archer-Hind in his note asserts) in the former proving the after-existence of the soul and the latter its pre-existence: the relation is more complicated than this. ἀνταπόδοσις had, as we saw, sought to establish that souls pass through an eternal cycle of alternating 'death' and 'life', thereby proving existence before birth equally with survival after death. But now that he comes back to it, Socrates does not speak of the eternal cycle; he merely refers to it as having shown that 'all that lives comes from the dead' (τὸ γίγνεσθαι πᾶν τὸ ζῶν ἐκ τοῦ τεθνεῶτος). Why is

---

[1] Socrates is an 'expert charmer' in the eyes of Cebes not merely because he can produce the 'good arguments' (καλοὶ λόγοι) with which Zalmoxis is said in the *Charmides* (157A) to have identified his ἐπῳδαί, but also because by his courage and serenity he has plainly shown himself devoid of the 'childish' fear which lurks in his friends.   [2] 77D5.

this? It is no doubt because what he wants now is to show that the soul *as conceived in the* ἀνάμνησις *argument*, the soul which apprehends the Forms, exists after death as well as before birth; he wants, in fact, something more than such survival as the former argument could establish. And this purpose he achieves by arguing, quite logically, that the principle πᾶν τὸ ʒῶν ἐκ τοῦ τεθνεῶτος justifies us in regarding the conclusion of the second argument, expressed in the words ἔστιν ἡ ψυχὴ καὶ πρότερον as necessarily involving the corollary ἔστιν ἡ ψυχὴ καὶ ὕστερον: for the time before birth *is* the time after death: *that* has become the important result of the ἀνταπόδοσις argument, and it is in virtue of that, and that alone, that ἀνταπόδοσις is regarded as complementary to ἀνάμνησις. Thus we reach the position that the two arguments together have established the existence of the soul and its possession of δύναμις καὶ φρόνησις (70B) both before its birth in the body and after death.

The rest of the section forms a short interlude preparatory to the next argument. What Socrates says at 78A may be taken to reflect Plato's recognition of the fact that culture and wisdom were not the monopoly of Athenians. He, unlike Socrates, had travelled widely in the years following 399, and had seen something of Egypt and Cyrene as well as of Sicily and Magna Graecia. Doubtless also he knew that Egyptians, Persians and Indians believed in the soul's immortality, and may well have thought that the wise men of those countries had something to contribute to philosophy. Whether, as some think, he came under strong Oriental influence in his old age is of course beside the point here.

The recommendation in the last three lines is, I should guess, a 'prophecy' that a worthy successor to Socrates may emerge from amongst his disciples. That this would offend modern standards of humility and good taste is irrelevant. If there is any probability in this conjecture, it is not (I submit) invalidated by the fact that Plato was not one of those present in the prison: Socrates may well be conceived as thinking of all his close followers, whether actually present or not.

IX

78B–80C THIRD ARGUMENT. THE KINSHIP
OF SOULS AND FORMS

Socrates now takes up the point raised by Cebes, that the soul may be dispersed at death. He urges that dispersal can only be suffered by composite objects, whereas the soul is not composite but of a single nature, like 'the beautiful itself', the equal itself' and Forms in general. Souls are akin to Forms, for both belong to the unseen order, whose attributes are changelessness and indestructibility, whereas body belongs to the visible order, whose attributes are the opposites of these. We may therefore believe that soul is 'altogether indestructible or nearly so'.

Socrates then resumed: 'Now the sort of question that we ought to 78 B put to ourselves is this: what kind of thing is in fact liable to undergo this dispersal that you speak of? For what kind of thing should we fear that it may be dispersed, and for what kind should we not? And next we should consider to which kind the soul belongs, and so find some ground for confidence or for apprehension about our own souls. Am I right?'

'Yes, you are.'

'Well now, isn't anything that has been compounded or has a com- C posite nature liable to be split up into its component parts? Isn't it incomposite things alone that can possibly be exempt from that?'

'I agree that that is so', replied Cebes.

'And isn't it most probable that the incomposite things are those that are always constant and unchanging, while the composite ones are those that are different at different times and never constant?'

'I agree.'

'Then let us revert to those objects which we spoke of earlier. What of that very reality of whose existence we give an account when we D question and answer each other?[1] Is that always unchanging and constant, or is it different at different times? Can the equal itself, the beautiful itself, the being itself whatever it may be, ever admit any sort of change? Or does each of these real beings, uniform[2] and indepen-

---

[1] I.e. in philosophical discussions; cf. 75 D 2.

[2] The term μονοειδές recurs at 80B in close conjunction with ἀδιάλυτον, and it is used of the Form of beauty at *Symp.* 211B. It has the same force as πᾶν ὅμοιον which Parmenides asserts of his ἓν ὄν, viz. the denial of internal difference or distinction of unlike parts.

dent, remain unchanging and constant, never admitting any sort of alteration whatever?'

'They must be unchanging and constant', Cebes replied.

'But what about the many beautiful things, beautiful human beings, E say, or horses or garments or anything else you like? What about the many equal things? What about all the things that are called by the same name as those real beings? Are *they* constant, or in contrast to those is it too much to say that they are never identical with themselves nor identically related to one another?'[1]

'You are right about them too,' said Cebes, 'they are never constant.'

79 'Then again, you can touch them and see them or otherwise perceive them with your senses, whereas those unchanging objects cannot be apprehended save by the mind's reasoning. Things of that sort are invisible, are they not?'[2]

'That is perfectly true.'

'Then shall we say there are two kinds[3] of thing, the visible and the invisible?'

'Very well.'

'The invisible being always constant, the visible never?'

'We may agree to that too.'

B 'To proceed: we ourselves are partly body, partly soul, are we not?'

'Just so.'

'Well, which kind of thing shall we say the body tends to resemble and be akin to?'

'The visible kind; anyone can see that.'

'And the soul? Is that visible or invisible?'

'Not visible to the human eye, at all events, Socrates.'

'Oh well, we were speaking of what is or is not visible to mankind: or are you thinking of some other sort of being?'

'No: of a human being.'

---

[1] Of two things called beautiful one may be to-day more beautiful, to-morrow less so, than the other; of two things called equal one may come to be greater, or smaller, than the other. But it seems possible that οὔτε ἀλλήλοις may be added simply because equality involves two terms. I do not see how ἀλλήλοις can, as Burnet supposes, refer to things appearing beautiful or ugly, equal or unequal *to different people*, as they were said to do at 74B8.

[2] The pleonasm ἀιδῆ καὶ οὐχ ὁρατά, though of a sort common enough in Greek, would be intolerable in English.

[3] As Prof. Grube has pointed out, the words εἶδος and ἰδέα are not used in a technical sense until 103 E, and thereafter become common. It is possible that this is due, or partly due, to the need to use εἶδος in its ordinary sense of 'class' or 'kind' here.

'Then what is our decision about the soul, that it can be seen, or cannot?'

'That it cannot.'

'In fact it is invisible?'

'Yes.'

'Hence soul rather than body is like the invisible, while body rather than soul is like the visible.'

'Unquestionably, Socrates.'   C

'Now were we not saying some time ago that when the soul makes use of the body to investigate something through vision or hearing or some other sense—of course investigating by means of the body is the same as investigating by sense—it is dragged by the body towards objects that are never constant, and itself wanders in a sort of dizzy drunken confusion, inasmuch as it is apprehending confused objects?'

'Just so.'

'But when it investigates by itself alone, it passes to that other world D of pure, everlasting, immortal, constant being, and by reason of its kinship thereto abides ever therewith, whensoever it has come to be by itself and is suffered to do so; and then it has rest from wandering and ever keeps close to that being, unchanged and constant, inasmuch as it is apprehending unchanging objects. And is not the experience which it then has called intelligence?'

'All you have said, Socrates, is true and admirably put.'

'Once again, then, on the strength of our previous arguments as well as of this last, which of the two kinds of thing do you find that soul resembles and is more akin to?'   E

'On the strength of our present line of inquiry, Socrates, I should think that the veriest dullard would agree that the soul has a far and away greater resemblance to everlasting, unchanging being than to its opposite.'

'And what does the body resemble?'

'The other kind.'

'Now consider a further point. When soul and body are conjoined, Nature prescribes that the latter should be slave and subject, the former 80 master and ruler. Which of the two, in your judgement, does that suggest as being like the divine, and which like the mortal? Don't you think it naturally belongs to the divine to rule and lead, and to the mortal to be ruled and subjected?'

'Yes, I do.'

'Then which is soul like?'

'Of course it is obvious, Socrates, that soul is like the divine, and body like the mortal.'

'Would you say then, Cebes, that the result of our whole discussion
B amounts to this: on the one hand we have that which is divine, immortal, indestructible, of a single form, accessible to thought, ever constant and abiding true to itself; and the soul is very like it: on the other hand we have that which is human, mortal, destructible, of many forms, inaccessible to thought,[1] never constant nor abiding true to itself; and the body is very like that. Is there anything to be said against that, dear Cebes?'

'Nothing.'

'Well then, that being so, isn't it right and proper for the body to be quickly destroyed, but for the soul to be altogether indestructible, or nearly so?'
c   'Certainly.'

The argument of this section is directed against Cebes's fear that the soul may be blown to pieces or dispersed at death.

(1) The first part (78 B 4–79 c 1), reduced to essentials, is as follows: only composite things can be dispersed, and that the soul is not a composite thing may be inferred from the fact that it belongs to the same order as the incomposite Forms; for like them it is invisible and changeless, in contrast to body which, belonging to the same order as sensible things, is visible and changing.

In thus associating the properties of simplicity (non-compositeness) and immutability Plato is influenced by Parmenides, whose One Being is changeless (*frag.* 8, 38–42 DK, where, as Cornford points out (*Plato and Parmenides*, p. 42) ἀκίνητον 'denies both locomotion and change of any sort'), indivisible and homogeneous (*ibid.* p. 22 οὐδὲ διαιρετόν ἐστιν, ἐπεὶ πᾶν ἐστιν ὁμοῖον. By πᾶν ὁμοῖον Parmenides intended to deny that his Being is made up of distinguishable parts, from which it followed that it could not be divided into *unlike* parts; nor indeed could it be divided into *like* parts, for any division would entail a void or gap of non-being; but the idea of division into *like* parts is not, I think, in Plato's mind when he speaks of τὸ ἀσύνθετον here.

Socrates expresses the conclusion of this first part at the end of 79 B in the words ὁμοιότερον ἄρα ψυχὴ σώματός ἐστιν τῷ ἀιδεῖ, τὸ δὲ τῷ ὁρατῷ. Now this is puzzling, since it has just been agreed, and is indeed

---

[1] The word ἀνόητος usually means 'foolish', but for using it to mean 'not the object of thought' Plato has the precedent of Parmenides 8, 17 DK. Burnet speaks of a 'play on words', but it is hardly that.

an obvious fact, that soul is invisible. If it *is* invisible, what sense is there in saying that it is more like what is invisible than body is? What we should expect is ὁμοιότερον ἄρα ψυχὴ σώματός ἐστι τῷ ἀεὶ κατὰ ταὐτὰ ἔχοντι, τὸ δὲ τῷ μή. But I think we can see why Plato has not written that: it is because he wishes to postpone this conclusion to a later point, namely until he has put forward a second argument (79 C 2–E 7); only then does Socrates admit that each of these arguments proves the same thing (καὶ ἐκ τῶν πρόσθεν καὶ ἐκ τῶν νῦν λεγομένων, 79 D 9). It is difficult, however, to see that anything is gained by this postponement; the two arguments do in fact establish the point independently of each other; but the illogicality of the conclusion at 79 B 15 is natural enough in view of the dichotomy of 79 A 6 τὸ μὲν ὁρατόν, τὸ δὲ ἀιδές: it amounts in fact to saying that soul belongs to the class of τὸ ἀιδές *and therefore* (in virtue of 79 A 9–10) to the class of τὸ ἀεὶ κατὰ ταὐτὰ ἔχον, while body belongs to the class of τὸ ὁρατόν *and therefore* (again in virtue of 79 A 10) to the class of τὸ μηδέποτε κατὰ ταὐτά.

(2) The second part of the section (79 C 2–E 7) is professedly a reminder of what was said a while ago (viz. 65 B ff.); but in point of fact it is a restatement or amplification of that in terms of what has just been established regarding the opposition of changeless Forms to mutable sensibles. We should here especially note the addition of συγγενέστερον to ὁμοιότερον at E 1: the soul is not merely like the Forms; in knowing them it has the intimate and satisfying relation of 'kinship', with all the emotional colouring that attaches to that word. The love of φρόνησις, of which Socrates has spoken earlier (68 A), is the union of the soul with that which is near and dear to it.

(3) The third and final argument (79 E 8–80 A 9) for the soul's affinity to the unseen order rests on its 'natural' right to rule the body. The unseen is now called 'divine', which to a Greek is no more than calling it 'immortal', as Socrates has already done (79 D 2); yet the new epithet helps to commend the argument, since rule is an appanage of divinity.

If we are to look for any earlier source of this argument, we should probably find it in Anaxagoras, for whom νοῦς is 'the finest and purest of all things, and has full knowledge of all, and is mightiest in power' (*frag.* 12 DK).

Socrates now draws the conclusion of the whole matter; from the affinities established we may infer that, whereas body must soon be broken up, soul is 'altogether indestructible or nearly so'. What is the reason for the disappointing limitation expressed in the words 'or nearly so'? It lies, I think, in the ambiguity of τὸ ἀιδές. If understood as the whole class of things invisible, this will, or may, include other members besides Forms, and the dichotomy of 79 A 6 certainly leads us to believe that Plato at least *begins* by giving it this sense; yet if that is so, he almost immediately narrows the meaning so as to include nothing but Forms, and the question becomes not 'which of the two orders of things does soul belong to?' but 'which of two kinds of things, Forms or sensibles, does soul resemble, and which does body?' Thenceforward the vague notion of likeness replaces the notion of membership of an order, all members of which have certain attributes; and Plato recognises in the end that, just because 'likeness' is a vague notion, his argument can at most establish approximate indissolubility of soul.

A possible criticism of this whole section must finally be taken into account. When Cebes suggests that the soul may be blown to pieces, why does not Socrates simply reply that the suggestion assumes the soul to be material, which it is not? The answer to this question is not that Plato has not fully grasped the conception of immateriality or spirituality, nor that he has any doubt that the soul is immaterial; the failure to grasp the conception and apply it to soul lies not with Plato, but with Cebes. Socrates (Plato) sees that Cebes's suggestion can only be refuted by showing him that there are things which are immaterial, namely Forms and souls; and this he shows in language which Cebes and other instinctive materialists can understand.

X

As an afterthought to the conclusion just reached, Socrates remarks that we can hardly suppose the soul to be less enduring than the bones and sinews of the body, which are virtually indestructible. He then proceeds to contrast the fate of the philosopher's soul, purified by the 'training for death', with that of others, whose future incarnations, some in human bodies, some in animal, are determined by the kind of training to which they have been subjected in this present life.

'Now you are aware that when a man dies his body, the visible part 80 c of him which belongs to the visible world, the corpse as we call it, which in the natural course is destroyed, falling to pieces and scattered to the winds, does not undergo any part of this fate immediately, but survives for quite a considerable time, indeed for a very long time if death finds the body in favourable condition and comes at a favourable season:[1] for that matter,[2] a corpse that has been shrunk and embalmed, in the Egyptian fashion, will remain almost entire for ages and ages; and some parts of the body, such as bones, sinews and so forth, even D when decomposition has occurred, are virtually immortal. Isn't that so?'

'Yes.'

'What then of the soul, the invisible thing which passes to an invisible region,[3] a region of splendour and purity, literally the "unseen"

[1] It seems to me certain that the words ἐὰν μέν...καὶ πάνυ μάλα describe what happens when conditions are specially favourable to preservation, for καὶ πάνυ μάλα must surely indicate a longer time than ἐπιεικῶς. If that is so, χαριέντως ἔχων τὸ σῶμα will not mean 'with his body in good condition' (though indeed this is the natural sense of the phrase, and is accepted by Burnet); for, as Burnet points out: 'a healthy body decomposes more rapidly than an old and withered one'; it will mean 'in a favourable condition' (*sc.* to preservation). I have been unable to find a parallel for this sense of χαριέντως or χαριείς: but it does not seem to me impossible. As to ὥρᾳ, I have little doubt that Burnet is right in translating 'season of the year': τοιαύτῃ I take to mean 'correspondingly favourable'.

Prof. G. C. Forsey (*C.Q.* 1926, p. 177) resorts to an emendation which I find unconvincing.

[2] γάρ is, as often, elliptical: ⟨'this is confirmed by a familiar occurrence'⟩ for....

[3] I cannot doubt that despite Burnet's note τοιοῦτον ἕτερον is equivalent to ἀιδῆ. In that case καὶ ἀιδῆ in line 6 is intolerable, and is probably a gloss by someone who thought that this adjective should come *immediately* before εἰς Ἅιδου ὡς ἀληθῶς.

world of Hades,[1] into the presence of the good and wise god,[2] whither, if god will, my own soul must shortly pass? Having found what its nature is like, are we going to say that when it quits the body it is immediately blown to pieces and annihilated, as most people maintain?[3] Far from it, E my friends: the truth of the matter is very different. Let us suppose that a soul departs in a state of purity, trailing nothing bodily after it inasmuch as during life it has had as little connexion as possible with the body, has shunned it and gathered itself together to be by itself—a state it has always been training for, training itself, in fact, to die readily: which is precisely 81 what true philosophy consists in, as I think you would agree?'

'I agree entirely.'

'Well, will not a soul in such condition depart into the world of the invisible which it resembles, where all is divine, immortal and wise,[4] and having come thither attain happiness, released from its wanderings and follies and fears, its wild desires and all the other ills that beset mankind? Will it not truly dwell, as the initiated are alleged to dwell, in the company of the gods for all time to come?[5] May we say that, Cebes, or may we not?'

'Yes, indeed we may', replied Cebes.

[1] Plato is ready to accept or reject popular etymologies according as they do or do not suit his momentary purpose. The etymology of 'Hades' here accepted is rejected at *Cratylus* 404 B.

[2] I doubt whether any allusion is intended to εὐβουλεύς as an epithet of Hades, as Burnet suggests. Socrates has spoken earlier (63 B) of his going to join θεοὺς ἄλλους σοφούς τε καὶ ἀγαθούς—in the plural, which he again uses at 81 A 9. Plato is notoriously indifferent about speaking of 'god' or 'gods' (see Cornford, *Plato's Cosmology*, p. 280), and Hades is brought in here simply for the sake of the etymology.

[3] This is a noteworthy assertion, but perhaps 'most people' (οἱ πολλοὶ ἄνθρωποι) should not be taken too literally; there was, no doubt, much variety of belief or half-belief about the soul's fate in the fourth century. 'The Classical Age', writes Prof. Dodds (*op. cit.* p. 179), 'inherited a whole series of inconsistent pictures of the "soul" or "self"—the living corpse in the grave, the shadowy image in Hades, the perishable breath that is spilt in the air or absorbed in the aether, the daemon that is reborn in other bodies.'

[4] The three adjectives θεῖον, ἀθάνατον, φρόνιμον should be taken as applying directly not to the place of the departed soul, but rather to the gods or god (already called φρόνιμον at 80 D 7) whose place it is. The collective neuter is due to the apposition with τὸ ἀιδές. Grammarians (or pedants) might say there is a 'slight zeugma' in the use of εἰς.

[5] According to this passage the philosopher's soul can escape from the 'wheel of birth' after a single incarnation; herein our dialogue differs from the *Phaedrus* (249 A), where it can only do so after three times choosing the philosophic life: cf. Pindar, *Ol.* II, 68 ff. ὅσοι δ' ἐτόλμασαν ἐστρὶς ἑκατέρωθι μείναντες ἀπὸ πάμπαν ἀδίκων ἔχειν ψυχάν κ.τ.λ. The discrepancy may be due to Plato's closer adherence in the later dialogue to the details of Orphic eschatology.

'But now let us suppose that another soul departs polluted, un- B
cleansed of the body's taint, inasmuch as it has always associated with
the body and tended it, filled with its lusts and so bewitched by its
passions and pleasures as to think nothing real save what is bodily,
what can be touched and seen and eaten and made to serve sexual
enjoyment; while it has grown to hate and shun with terror the things
that are invisible, obscure to the eyes but to be seized by philosophic
thought. Do you believe that a soul in such condition as that will
depart unsullied, alone by itself?'   C

'That could never be so.'

'No: it would be interspersed, I think, with a bodily element which
had been worked into its substance by unceasing commerce and association with the body, and by long training.'[1]

'Just so.'

'Yes, my friend; and we must think of that element as a ponderous,
heavy, earthy and visible substance; and the soul that carries it is
weighed down and dragged back into the visible world; you know the
stories about souls which, in their dread of the invisible that is called
Hades, roam about tombs and burying-places, in the neighbourhood of D
which, it is alleged,[2] ghostly phantoms of souls have actually been
seen—just the sort of wraiths that souls like that would produce, souls
which are not pure when they are released but still retain some of that
visible substance, which is just why they can be seen.'

'It may well be so, Socrates.'

'It may indeed, Cebes, and it is certainly not the souls of the righteous,
but those of the wicked that are compelled to wander about such places,
as the penalty for bad nurture in the past. And they must continue to
wander until they are once more chained up in a body, by reason of the
desires of that bodily attendant which is ever at their side; and naturally E
they will be chained to the type of character that they have trained
themselves to exhibit in their lifetime.'

'What types have you in mind, Socrates?'

'I mean, for example, that those who have trained themselves in
gluttony, unchastity and drunkenness, instead of carefully avoiding
them, will naturally join the company of donkeys or some such creatures, 82
will they not?'

---

[1] The opposite of the μελέτη θανάτου spoken of above.
[2] By ὥσπερ λέγεται and δή (semi-ironical) Socrates maintains a non-committal
attitude on these ghostly apparitions.

'Yes, very naturally.'

'Whereas those who have set more value upon injuring and plundering and tyrannising over their fellows will join the wolves and hawks and kites. Or should we give such souls as these some other destination?'

'By no means', said Cebes; 'leave them where you have put them.'

'Then it is obvious, I take it, where all the other types will go conformably to the roles in which they have severally trained themselves.'

'Quite obvious, I agree.'

'Now if we may call any of these happy, the happiest, who pass to the most favoured region, are they that have practised the common B virtues of social life, what are called temperance and justice, virtues which spring from habit and training devoid of philosophic wisdom.'

'Why are they the happiest?'

'Because they will naturally find themselves in another well-conducted society resembling their old one, a society of bees, perhaps, or wasps or ants; and later on they may rejoin the human race they have left, and turn into respectable men.'

'Naturally enough.'

'But the society of gods none shall join who has not sought wisdom C and departed wholly pure; only the lover of knowledge may go thither. And that is the reason, dear friends, why true philosophers abstain from the desires of the body, standing firm and never surrendering to them; they are not troubled about poverty and loss of estate like the common lover of riches;[1] nor yet is their abstinence due to fear of the dishonour and disgrace that attach to an evil life, the fear felt by the lovers of power and position.'

'No, that would be unworthy of them, Socrates', remarked Cebes.

D   'Most certainly it would', he replied. 'And that of course, Cebes, is why one who is concerned about his own soul, instead of spending his life getting his body into good shape,[2] says good-bye to all that sort of thing; and while the rest follow a road which leads them they know not whither, he takes another one: holding that he must never act against philosophy and that deliverance and purification which philosophy achieves, he proceeds in the direction whither philosophy points him.'

---

[1] Socrates himself was untroubled by the πενία μυρία (*Apol.* 23 c) to which the pursuit of his vocation had reduced him.

[2] Reading σώματα with T and W. σῶμα πλάττειν, 'to mould the body', is implicitly contrasted with ψυχὴν πλάττειν: cf. *Tim.* 88 c and Taylor's note *ad loc.*

We have been told already of Socrates's faith that he will pass at death into the keeping of 'wise and good gods' (63B); we have been told too that he has practised the philosophic life to the best of his ability (67C, 69D). Latent in the account of the philosopher's future blessedness we may have discerned the converse picture of a less happy destiny for those who have failed to practise the 'training for death'; and it is now that this comes to the surface.

That the picture, which includes the transmigration of human souls into animal bodies, is not intended to be taken as established truth or matter of certain knowledge is evident, if from nothing else, from the repeated use of the word εἰκός, 'probable' (81D, E; 82A, B). Clearly too there are elements of light satire, especially in the passage (82A–B) describing the destiny of those who practise δημοτικὴ καὶ πολιτικὴ ἀρετή.[1] It is the only passage in Plato outside the myths where transmigration into animal bodies (as distinct from human reincarnation) is affirmed; and Frutiger, partly for this reason, regards the whole section 80D–84B as mythical;[2] this seems to me to go too far; it is speculative and imaginative, yet in form at all events it is dialectical. If we take into account what Socrates says later (114D), after recounting an elaborate myth which reaffirms transmigration, albeit very briefly, (113A), I think we must admit that this, as well as human reincarnation, is a religious belief which Plato held in the period of the great middle dialogues, though it may well be that he abandoned transmigration in later years.[3]

However that may be, Plato is completely serious in arguing that if the soul is reincarnated its new life in the body, whether human or animal, will be such as it has fitted itself for in its present life; and it is upon this that he is concerned here to insist. As to pains and penalties to be endured between incarnations, there is bare mention of them, but no more; there is nothing like the vivid picture of torments in the myth of Er (*Republic* X); there is no hint of the incurable sinners of the *Gorgias* myth (525B), though these reappear in the myth of the present dialogue (113E); nor again is there any suggestion of souls choosing their new lives, as they do in *Rep.* X, 617E ff. and *Phaedrus* 249B. From these silences, however, it would not be legitimate to infer anything as to Plato's beliefs in these matters: we should not expect him always to say all that he might say on a given topic: indeed it would be inappropriate to the dialogue form that he should do so.

---

[1] On Plato's varying estimate of non-philosophic goodness Archer-Hind's valuable Appendix 1 to his edition of the dialogue should be consulted.

[2] *Op. cit.* p. 61.

[3] Cf. my commentary on *Phaedrus*, pp. 88 ff.

XI

82D–85B SOCRATES DESCRIBES THE PHILOSOPHER'S
PROGRESS AND DECLARES HIS SWAN-SONG
TO BE A SONG OF JOY

Recalling philosophy's task of delivering the soul from its bodily prison,
Socrates maintains that the greatest evil of attachment to the body is
a false estimate of reality. Once the deliverance is begun, the true philo-
sopher will not slip back, but will continue in contemplation of divine truth
until death releases him from all human afflictions.

A long silence ensues, after which it appears that Cebes and Simmias
still harbour doubts, but are reluctant to trouble Socrates further in his
'sad situation'. For this expression he gently rebukes them, adding that
just as the dying swan sings not, as men suppose, for sorrow but for joy, so
he who, like the swan, is a servant of Apollo and endowed by him with
prophetic power, joyously foresees a happy deliverance from this life.

82D 'How so, Socrates?'

'I will tell you', he replied. 'The lover of knowledge recognises that
E when philosophy takes over his soul it is a veritable prisoner fast bound
within his body and cemented thereto; and that instead of investigating
reality by itself and through itself it is compelled to peer through the
bars of its prison, wallowing in utter ignorance; moreover the philosopher's eye discerns the ingenuity of a prison in which the prisoner's
desire can be the means of ensuring that he will co-operate in his own
83 incarceration.[1] So then, the lover of knowledge, as I was saying,
recognises that such is the plight of his soul when philosophy takes it
over, and whispers a word of comfort, essaying its release and showing
how utterly deceitful are the senses, whether it be through eye or ear or
any other organ that one seeks to comprehend: urging and exhorting
the soul to withdraw from these, so far as that is possible, and to assemble
B and gather itself together, putting its trust in itself and in nothing else

---

[1] Archer-Hind, Burnet and Robin all put a comma after ἐστίν, taking the
subject to be ὁ εἱργμός. But I do not believe that any satisfactory sense can be
got out of ὁ εἱργμὸς δι' ἐπιθυμίας ἐστίν, and I take the literal meaning to be 'discerning
the ingenuity of the prison, consisting in the fact that the way in which the prisoner
would be most likely to co-operate in his own incarceration is through his desire'.
The prison is of course the body, regarded as the seat of ἐπιθυμίαι, and the
ἐπιθυμίαι serve as chains.

whensoever it conceives by itself its several objects by themselves, but deeming no truth to dwell in any of those fluctuating objects which it studies through external aids; of which latter sort are all things sensible and visible, while the object of the soul's own eye is intelligible and invisible. Wherefore the soul of the true philosopher, believing that it must not resist this deliverance, abstains, as we have seen, from pleasures and desires and pains so far as may be; and reflects that, when a man is violently stirred by pleasure or fear or desire, there comes upon him not merely some such lesser evil as might be expected, sickness maybe, c or loss of money spent on satisfying his desires, but the greatest and worst of all evils, though indeed he does not reflect upon it.'

'And what is this greatest evil?' asked Cebes.

'It is this, that no man's soul can feel intense pleasure or pain in anything without also at the same time believing that the chief object of these his emotions is transparently clear and utterly real, though in fact it is not; this is especially the case with visible objects, as you may agree.'

'I certainly do.'

'Well, when that happens, isn't the soul more than ever fast bound D by the body?'

'How do you mean?'

'Every pleasure and every pain drives as it were a rivet into the soul, pinning it down to the body and so assimilating it thereto that it believes everything to be real which the body declares so to be. Indeed it seems to me an inevitable result of sharing the body's beliefs[1] and joys that the soul should adopt its habits and upbringing, and so be destined never to reach Hades in a pure condition, but always to depart with much taint of the body, and therefore to fall back again soon into E another body, like a seed replanted in new soil; a fate which denies it all converse with that which is divine and pure and single of form.'

'What you say is perfectly true, Socrates', Cebes remarked.

'So that, Cebes, is the reason why genuine philosophers are orderly and brave; it is not for the reasons which weigh with the multitude;[2] or do you think it is?'

---

[1] ὁμοδοξεῖν τῷ σώματι is a loose phrase, which taken literally would imply that the body can have beliefs or opinions; but it is intelligible enough in the context.

[2] I follow the papyrus (Arsinoitica) and Hermann in excising φασί in E6; for the complement to be understood with φασί could, in my judgement, only be αὐτούς (viz. τοὺς φιλομαθεῖς) κοσμίους εἶναι, not αὐτοὶ κόσμιοι εἶναι: but we have not been told anything about the motives alleged by the multitude for the philosopher's virtues, whereas we have heard much (68 D ff.) about the motives which account for the so-called virtues of the multitude.

84   'No indeed, I do not.'

'No: the soul of a philosopher will reflect as we have said, and will not suppose that, while it is the task of philosophy to secure its release, it should thwart that task by surrendering itself to pleasures and pains, and so relapse into its old imprisonment, like Penelope at the interminable task of undoing her web; rather will it abate the storm of desire by taking reason as its guide and constant companion, by contemplating the utter certainty of divine reality and finding sustenance
B therein. After this manner the soul deems that all its earthly life should be lived, and that when that is ended it will pass into the presence of a kindred being like unto itself, quit of all human evils. Surely if that be the manner of its sustenance, my friends, we need not be alarmed about its having to fear that on its release from the body it may be dissipated, blown to pieces by the winds, vanishing into thin air and existing no longer anywhere.'

C   When Socrates had finished there was a long silence; to judge from his look he was pondering on what he had just said, as indeed were most of us others; Cebes and Simmias were having a few words[1] with each other, and Socrates observing this asked, 'What is it? Can it be that you find something unsatisfactory in the argument? No doubt a thoroughgoing examination would still find plenty of dubious points and grounds for objection. Of course if you two have something else in mind, that is no affair of mine: but if you do feel difficulties about the present question, do not hesitate to state them in your own words and expound
D any views you may have that seem more correct; and if you think you will clear things up better with my help, take me into your counsels once again.'

'Then here', replied Simmias, 'is the plain truth: Cebes and I have for some time been worried, each of us egging the other on and urging him to raise his point; we want to hear your answer, but we hesitate to trouble you with anything which in your sad situation you may find distasteful.'

At this Socrates smiled and proceeded: 'Dear me, Simmias. It looks as if I should have a hard job to convince the world in general that
E I don't consider my present situation a sad one, when I can't convince even you two, who are so afraid that I am in a more disagreeable plight

---

[1] This seems to me the natural meaning of σμικρὸν διελέγεσθην and I do not think Burnet supplies any real evidence for the meaning 'went on talking in a low voice'.

now than I ever was before. And I fancy you must think me a poorer sort of prophet than the swans; for they, when they realise that they have to die, sing more, and sing more sweetly than they have ever sung 85 before, rejoicing at the prospect of going into the presence of that god whose servants they are; though indeed human beings, because of their own fear of dying, malign them, making out that their departing song is a painful lament for death; they fail to reflect that no bird sings when it is hungry or cold or feels any sort of pain, not even the nightingale itself, nor the swallow nor the hoopoe; of course the story is that these birds sing a lament because of their pain, but I don't believe that is true either of them or of the swans: what I think is that belonging as they do to Apollo, they are prophetic creatures who foresee the blessings B in store for them in Hades, and therefore sing with greater delight on that last day than ever before. And as for me, I count myself a fellow-servant of the swans, dedicated to the same god, and favoured by my master with prophetic power equal to theirs; nor am I more sorrowful than they in departing this life. No; so far as that goes, you should say what you will and ask what you will, so long as the prison authorities of Athens permit you.'

Socrates here continues to dwell on the contrast of the two orders and the two corresponding ways of life, with an increasing eloquence and perhaps a deeper feeling than before. Philosophy is in the earlier part of the section personified for a moment in a way that makes us think of that sustained personification which we find nearly a thousand years later in the *Consolatio Philosophiae* of Boethius.

One notable point is the declaration that the greatest evil resulting from excessive pleasures or other emotional disturbances is a false estimate of truth or reality (83C). We, with our modern labels and distinctions of moral and intellectual, of ethics and metaphysics, tend to feel surprised at this, and to object that the greatest evil springing from uncontrolled emotion or undue indulgence in the pleasures of sense lies not in intellectual error but in wrongdoing. From the Socratic and Platonic standpoint, however, the antithesis is unreal; the falsity which they have in mind is a reversal of values which is both intellectual and moral; to deem the beauties of the visible world more real than those of the invisible is not mere intellectual misjudgement, but a misdirection of the will, an avoidable blindness of the soul. This Socrates himself implies when he goes on to say that the soul of one in this condition is more than ever imprisoned, or (varying his metaphor) that pleasure and pain—that is to say intemperate lust for physical pleasures and immoderate aversion from physical pains—rivet the soul to the body, and then adds in the same breath (in a dependent participial clause) 'when it believes everything to be real which the body declares so to be'.

His last speech before the silence which ensues at 84 c is one of those massive and magnificent periodic structures in which Plato can harness rhetoric in the service of his own deep feeling and conviction. It ends with his scouting once more as incredible the notion that the soul is torn apart or blown to pieces when it quits the body.

It is fitting that this should be followed by a long silence; and the reader's own emotion is quietened by the narrator's report of Cebes and Simmias talking to each other, and of their reluctance to trouble the master any further in his 'sad situation'. After a gentle rebuke for this expression, Socrates declares that his confidence of happiness beyond the grave rests on the prophetic power conferred upon him by Apollo, whose servant he is. It is quite possible that he did in fact say something of the sort on this last day; we have seen already (p. 29 *supra*) that he regarded himself as the servant of Apollo; and in the *Apology* (40 A) he speaks of his 'sign' as 'my customary prophetic power'. But there is a curious discrepancy between *Apology* and *Phaedo* in this connexion: in the former Socrates interprets the silence of his 'voice' on the morning of the trial as evidence that a good thing is about to befall him (40 A–C), whereas in the latter nothing is said about the 'voice' or 'sign', but he claims the power to foresee the same good. I have called this a discrepancy, but the two reports are not contradictory, and it is quite possible that Plato has given the substance of what his master said on the two occasions. The striking comparison of himself to the swans, however, is in my judgement more likely to be Platonic than Socratic.[1]

---

[1] I do not know of any modern discussion of this point, nor was any to be expected: it must remain a matter of opinion.

XII

Simmias, after some general reflexions on the right attitude to problems of this sort, proceeds to elaborate a theory of the soul as an 'attunement' (ἀρμονία) of the bodily constituents. Then Cebes argues that, despite the fact that any soul endures longer than any body, we cannot be sure that it can outlast the whole series of bodies which (as he contends) succeed one another throughout a man's lifetime, any more than a weaver can outlast the whole series of cloaks that he weaves and wears.

'Thank you', said Simmias. 'Then I will tell you my difficulty, and 85 B Cebes here in his turn will say what he finds unacceptable in the argu- C ment. What I feel, Socrates—and perhaps you feel the same yourself— is that certainty of knowledge on matters like this is either impossible of attainment in this life or very difficult; nevertheless he would be a very feeble-spirited person who failed to subject current opinions about them to the closest scrutiny; one should not desist until he has worn himself out in a thoroughgoing inquiry. In fact we ought to achieve one of two things: either to find for ourselves, or learn from some other, the truth about these matters: or else, if that is impossible, to seize upon the best and most irrefutable doctrine that mankind can offer, and take it as a raft on which to accomplish the dangerous voyage D of life; unless indeed we can come to harbour in a safer and less dangerous fashion, resting on the firmer support of doctrine divinely revealed. That being so, I shall not scruple to put my question, as you indeed bid me, and I shall not have to blame myself later on for failing to say what I think. The fact is, Socrates, that on reflecting by myself and with our friend here on what has been said, I don't feel altogether satisfied.'

'Maybe you are right in that, my friend', replied Socrates; 'but tell E me on what point you are dissatisfied.'

'The point is this', said Simmias. 'One could apply the same argu- ment to the attunement[1] of a lyre and its strings: one could say that the

---

[1] The primary meaning of ἀρμονία is right adjustment, the fitting together of two or more things, and in particular of the strings of a lyre. The right adjust- ment of the strings is an attunement, that is to say it is such adjustment as will enable a player to produce a succession of notes separated by precise intervals. The term naturally came to be used of these successions, or scales, and it is in

attunement in the tuned lyre is something invisible, incorporeal, lovely
86 and divine; whereas the strings are bodies, corporeal, composite,
earthy and akin to all that is mortal. Now suppose the lyre came to be
smashed or split, or its strings to be broken: somebody might adopt
your argument and insist that the attunement had not been destroyed,
but must still exist: for, he would argue, it is impossible for such mortal
objects as the lyre with its strings broken, and the strings themselves,
still to exist, and yet for the attunement to have perished; how could
B this thing of such close kinship with the divine and the immortal
perish sooner than that mortal object? No, he would say: the attunement must still exist somewhere, and before anything happens to it the
wooden frame and the strings will have rotted away. And in point of
fact I fancy that you yourself are well aware, Socrates, that we mostly
hold a view of this sort about the soul: we regard the body as held
together in a state of tension by the hot, the cold, the dry and the moist,
and so forth, and the soul as the blending or attunement of these in the
C right and due proportion.[1] Now if the soul really is a kind of attunement, plainly when our body is unduly relaxed or tautened by sickness
or some other trouble, the soul, for all its divine nature, is bound forthwith to be destroyed, just as much as any other attunement or adjustment—in musical notes, for instance, or in a craftsman's product;
whereas the bodily remains will last for a considerable time, until they
D are burnt or rot away. So see what answer you can find for us to this
argument, which insists that the soul, being a blending of the bodily
constituents, is the first thing to perish in what is called death.'

At this Socrates stared broadly, as his habit was, and then smiled and
remarked: 'Certainly Simmias's request is fair enough. Well now, if
anybody here present is readier with a solution than I am, why doesn't

virtue of this secondary meaning, and of the fact that scales are, so to speak, the
raw material of all melodies, that ἁρμονία is here called πάγκαλόν τι καὶ θεῖον. Nevertheless, in the conception of soul as a ἁρμονία it is the primary meaning of
adjustment, or being in tune, that is before us.

[1] The 'opposites' composing the body correspond to the strings of a lyre,
whose attunement is secured by the right degree of tension. The use of the word
'blending' (κρᾶσις) and the corresponding verb in B9, C2 and D2, as synonymous
with or explanatory of ἁρμονία is natural enough in the case of the body, for the
opposites can be indifferently thought of as mixed or as adjusted; in fact the two
notions, mixing and adjustment, are indistinguishable whether we think of one
pair only (e.g. hot and cold) or of all the pairs (indefinite in number, καὶ τοιούτων
τινῶν, B9) taken together. But in the case of the lyre there is no κρᾶσις, only
ἁρμονία of the strings: hence as we should expect, when we come to the refutation
of Simmias's theory (92Aff.) the words κρᾶσις and κεράννυσθαι do not reappear.

he reply? The fact is our friend seems to argue very ably. However, before we answer him I suggest that we should first hear what objection E Cebes here has to make; then we could have an interval for considering our reply; and having listened to them both we shall either decide that they have hit the right note,[1] and adopt their views, or else we shall deem it the proper moment to plead for our own theory. So come now, Cebes: it is your turn to tell us what was troubling you.' 'Very well,' said Cebes, 'I will. It seems to me that we are still just where we were:[2] the theory is open to the same objection as was made a while back. As 87 to the existence of our souls before they entered this bodily frame, I do not withdraw my assent: I think that has been very neatly and, if it isn't presumptuous to say so, very cogently shown; but I do not think the same about their still existing somewhere after our death. I don't indeed doubt that a soul is something stronger and longer-lasting than a body: as to that I dissent from Simmias's criticism; in all that field I regard soul as far and away the superior. "Why then", the question will be put, "are you still in doubt, when you observe the weaker part of the dead man still in existence? Don't you believe that the longer-lasting part must necessarily be preserved so long as the other is?" B Well, see if there is any substance in my reply to that; for I feel I too need to employ an illustration, no less than Simmias did.

'I think this would be an analogy to what we have been saying: an elderly weaver dies, and someone argues that the man has not perished, but is still in existence somewhere; as evidence for this he points to the fact that the cloak which he had woven for himself and was wearing still exists, and has not perished; and if anybody doubts his word, he will ask him which lasts longer, a human being or a cloak that is constantly c being worn; and when the objector replies that a human being is far the longer-lived of the two, he thinks he has proved that beyond all doubt the weaver is still in existence, inasmuch as his shorter-lived cloak has not perished. But in fact, Simmias, I think that is not so: I want you too to consider my point. Anyone might retort that the author of this argument is being stupid: for the weaver in the story, after having woven and worn out cloak after cloak, perishes after all of them, I grant, except the last of all: he perishes before that one, but it doesn't D follow from that that a human being is feebler or weaker than a cloak. Now this same illustration can, as I think be applied to body and soul:

---

[1] With προσᾴδειν I understand τῷ ἀληθεῖ.
[2] I.e. at 77E, before the argument based on the affinity of souls and Forms.

exactly the same might be said, and in my opinion rightly said, in respect of them, namely that the soul lasts longer and the body is weaker and lasts less long; but of course the critic would maintain that any soul can wear out a number of bodies, especially in the case of a long life; the body may well stream and waste away while its owner E still lives, yet the soul will always replace the worn-out tissue with new-woven material: but for all that, when the soul does perish, it must needs be wearing its last garment, and perish before that, though it has survived all the others; and it will only be when the soul has thus perished that the body will reveal its inherent weakness and vanish in swift corruption.

'Consequently we cannot properly rely on our present argument; we cannot as yet feel confident that when we die our souls still exist some-88 where. No: for (my critic continues)[1] suppose we make yet further concession than you make to the author of the argument: suppose we grant him not only that our souls existed in the time before we were born, but that quite possibly some souls still exist after death, and will continue to exist, and will be born again and die again time after time—the soul's nature being so strong that it can endure a number of births; suppose we grant all that, yet unless we go on to make the final concession, namely that it is not wearied with its repeated births and does not finally perish altogether in one of its deaths—a point that might be supported[2] by arguing that no one has knowledge of this final death, B or of a dissolution of the body which brings destruction upon the soul, a thing which none of us can possibly perceive: if, I repeat, our position is what I have stated, and this final concession is not made, then nobody is entitled to a rational confidence in face of death unless he can prove that the soul is absolutely incapable of death or destruction;[3] if

[1] I have no doubt that Burnet is right in saying that the imaginary critic is still speaking, and that consequently σύ refers to Cebes, who has made the concession in question at 87A 1–4. Formally it is the critic by whom everything is said down to the end of 88B, but he is in fact only a polite disguise for Cebes himself: and long before the end of the paragraph the reader—and perhaps the writer too—will have forgotten his existence.

[2] The words τοῦτον δέ...ἡμῶν (88A10–B3) are part of the argument which might be advanced by one who refused to believe that the soul finally 'wearies' or wears itself out—one who, in other words, *does* make the final concession which Cebes regards his audience as unlikely to make.

[3] ἀθάνατον and ἀνώλεθρον will later (106Aff.) be distinguished in meaning, and it is possible that the distinction may be already in Plato's mind here: but I am inclined to think that as yet they are used synonymously. The same question arises at 95B, where Socrates is recapitulating Cebes's demand.

he cannot, he must admit[1] that anyone about to die will inevitably fear that his soul may be utterly destroyed at the moment of severance from his body.'

Simmias's long opening speech in this section indicates his own attitude to the general problems of life and philosophy, and we may, I think, believe that Plato means his readers to approve that attitude as right and reasonable. In effect, it rejects both the existence of revealed truth (λόγος θεῖος) and the possibility of attaining certain knowledge by human reason; but it also condemns passive agnosticism, and recommends the adoption of such probable conclusions as careful and exhaustive investigation may reach.

It may be objected that this undogmatic rationalism is unsatisfying, and that neither Socrates nor Plato was an out-and-out rationalist: both were deeply religious men, even if they could not be said to accept a λόγος θεῖος: both were convinced from the outset, and not as the result of reasoned argument, that the universe and the life of man have a meaning and a purpose; both believed in objective moral values. All that is true, yet it may well be true also that Plato at least (I would not say Socrates also) conceived himself to be a pure rationalist[2] just because he could find reasons for the faith that was in him. Simmias's philosophy implies the completely open mind which few men, if any, possess, but which many suppose themselves to possess.

As for the uncertainty of human knowledge, what Simmias says is in conformity with such earlier passages as 66E–67A, and is re-echoed at 107B: though it can hardly be reconciled with the account of the philosopher in *Republic* VI–VII.

The theory of soul as attunement (ἁρμονία) which Simmias now puts forward is a thoroughly rationalist theory, utterly opposed to the mystical and religious conceptions characteristic of Orphics and Pythagoreans. What its origin is it is impossible to say with certainty. On the one hand, despite its incompatibility with the soul's immortality, with reincarnation and transmigration, the very word ἁρμονία suggests Pythagorean origin, or at least influence; and that suggestion is borne out by the facts that Echecrates, who expresses his adherence to the

---

[1] The syntax of ἀνάγκην εἶναι is difficult to explain. Burnet says it depends on φαίη in B2, the oblique construction having been dropped for a moment at B4 (προσήκει) but now reasserting itself. This I find difficult to accept; more probably it depends on something like πᾶσι προσήκει ἡγεῖσθαι felt as the implied opposite of οὐδενὶ προσήκει…θαρρεῖν. But it may be doubted whether the complicated structure of all this long passage (88A–B) is susceptible of strict grammatical analysis.

[2] Yet Prof. Dodds (*op. cit.* ch. VII) has made out a strong case for an increasing irrationalism in Plato's latest period.

theory[1] later on (88 D), was himself a Pythagorean (Diog. Laert. VIII, 46), and that Simmias, though nowhere stated to belong to the school, had at least studied under the famous Pythagorean, Philolaus (61 D). Furthermore, the theory is partly of a medical character,[2] and Philolaus, as we learn from the papyrus[3] whose author is known as Anonymus Londinensis, wrote on medicine.

Hence there is attractiveness in Burnet's suggestion[4] that 'such a doctrine would naturally arise from the attempt to adapt Pythagoreanism to the views of the Sicilian school of medicine, which were based on the Empedoclean doctrine of the four "elements" identified with the "opposites" hot and cold, wet and dry'. Burnet would accordingly explain the 'we', the first person plural of ὑπολαμβάνομεν (86 B 6), as meaning that Simmias belongs to the Pythagorean (or perhaps we should say ex-Pythagorean) group who have made or were making such an attempt.

On the other hand there is no direct evidence for any such development within the Pythagorean school; and that the doctrine cannot be that of Philolaus himself follows from the statement in the Anonymus (the only authority for Philolaus's medical interests) that he expressly excluded 'the cold' as a factor in the human body, whereas Philistion (Anon. XX, quoted in Burnet's note on 86 B 8), like Simmias himself, included all four 'elements', with their respective powers (δυνάμεις) the hot, cold, dry and moist, in its composition.

Moreover, as Prof. G. C. Field has pointed out,[5] Aristotle, when he has occasion in the de anima (407 B 27) to mention what appears to be this very theory of Simmias, says nothing about its Pythagorean origin, while elsewhere[6] in the treatise he attributes to that school an utterly different theory of the soul. Both the Phaedo (92 D) and the de anima use very similar language about the popularity of the doctrine, and Field's conclusion seems to me, on balance, highly probable, namely that 'it was a popular view originating from some other source' (sc. than Pythagoreanism) 'at which we can only conjecture, and appealing

---

[1] A. Cameron (The Pythagorean Background of the Theory of Recollection, pp. 45 f.) deduces from 88 C–D that Echecrates believed in a ψυχὴ ἁρμονία doctrine other than that expounded by Simmias. That cannot be so: it is because of the theories of Simmias and Cebes, which he has heard Phaedo reporting, that he, like the audience in the prison, feels Socrates's earlier arguments to be unconvincing. If Echecrates had been a lifelong believer in a doctrine to the effect that soul is (in Cameron's phrase) 'a Harmonia antecedent to incarnation' he would have been quite unmoved by Simmias's exposition, though of course Cebes's argument might still have worried him.

[2] The idea of a ἁρμονία καὶ κρᾶσις of opposites in the body appears in the speech of the physician Eryximachus in Symp. 188 A.

[3] Chapter XVIII (p. 70 in the edition of W. H. S. Jones).

[4] In his note on 86 B 6; see also E.G.P.[3] pp. 295 f.

[5] Plato and his Contemporaries, pp. 179 f.   [6] 404 A 16 ff.

to individual Pythagoreans, but having no special connexion with the school'. Yet it should be added that Alcmaeon, who though not a Pythagorean appears to have had connexions with the school, made health consist in the 'balance of power' (ἰσονομία) between an indefinite number of opposites, and it is no great step to apply this to life itself.[1]

With whom then, it remains to ask, are we to understand Simmias as associating himself in the word ὑπολαμβάνομεν? I would answer, with people in general:[2] μάλιστα ὑπολαμβάνομεν would then be just another way of saying what he says at 92 D, τοῖς πολλοῖς δοκεῖ ἀνθρώποις. Of course he is exaggerating in both places; most people would never have heard of the theory; but such looseness of expression is natural enough in all ages: might not one well say to-day, 'Most people regard the second Platonic Epistle as spurious'?

It is no doubt possible, indeed it may seem probable, that a doctrine that the human soul is *in some sense* a ἁρμονία was held by the school which said that the whole universe is ἁρμονία καὶ ἀριθμός (Ar. *Met.* 986 A 2)—in some sense compatible with its immortality, e.g. the right adjustment not of the bodily constituents but of its own parts. This is suggested by A. E. Taylor (*Comm. on Timaeus*, p. 136) and by F. M. Cornford (*C.Q.* xvi, p. 146). The only positive evidence on the point is that of Macrobius (DK 44 A 23) in the fourth-fifth century A.D., and it is perhaps strange that Aristotle appears to know nothing of it. In any case a commentator on the *Phaedo* may be content to leave this particular aspect of the question open, as indeed I suspect it must be left.

The essence of Cebes's argument is not simply that showing the soul to be more enduring than the body is no proof that it survives for all time; rather it is that the whole of Socrates's answer to the doubt of the 'child within us' has tacitly assumed that there is one single body persisting throughout a man's lifetime, and that the falsity of this assumption vitiates the conclusion based on it. The general proposition that soul is more enduring than body cannot properly be taken to mean that a single soul can outlast an indefinite number of bodies succeeding one another through a lifetime, as in fact (so Cebes maintains) they do. And the perishing of the last of this series is not merely compatible with the soul having perished before it, but is actually due to that: it comes about simply because there is no longer a soul to

---

[1] Diog. Laert. (IX, 29) asserts that Zeno the Eleatic made the soul a mixture (κρᾶμα) of hot, cold, moist and dry, in which none of them was dominant; but the statement is unsupported by other evidence.

[2] The use of the first plural without ἡμεῖς rules out, I submit, the meaning 'the group to which I belong'. If it does not mean 'people in general' (a very common use) it could only mean 'Cebes and I' (a meaning excluded by 87 A 5–7) or 'you (Socrates) and I', which is obviously impossible.

effect the replacement, in other words to make good the wastage or flux which every body continuously experiences.

Up to this point (88 A 1) Cebes has left out of account the possibility of reincarnation; he now adds that even if this be granted the same argument applies in principle: the soul may last out many incarnations, but not the final one; and since no man can be sure that this his present life is not his soul's final incarnation, no man can be justified in facing death with the confidence that his soul will not perish then and there. The only real ground for such confidence is to be won not by considering the relation of souls to bodies, but by 'proving that the soul is absolutely incapable of death or destruction' (88B), by which is meant a proof establishing immortality and indestructibility as essential properties of the soul; and it is to the attempt to furnish such proof that Cebes's criticism leads on. Burnet maintains that in the illustration with which Cebes begins it is unnecessary to the argument to make the old man weave his own cloaks, and indeed to make him a weaver at all. With this I cannot agree: the whole argument turns on the soul being related to its series of bodies in the same way as a weaver to the cloaks which he both weaves and wears; the last body, like the last cloak, is still in existence when the soul, like the weaver, perishes, but itself soon falls to pieces because there is no longer a weaver to make good the wear and tear by patching or replacement. The simile fails, it is true, in one point, namely that the patching of an old cloak is different from the weaving of a new one, whereas in the soul's case the two processes are one; but this is of no importance.

What is the origin of Cebes's theory? The notion of the body as the soul's garment is no doubt, as Burnet says, primitive, and is natural enough; but whence comes the notion of the soul weaving its own garment?[1] Again, the flux-idea is of course Heraclitean, but where in earlier thought or literature do we find it applied, as Cebes applies it, to the human body, or combined, as Cebes combines it, with the soul's function of replacement? It seems to me not improbable that Plato's own genius is at work here. Nobody, I imagine, would give the credit to the historical Cebes; and there is no suggestion, as in Simmias's theory, of a widely accepted doctrine; on the contrary, phrases such as τόδε ἐπίσκεψαι εἴ τι λέγω (87B) or σκόπει γὰρ σὺ ἃ λέγω (87C) suggest that 'Cebes'—that is to say Plato—is offering something original, in the sense of a new combination and application of earlier ideas.

[1] Not from Empedocles *frag.* 126, where it is a goddess who περιστέλλει σαρκῶν χίτωνι.

XIII

An interlude now follows in which the disquiet caused to the company by the foregoing criticisms is first described. This is followed by some by-play between Socrates and Phaedo, but the greater part of the section consists of an impressive warning against 'hatred of arguments' or intellectual apathy and excessive scepticism. Finally Socrates rallies himself and his friends to resume the discussion with a good heart.

These remarks by Simmias and Cebes had a disquieting effect on all 88 c of us; indeed we afterwards admitted to each other that, having been completely convinced by the argument preceding, we now felt disturbed and reduced to scepticism not only about what had been already asserted but as regards future arguments as well. Were we perhaps quite incompetent to judge? Did the problem, of its very nature, admit of no certain solution?

[*Phaedo's narrative is now broken off, and we return to the conversation between him and Echechrates with which the dialogue opened.*]

Ech. Upon my word, Phaedo, I sympathize with you all; now that I have heard your account, the sort of question that comes into my mind is 'What argument shall we ever rely on after this? How com- D pletely persuasive was that put forward by Socrates, yet how deeply has it been discredited!' In point of fact, this theory of the soul being an attunement has always had a hold on me, and your statement of it served as a reminder that I had myself already come to the same conclusion. Hence I am most anxious to start all over again with some new argument which will convince me that the soul of a man who has died does not die with him. So tell me, I beg and beseech you, how Socrates next proceeded. Was he plainly troubled, as you say you and the others E were, or did he quietly muster his forces? And if so, was it with complete or only partial success? Please let us have your account of the whole matter, and make it as precise as you can.

Phaedo. I would have you know, Echecrates, that though I have admired Socrates on many occasions, I never found him more wonderful than at that moment. That he should not be at a loss for a reply is 89 perhaps not surprising; but what I especially admired was, first, the pleasure, the kindness, the respect with which he received those young men's observations, and secondly his swift perception of the effect upon us of their words and the success with which he healed our distress, rallying the routed battle-line and encouraging us to follow where he led in a re-examination of the question.

Ech. How was it done?

Phaedo. I will tell you. It so happened that I was sitting beside the
B couch on a low stool at his right, he being some way above me: so he began to stroke my head and squeeze the hair on my neck, for it was a habit of his, now and then, to make fun of my hair,[1] and remarked:

'To-morrow, I daresay, Phaedo, you will clip[2] these fair tresses.'

'I suppose so, Socrates', I replied.

'But if you take my advice, you won't.'

'Oh, why not?' I asked.

'Because this very day we will both of us clip our hair if our talk comes to a dead end and we can't bring it back to life. If I were in your
C place, and found the problem baffling me, I should do as the Argives did,[3] and swear I would never let my hair grow again until I had counter-attacked the theories of Simmias and Cebes and laid them low.'

'Yes', I replied: 'but there's a saying that two against one was too much even for Heracles.'

'Well then,' said he 'call me in as your Iolaus,[4] while the daylight lasts.'

'Yes, I will,' I replied, 'but it will be the other way round, Iolaus calling in Heracles.'

'That will make no difference', said he; 'but first there is a danger that we should be on our guard against.'

'Oh, what is that?'

D 'The danger of coming to hate argument in general, even as some people come to hate mankind in general. Such 'misology' is the worst thing that can befall a man, and it springs from the same source as

---

[1] I follow Robin's interpretation (Introd. p. x) of this incident; Athenians wore their hair long when young men, and Socrates is rallying Phaedo of Elis, making mild fun of his habit of still doing so though he is no longer young. Doubtless, however, we are meant to regard Socrates's action as exhibiting affection as well as raillery.

[2] In sign of mourning; see Isaeus IV, 7.

[3] The reference is to a vow made by the Argives after their unsuccessful attempt to recover a town lost to the Spartans (Hdt. I, 82: the date is uncertain).

[4] Heracles, while attacking the Hydra, was himself attacked by a large crab, and called on his nephew Iolaus for help (see *Euthyd.* 297c).

misanthropy. This latter creeps upon us as the result of our having naïvely put excessive trust in someone or other, and having come to regard him as perfectly true and sound and reliable, and shortly afterwards finding him an unreliable scoundrel—and then repeating the experience in another case. When this has happened a number of times, and particularly with people whom one thought one's closest and dearest friends, the repeated knocks we have taken leave us hating E everybody, and believing everybody to be completely and utterly rotten. I expect you have come across this sort of thing.'

'Yes indeed', I said.

'Well now, isn't it something to be ashamed of? Isn't it plain that people who feel like that have been attempting to deal with human beings without any practical knowledge of human life? For surely the possession of such knowledge would have led them to believe what is the fact, namely that very good people, and very bad ones too, are few 90 in number,[1] and the intermediate sort form the great majority.'

'How do you make that out?' I asked.

'By analogy with the very small and very big. Can you think of anything rarer to discover than a very big or very small man, or dog, or what not? Or a very swift or very slow, or ugly, beautiful, white, black one? Don't you realise that in all such cases the extreme instances at either end of the scale are rare and few in number, while the intermediates are forthcoming in abundance?'

'Yes, of course', I replied.

'Then if a competition in wickedness were to be advertised, those B in the first class would similarly be quite few?'

'Probably', I said.

'Yes, probably. However, that is not the real point of resemblance between arguments and men:[2] I was merely following the lead you gave me just now. The resemblance is rather to be found when someone

---

[1] It is clear from the words περὶ τῶν σφόδρα σμικρῶν καὶ μεγάλων in A4 that σφόδρα is needed with χρηστοὺς καὶ πονηρούς: on the other hand it seems impossible to dissociate it from ὀλίγους. Either, then, we should follow Heindorf in inserting a second σφόδρα before ὀλίγους, or put one before χρηστούς. That σφόδρα was in fact repeated is made probable by Apuleius, de doctr. Plat. II, 246 (Thomas): sed adprime bonos et sine mediocritate deterrimos paucos admodum rarioresque et, ut ipse ait, numerabiles esse.

[2] Socrates is perhaps hinting, with a touch of irony, that in a context λόγων πονηρίας there would probably be plenty of first classes. It is not easy to see how Phaedo had led Socrates on, unless it was by the readiness of his assent to what Socrates had been saying; perhaps continued irony is sufficient explanation.

relies on an argument as being true without knowing how to assess arguments, and then a little later decides that it is false—which it sometimes is, sometimes isn't—repeating the experience with one argument c after another. More especially, as you know, people who have spent their time in arguments both for and against some theory¹ come in the end to think they have attained the height of wisdom, and the unique discernment that nothing sound and nothing solid is to be found in any object or any argument; everything in existence, according to them, is fluctuating this way and that just like the tide in the Euripus: nothing abides for a moment in one stay.'²

'What you say', I remarked, 'is perfectly true.'

'Then, Phaedo, wouldn't it be a lamentable event if there were in fact a true, solid argument capable of being discerned, and yet as the result d of encountering the sort of arguments we were speaking of, which seemed true at one moment and false at the next, one were not to find the fault in oneself or one's own lack of address, but to find a welcome relief for one's distress in finally shifting the blame on to the arguments, and for the rest of one's life to persist in detesting and vilifying all discussion, and so be debarred from knowing the truth about reality?'

'Yes,' said I, 'most assuredly that would be lamentable.'

'Then let us before all things be on our guard against that: let us e never entertain the idea that all arguments are probably unsound; let us rather believe that it is we ourselves who are not yet sound, but should manfully exert ourselves to become so; you, Phaedo, and you

---

¹ The word ἀντιλογικός is used by Plato in various senses. At *Soph.* 225 B τὸ ἀντιλογικόν is formally defined as 'that species of disputation which occurs in private discussions and is chopped up into questions and answers', and Eristic is a sub-species of it. In *Phaedrus* 261 D it includes the public disputation of assembly and law-court, and also the argumentation of Zeno, which sought to draw contradictory conclusions from an opponent's thesis. R. Robinson (*Plato's Earlier Dialectic²*, p. 89) remarks that Plato 'has two chief names for this shadow or reverse of dialectic, antilogic and eristic. By "eristic" or the art of quarrelling, he indicates that the aim of this procedure is to win the argument, whereas the aim of dialectic is to discover truth. By "antilogic", or the art of contradiction, he indicates that it is a tendency to contradict, to maintain aggressively whatever position is opposite to that of one's interlocutor.' But there is evidence, as the commentary below shows, that one and the same speaker or writer could and did employ ἀντιλογικοὶ λόγοι, and I follow A. E. Taylor (*Varia Socratica*, p. 91) in interpreting the expression here in the light of the antinomies of the so-called Δισσοὶ Λόγοι and other evidence of the same practice.

² The language here is reminiscent of *Crat.* 440 C and *Theaet.* 179 E ff.; but Plato does not necessarily mean to include Heracliteans amongst the ἀντιλογικοί: he need mean no more than that both sorts arrive ultimately at the same complete scepticism.

others out of regard for your remaining lifetime, I out of regard for death itself; for very possibly it is not a love of wisdom that I am 91 showing on this present issue, but that love of defeating an opponent which goes with utter lack of culture. I am thinking of those people who are quite unconcerned about the truth of any question which may come up in debate, but devote all their effort to persuading the company to adopt their own thesis.

'The only point, I think, in which I shall on this occasion differ from such people is this, that my endeavour will not, save perhaps incidentally, be to convince my companions of the truth of my statements, but so far as possible to convince myself. The way I look at it (and B observe how I mean to score)[1] is this: if what I maintain is indeed true, then it is well that I have come to believe it; if on the other hand there is no future for the dead, then at all events I shall be less likely to distress everyone here with lamentations during the time still remaining before death comes, and moreover this foolish belief of mine[2] will not survive with me—which would have been a pity—but will very soon be over and done with.

'There then, Simmias and Cebes, is the prepared position from which I advance to the discussion; but if you will take my advice, you will pay heed not so much to Socrates, but rather to the truth; and if you think C what I say is true, then accept my conclusions; if not, you must oppose me with every argument you can muster; otherwise I might lead both you and myself astray through my enthusiasm, like a bee that wouldn't disappear until it had left its sting.'

Plato has chosen a fitting place for his digression on 'misology'. We are almost exactly at the middle of the dialogue; we have reached a point where the two weighty arguments against Socrates's thesis have been set forth, and the audience in the prison, like ourselves, are wondering whether they may not be fatal. An interval before the resumption of close argument is welcome to them as to us, and the artistry of Plato fills the interval in a most satisfying way. First the tension is momentarily increased by Echechrates's interruption of the narrative, then it is eased, partly by Phaedo's words of warm admiration for the Master, partly by the incident of Socrates stroking

[1] This sentence pursues, half ironically, the theme of *selfishness* suggested by Socrates's preceding remark that he cares only (or chiefly) about convincing himself. To continue the discussion will be to his own advantage, whether his view is true or false. Why this is so he proceeds to explain.

[2] ἄνοια perfectly suits the irony of the passage, as neither ἄγνοια nor διάνοια would.

Phaedo's hair—an incident combining raillery and pathos, evoking
both a smile and a tear. By this time Socrates's companions and Plato's
readers are braced for a vigorous warning against intellectual defeatism,
a warning dramatically opportune but doubtless intended for Plato's
readers whether in his own or a later day. That it was needed in his
own day we may well believe; and there is no reason to suppose that
it was either more or less needed at the dramatic date. Since about the
middle of the fifth century the Greek world, and especially Athens,
its intellectual centre, had been buzzing with λόγοι—speeches, arguments, debates—from the lips of men calling themselves sophists and
rhetors, to an extent of which the surviving literature can give us only
a faint idea. Some of the speakers and writers were men of intellectual
ability and high moral purpose; others were political propagandists
or purely self-seeking demagogues; others again had no higher aim
than to tickle the ears of an audience by verbal dexterity and clever
paradox; there were indeed innumerable ways of exploiting the 'art
of words'. But to Plato's eye neither sophistry nor rhetoric (and he
uses these two terms to cover between them the whole field of persuasive speech and writing designed to influence hearers or readers)
was a true art, a τέχνη. The main ground of his condemnation, which
is prominent in the *Gorgias* and *Phaedrus*, was their indifference to
truth and knowledge, for which were substituted opinion and plausibility; but it was not always a case of deliberate falsification: often it
was a negative defect, the lack of a *method*, an orderly procedure for
attaining truth. In default of such method, for which Plato's word is
'dialectic', no λόγος could be assured of validity, and everyone was
at the mercy of the plausible speaker, whose thesis, however, could be
countered next day by one more plausible.

It is this lack of method, this absence of τέχνη four times referred
to (89 D 5, E 7, 90 B 7, D 3), that is uppermost in Plato's mind in the
present section; later in the dialogue[1] he will let Socrates describe his
own method of seeking truth. Misology, we are told, is more particularly the effect produced by 'those who spend their time in arguments both for and against some theory' (οἱ περὶ τοὺς ἀντιλογικοὺς
λόγους διατρίψαντες, 90 c). The best example of ἀντιλογικοὶ λόγοι
which we possess is the sophistical treatise known as Δισσοὶ Λόγοι,[2]

---

[1] 99 D ff. Socrates does not call his procedure here either a μέθοδος or a τέχνη,
but it is commonly and rightly referred to nowadays as his 'hypothetical method',
and in the account of dialectic in *Rep.* VII, which is a development of the *Phaedo*
procedure, we find ἡ διαλεκτικὴ μέθοδος at 533 c (cf. ἄλλη τις μέθοδος, 533 B).
Plato never perhaps actually calls dialectic a τέχνη, chiefly because the feminine
adjective implied the word; but R. Robinson (*op. cit.* p. 74) is obviously right in
saying 'Dialectic is an art or τέχνη as well as a method.'
[2] For a full account of the work see A. E. Taylor, *Varia Socratica*, ch. III,
and H. Gomperz, *Sophistik und Rhetorik*, pp. 138–79.

which belongs to the last few years of the fifth century; it consists mainly of a series of antinomies, in which a 'thesis' maintaining that two things are the same is followed by an 'antithesis' maintaining that they are different; the things in question include good and bad, just and unjust, honourable and base, and so forth. In some places the writer, though in general of little merit, shows a certain logical acumen, and it is easy to understand the despairing bewilderment of the plain man faced with this sort of thing. Behind this author, and clearly influencing him, stood Protagoras, who had asserted that 'there are two λόγοι about everything, opposed to each other' (Diog. Laert. IX, 51), and to whom are attributed two books of ἀντιλογίαι: and that Protagoras had plenty of imitators may be inferred from a fragment (189 N) of the *Antiope* of Euripides, ἐκ παντὸς ἄν τις πράγματος δισσῶν λόγων | ἀγῶνα θεῖτ' ἄν, εἰ λέγειν εἴη σοφός.

Towards the end of the section Socrates turns from warning against misology to exhortation to positive effort: ἀνδριστέον καὶ προθυμητέον ὑγιῶς ἔχειν: and this, he adds, applies as much to himself as to the others: he is, maybe, in an unhealthy, unphilosophic condition, inasmuch as he is in peril of arguing for the sake of overcoming his opponents rather than of finding the truth. These words may indicate Plato's realisation that a practitioner of Socratic dialectic was always in danger of degenerating into eristic,[1] but it soon becomes clear that Socrates himself is not really in peril; his procedure will show a trifling difference from that of the eristics, by being an attempt primarily to convince himself, and only secondarily his friends and critics.

The section ends half playfully: Socrates will get something for himself out of the argument, whether he be right or wrong; and now his forces are ready to resume the attack.

[1] See F. M. Cornford, *Plato's Theory of Knowledge*, p. 190; also R. Robinson, *op. cit.* p. 86: 'Part of Plato's antagonism to eristic is vigilance against an evil to which the Socratics were more liable than anyone else, against the enemy within their own gates.'

XIV

Socrates briefly recapitulates the theories advanced by Simmias and Cebes, and proceeds to develop three arguments against the former. First, it is incompatible with the doctrine of Recollection, to which both the interlocutors proclaim their continued adherence. Secondly, the theory leads to ethical consequences plainly unacceptable. Thirdly, soul can control the bodily feelings, as it could not do if it were merely something that resulted from the 'attuning' or adjustment of the bodily parts.

91 C   'And now to proceed', said Socrates. 'First of all remind me of what you were saying, in case I prove not to have remembered. Simmias, I think, is sceptical, and fears that the soul, despite its being a fairer and more divine thing than the body, may nevertheless perish before it, D because it is a sort of attunement. Cebes, on the other hand, seemed to agree with me on that point: he thought that the soul is longer-lasting than the body, but that nobody could be sure that it might not wear out a whole series of bodies, yet itself perish with the last one left behind: death might really be just this destruction of the soul, not of the body, for of course the body is incessantly and always perishing. Am I right, Simmias and Cebes, in thinking these to be the points for our consideration?'

E   They both agreed that they were.

'Well now, do you reject all the previous arguments, or only some of them?'

'Only some', they replied.

'Then what have you to say about our assertion that learning is recollection, together with its corollary, that our souls must have 92 existed somewhere else before being imprisoned in our bodies?'

'For my part,' said Cebes, 'I found it wonderfully convincing at the time; and I still abide by it as outstandingly true.'

'And let me assure you', said Simmias, 'that that is my position too, and I should be much surprised if we ever changed our belief on that point.'

To this Socrates rejoined: 'My Theban friend, you will have to change your belief if you continue to think that an attunement is something composite,[1] and that the soul is a sort of attunement resulting from the corporeal components held in tension; for you would hardly B permit yourself to say that the attunement existed as a composite whole before the parts from which it was to be composed were in existence; or would you?'

'No indeed, Socrates.'

'Then do you realise that that is what you are in effect maintaining, when you say that the soul exists before entering the human frame or body, and yet that it exists as a whole composed of parts not yet existent? The fact is, of course, that an attunement is not the same sort of thing as that to which you are comparing it: lyre and strings and notes can be there as yet untuned: the attunement comes into existence C last of all, and perishes first of all. So how is this theory of yours going to harmonise with the other one?'

'It never can', said Simmias.

'But surely, if there is any theory that ought to be in tune, it is a theory about attunement.'

'It certainly ought.'

'Well, this one of yours isn't. But which of the two theories, on reflexion, do you prefer? That learning is recollection, or that the soul is an attunement?'

'I find the former far preferable, Socrates; the latter I have adopted without any proof, merely because it seemed likely[2] and plausible, D which is indeed the general ground for its acceptance. I am well aware that theories which rest their proofs on a basis of what is likely are

___

[1] The expression σύνθετον πρᾶγμα, as also the use of συγκεῖσθαι in A9 and B6, of συνίστασθαι in C2, and above all the reference to 'parts' (μέρη) of a ἁρμονία at 93A9, are all likely to suggest something concrete and material. It is plain, how- ever, from Simmias's general exposition of his theory, and in particular from his language at 85E, that he did not so conceive it. The abstract noun σύνθεσις, used at 93A1, is more correct.

[2] The theory of Simmias was supported, it is true, by an analogy: but I doubt whether εἰκός τι could mean 'an analogy', and the parallels at *Theaet.* 162E and *Euthyd.* 305E, quoted by Burnet, are strongly in favour of it meaning 'something probable'. Moreover it does not seem likely that one who used εἰκόνες so com- monly as Plato would make Simmias speak so contemptuously of εἰκότα as he does in the next sentence if εἰκότα meant εἰκόνες: nor again is it easy to attach any meaning to arguing by analogy in geometry. It is possible that Aristotle had this passage in mind at *E.N.* 1094B25 παραπλήσιον φαίνεται μαθηματικοῦ τε πιθανο- λογοῦντος ἀποδέχεσθαι καὶ ῥητορικὸν ἀποδείξεις ἀπαιτεῖν: if so, he clearly took εἰκός as equivalent to πιθανόν. Burnet's note on that passage cannot be reconciled with his note on this.

On ὅθεν . . . ἀνθρώποις see p. 103 *supra*.

tricksters; unless one is careful about them they cheat one completely, whether it be in geometry or anything else. But the theory about recollection and learning has proceeded from a postulate that deserves acceptance;[1] we said, I think, that the existence of our souls before their entry into the body was just as certain as the existence of that very reality[2] which bears the title of "the thing itself". That is a postulate

E which, I feel sure, I am fully justified in accepting; and consequently I am bound, it seems, to refuse to accept the theory, whether advanced by myself or anyone else, that the soul is an attunement.'

'Now look at it from another angle, Simmias. Do you consider it

93 befits an attunement or any other compound to be otherwise qualified than the elements of which it is the product?'

'Certainly not.'

'Nor, I imagine, to do anything, or have anything done to it, other than that which those elements do or have done to them.'

He assented.

'Hence it doesn't befit an attunement to direct its elements: it must follow them.'

He agreed.

'Then it is out of the question for an attunement to have a movement or produce a sound, or do anything else, contrary to its own parts.'

'Utterly out of the question.'[3]

'Now another point: will not any attunement naturally correspond to the way in which the tuning has been done?'[4]

---

[1] For a good discussion of ὑπόθεσις and ὑποτίθεσθαι in Plato see R. Robinson, *op. cit.* ch. VII. As he well puts it (p. 95) 'ὑποτίθεμαι or "hypothesise" is to posit as a preliminary. It conveys the notion of laying down a proposition as the beginning of a process of thinking, in order to work on the basis thereof.'

The ὑπόθεσις here referred to is of course the existence of the Forms; and that Simmias should call this 'deserving of acceptance' simply reflects his attitude throughout the dialogue, e.g. at 65 D, 74 B.

[2] I accept Mudge's αὐτή for αὐτῆς, since the sentence is parallel in structure as well as in substance to 76 E 2–4 οὕτως ὥσπερ καὶ ταῦτα ἔστιν, οὕτως καὶ τὴν ἡμετέραν ψυχὴν εἶναι κ.τ.λ. It would not be relevant here to remark that the Forms are apprehended by the soul, and if it were, αὐτῆς ἐστιν (possessive genitive) would be an unnatural way of saying so.

[3] The point made at 92 E 4–93 A 10 is held in reserve, to be made use of at 94 B 4 ff.

[4] Burnet's explanation of 93 A 11–12, 'i.e. according as it is tuned to the fourth (διὰ τεσσάρων), the fifth (διὰ πέντε) or the octave (διὰ πασῶν)' is irreconcilable with Socrates's own explanation at A 14–B 2. It would involve understanding either μᾶλλον or ἐπὶ πλέον or both as 'to a wider interval': and since it obviously *is* possible for one tuning to produce a wider interval than another, the words εἴπερ ἐνδέχεται τοῦτο γίγνεσθαι would be unmeaning.

'I don't understand.'

'If the tuning has been done more completely, more fully (supposing that to be possible), won't there be more of an attunement, a fuller B attunement; whereas if it has been done less completely, there will be less of an attunement;[1] don't you agree?'

'Quite so.'

'Well, will that apply to a soul? Can there possibly be such a distinction between two souls that one is, even to a fractional extent, more or more fully itself,[2] that is to say more or more fully soul, while the other is less or less fully soul?'

'No, that is quite impossible.'

'Then look here, will you please! We speak of one soul as possessing wisdom and virtue, and being good, and of another as possessing folly and wickedness, and being bad; and we are, I suppose, right in so speaking.'

'Certainly we are.'   C

'Well, how will an adherent of the attunement doctrine conceive of this soul-content, this virtue and vice? Will he say that they are respectively a second attunement and a non-attunement? Will the good soul be tuned, and have a second attunement within the first one, that is to say within itself, while the bad soul is itself untuned and devoid of any attunement within itself?'[3]

'I really can't answer, Socrates: but plainly he would have to have some such theory.'

'But we are already agreed that one soul cannot be more or less a soul D than another; and that amounts to agreeing that, on the theory under discussion, one cannot be more or more fully, or again less or less fully, an attunement than another; does it not?'[4]

[1] Despite Olympiodorus (see Burnet's note) I do not believe that any difference of meaning is intended between the two terms in the four pairs, viz. μᾶλλον and ἐπὶ πλέον, μᾶλλον and πλείων, ἧττον and ἐπ' ἔλαττον, ἧττων and ἐλάττων.

[2] It is just possible that Plato wrote μᾶλλον twice in this line, but if so it was a slip, and I am disposed to follow Heusde in bracketing its first occurrence.

[3] Plato does not reject the notion of one ἁρμονία containing another as unmeaning or impossible: what he does is to make Socrates argue that it is incompatible with the point already agreed upon, viz. that there are no degrees of soul. This argument seems to me fallacious, for the reason given in my commentary below (p. 120).

[4] The words 'on the theory under discussion' are not in the Greek, but they must be implied, and I add them for greater lucidity. Burnet (as also Robin in his translation) apparently understands Socrates as here saying that to agree that no soul can be more or less soul than another is, for adherents of the ἁρμονία

'Certainly.'

'And that what is not more or less of an attunement cannot be more or less tuned.[1] Is that so?'

'It is.'

'And what is neither more nor less tuned than something else cannot partake of attunement to a greater or less degree than that other, but only to an equal degree.'

'Yes, to an equal degree.'

E   'Then since one soul cannot be more or less itself, that is to say more or less soul, than another, it clearly cannot be either more or less tuned.'

'No.'

'And that being the case, it cannot partake either of attunement or of non-attunement to a greater degree than another.'

'No, it cannot.'

'Then in that case again, and if we allow that virtue is an attunement and vice a non-attunement, one soul cannot partake of virtue or vice to a greater degree than another.'

'No.'

94   'But indeed it would be more logical surely to say that, if soul is an attunement, no soul will ever partake of vice: for of course an attunement that is really and truly an attunement can never partake of non-attunement.'

'No indeed.'

'And similarly, I imagine, a soul that is really and truly soul can never partake of vice.'

'Not on our premisses, certainly.'

theory, to agree that no ἁρμονία can be more or less ἁρμονία than another. Certainly this is what the Greek text, as it stands, would most naturally mean, if these lines were taken in isolation; but to understand it thus is to ignore the fact that 93 B has not *assimilated*, but *distinguished* souls and ἁρμονίαι in this very point. It is true that the distinction rests only on a provisional assumption, viz. that there are degrees of ἁρμονία: but Burnet argues, or makes Socrates argue, as if provisionally assuming something were the same as denying it.

We must, however, in my opinion, follow Madvig, Wohlrab, Schmidt and Schanz in bracketing ἁρμονίας in D4; it might well have been inserted under the influence of ψυχὴν ψυχῆς above by someone who failed to understand the argument. Archer-Hind refuses to bracket on the ground that 'this prematurely anticipates the conclusion in E, οὐκοῦν ψυχή...ἥρμοσται': my reason for disagreeing with him will, I hope, be evident from the translation taken together with my comment below.

[1] The gender of τὴν and οὖσαν in D6 is not due to ψυχήν being understood, but to normal attraction to the gender of the predicate ἁρμονίαν. The logical, unidiomatic Greek would be τὸ δέ γε μηδὲν μᾶλλον μηδὲ ἧττον ἁρμονίαν ὄν.

'So we reach the conclusion that inasmuch as it is the nature of every soul to be just as much of a soul as every other, all souls of all living beings will be equally good.'

'That seems to me to be our conclusion, Socrates.'

'And does it seem to you a satisfactory one? Do you think we should have reached this position if the suggestion that soul is an attunement B were correct?'

'I certainly do not.'

'And now for another point. Is it a man's soul that controls every part of him, more especially if it be intelligent, or can you point to something else?'

'I cannot.'

'And does it do so by conforming to the feelings of the body, or by opposing them? For instance, when a man feels hot and thirsty, don't we find his soul pulling him away from drinking, when he feels hungry pulling him away from eating; and don't we observe countless other instances of the soul opposing the bodily feelings?'[1]   C

'Yes indeed.'

'But then didn't we agree just now that the soul, if it is an attunement, could never utter a note that was opposed to the tension or relaxation or the manner of striking the strings or anything else that was done to those alleged sources from which it sprang? Didn't we agree that it must follow them and could never dominate them?'

'To be sure, we did.'

'Well now, don't we find the soul in fact achieving the exact opposite of this? Dominating all these alleged sources of its existence, opposing them almost incessantly for a whole lifetime, mastering them in this D way and that, sometimes inflicting severe and painful punishment in the course of physical training or medical treatment, sometimes proceeding more gently; threatening here and admonishing there; speaking to a man's desires and passions and fears after the fashion of a visitor from without, a fashion reminding us of Homer's description of Odysseus:

Then did he smite his breast, and spake to his heart with a chiding:[2]
'Heart, I bid thee endure: worse ills ere now thou enduredst.'   E

[1] This opposition of the soul to the 'feelings of the body' becomes in *Rep.* 439 B an opposition of one part of the soul (τὸ λογιστικόν) to another (τὸ ἐπιθυμητικόν), the same example, of desire and restraint in thirst and hunger, being used in both places. For similarity of language compare ἐπὶ τοὐναντίον ἕλκειν here with ἀνθέλκει there.

[2] *Odyssey* XX, 17f. At *Rep.* 441 B the first line is again quoted to support Socrates's distinction between τὸ λογιστικόν and τὸ θυμοειδές.

'Do you suppose that the poet would have written thus if he had regarded the heart as an attunement, as something that could be guided by the feelings of the body, instead of guiding those feelings and mastering them, being much too divine a thing to be conceived as an attunement?'

'Upon my word, I think you are right, Socrates.'

'Then, my good friend, we by no means approve the doctrine that
95 the soul is a kind of attunement: it would involve, it seems, contradicting both the divine Homer and ourselves.'

'That is so.'

In this section we have three arguments against Simmias's theory that soul is an attunement. The first and third of these, namely (1) that it is inconsistent with the belief in Recollection, and (3) that the soul can oppose and control the body, are quite straightforward and need no comment, except perhaps for the very strong terms in which Cebes and Simmias reaffirm their belief in ἀνάμνησις at 92A; this I take to be a hint that nothing later in the dialogue is to be understood as impairing the truth and importance of that doctrine as a proof of the soul's pre-natal existence and power of apprehending truth.

We might guess that the adherents of the ἁρμονία theory would reply that Socrates's third argument leaves them unshaken, since ψυχή there is taken to mean 'mind', whereas for them it meant no more than the principle of life, that which differentiates a living body from a dead one. But if so, Plato would have a prompt retort: everyone agrees that (1) a living creature is a union of σῶμα and ψυχή, and (2) a man has a mind; hence to exclude mind from ψυχή is either to make it a part of σῶμα or to deny its existence—two equally impossible alternatives.

The second of the three arguments, however, is far from straightforward; it is indeed one of the most difficult passages in the dialogue, and needs detailed interpretation and comment beyond what I have given in footnotes. It extends from 93A11 to 94B3. The character of an attunement, Socrates begins, depends on the way in which it has been produced: if the strings of a lyre have been more completely or precisely tuned, there is a greater degree of it; if less completely, a lesser degree. He assumes provisionally (εἴπερ ἐνδέχεται τοῦτο γίγνεσθαι) that one *can* tune a lyre more or less exactly, and hence that attunement can exist in different degrees of completeness. Then he asserts that this obviously cannot be true of a soul: a soul is always fully a soul—that, as Simmias's οὐδ' ὁπωστιοῦν indicates, is taken as needing no proof.

Hence the theory of Simmias is, in fact, *provisionally* refuted; but Socrates does not actually say so, the reason being (so I think) that

he (or Plato) is suddenly struck (φέρε δὴ πρὸς Διός) by a further consequence, more damaging still to the theory, namely that whether we
retain the provisional assumption or reject it—as Socrates in the end
(94A) decides that we should—in either case we are led to unacceptable
ethical consequences, namely either (if we retain it) that no soul is
more virtuous or more vicious than any other, or (if we reject it) that
there cannot be such a thing as a soul that partakes of vice.

These ethical impossibilities are naturally enough felt by Plato to
provide a more cogent refutation of the theory under examination than
the point made at 93A14–B7, resting as it did on an assumption dubious
at best (in his view), and in the upshot to be discarded. The steps of
this ethical argument (as we may call it) may be set out as follows:

(93B8–C10)   How will the adherents of ψυχὴ ἁρμονία account for
the presence of virtue and vice in the soul? Presumably by saying
that a good soul is an attunement which is itself tuned *qua* containing
another attunement within itself, whereas the vicious soul is not tuned,
in the sense that it contains no attunement within itself. Socrates
proceeds to examine the consequences of this.

(93D1–5)   Now it has been agreed that any soul is just as much
soul as any other: and this, in terms of the ψυχὴ ἁρμονία theory, means
that any soul is as much of an attunement as any other.

(93D6–11)   Now if one thing *A* is just as much (or as little) of an
attunement as another thing *B*, they cannot have been subjected to
different degrees of tuning; in other words, they must partake in
attunement equally.

(93D12–E6)   What has just been established generally of any two
things *A* and *B* that are attunements must of course apply to two souls,
i.e. two soul-attunements. Since one is just as much of an attunement
as the other, they cannot have been subjected to different degrees of
tuning ⟨as was supposed in C6–8⟩. In other words, they must partake
in ἁρμονία (or of course in ἀναρμοστία) equally.

[The essential thing to understand here is that *being subjected to*,
or *partaking of*, different degrees of tuning is to be interpreted in terms
of the 'containment' hypothesis of 93C. Socrates is arguing that the
varying degree of attunement postulated by the containment theory
is incompatible with the ὁμολόγημα of D1–4, the ὁμολόγημα originally
made at B4–7.]

(93E7–9)   And since virtue and vice are admitted to be respectively
ἁρμονία and ἀναρμοστία, it follows that any two souls must partake
equally with each other in virtue and in vice.

[Thus the 'containment' theory, which appeared as a necessary
corollary of the main theory, has led to a paradoxical, indeed an
impossible, ethical conclusion.]

(94A1–B3)   Though indeed it would be truer to say that no soul will ever partake of vice at all, on the theory of Simmias. For though we provisionally assumed that there can be degrees of ἁρμονία, yet in fact that was a false assumption, since it would mean that ἁρμονία can partake in ἀναρμοστία.

[This is taken as a *reductio ad absurdum* of Simmias's theory.]

It is difficult to feel sure that I have interpreted this argument correctly; but if I have, it seems to contain two fallacies, one in 92 D–E, the other at 94 A.

(i) To argue that two souls cannot differ in respect of their contained ἁρμονίαι without differing in respect of the ἁρμονίαι which they themselves *are* involves ignoring the fact that the containing and contained ἁρμονίαι are adjustments of wholly different terms: the former is of physical bodies (or quality-things), the latter of non-physical terms (exactly how these non-physical terms are conceived is not clear, but does not matter). When this is realised there seems no impossibility in two souls which are equally exact attunements containing attunements which differ in exactness.

(ii) ἁρμονία is a term like 'purity' which can quite properly be used in a non-absolute sense. One specimen of water can be purer than another, and similarly one ἁρμονία more exact than another. The provisional assumption of 93 B should not have been withdrawn. In Platonic doctrine all particular ἁρμονίαι must necessarily μετέχειν ἀναρμοστίας: only of the Form, αὐτὸ ὃ ἔστιν ἁρμονία, is this untrue.

According to Cicero (*de Fin.* IV, 75) the Stoics supported their paradox that all sins are equal by arguing that a number of lyres of which none is in tune are all equally out of tune; a fallacy which Cicero himself neatly exposes: 'hic ambiguo ludimur: aeque enim contingit omnibus fidibus ut incontentae sint: illud non continuo ut aeque incontentae.'

XV

The theory of Simmias has now been disposed of, and Socrates turns to the contentions of Cebes, of which he gives a clear and forceful recapitulation, culminating in the expression of his conviction that to answer them it will be necessary to investigate the whole question of coming-to-be and perishing. To this end he makes a proposal, readily accepted by Cebes, that he should narrate his own experiences in early life as a student of 'natural science'. The narrative, notable amongst other things for the mention by name of Anaxagoras, and of the initial delight and subsequent disappointment which Socrates had felt on becoming acquainted with that philosopher's work, ends with the announcement of his total dissatisfaction with the methods of the scientists, and his adoption of a 'second-best' course of his own.

'Very well, then', said Socrates; 'we seem to have more or less 95 A propitiated the tuneful goddess of Thebes; but now comes the question of Cadmus:[1] What sort of argument shall we use to propitiate him, Cebes?'

'I expect you will discover one', replied Cebes; 'at all events your argument against the tuneful lady came as a wonderful surprise to me; for while Simmias was telling us of his difficulties[2] I was wondering very much whether anyone would be able to cope with his argument, and so B I was quite taken aback by his apparent inability to withstand your first attack for a moment. Hence it wouldn't surprise me if the theory of Cadmus were to suffer the same fate.'

'No boasting, please, my good sir,' rejoined Socrates, 'or we shall find some malign power making havoc of our next argument. However, that possibility must be left to heaven; what we must do is to come to close quarters, in Homeric fashion, with your contention, and try to see whether there is anything in it. Now your problem may be summed up

---

[1] This banter rests merely on Cadmus, the reputed founder of Thebes, having been the husband of Harmonia. No offence was intended to the lady, and none (Socrates hopes) taken.

[2] I agree with Burnet that we have no right to alter ὅτε into the more natural ὅτι (indirect interrogative); the literal meaning is 'when Simmias was speaking at a moment of perplexity'.

like this: you require it to be proved that our souls are indestructible
c and immortal,[1] if the confidence shown by a philosopher at the point
of death, who believes that he will be far better off in the other world
than if he had lived a different sort of life, is not to be an irrational,
foolish confidence. To show that the soul is something strong and
godlike, and that it existed even before we were born as men—all that,
you urge, may well be a revelation not of its immortality, but of its
being long-lasting, of its having existed somewhere for ever so long,
knowing much and doing much; but that leaves it as far as ever from
d being immortal, and indeed its very entry into a human body was the
beginning of a sickness which would end in its destruction; its life here
is a life of distress, and it finally perishes in what men call death. And
in respect of our individual fears it makes no difference, you argue,
whether it enters a body once or many times; anyone who is not a fool
will naturally be afraid if he doesn't know, and cannot give a ground
for believing, that it is immortal.

e 'That, I think, Cebes, is more or less what you maintain; and I am
deliberately going over it again and again in order that no point may
escape us, and that you may add or subtract anything that you wish.'

To this Cebes replied, 'There is nothing that I want to subtract or
add at the moment; my contention is what you have said.'

At this point Socrates paused for a long time in meditation; finally he
resumed: 'The problem you raise, Cebes, is no light one: we have got
to have a thorough inquiry into the general question of the cause of
96 coming into being and perishing. I will therefore, if you like, narrate
my own experiences bearing on the matter; and then, if anything I have
to say should appear to you helpful, you can make use of it to settle the
points you have been raising.'

'Why of course', said Cebes, 'I should like that.'

'Then listen and I will tell you. When I was young, Cebes, I had a
remarkable enthusiasm for the kind of wisdom known as natural science;
it seemed to me magnificent to know the causes of everything, why
a thing comes into being, why it perishes, why it exists.[2] Often I used
b to shift backwards and forwards trying to answer questions like this,
to start with: Is it when the conjunction of the hot and the cold results

---

[1] See note on 88B, p. 100 *supra*.

[2] διὰ τί ἔστι, distinguished from διὰ τί γίγνεται, perhaps expresses the idea
of purpose or Final Cause, although in the sequel this is said to have been first
suggested to Socrates by his hearing about the νοῦς of Anaxagoras.

in putrefaction that living creatures develop?[1] Is it blood that we think with, or air or fire?[2] Or is thought due to something else, namely the brain's providing our senses of hearing, sight and smell, which give rise to memory and judgement, and ultimately, when memory and judgement have acquired stability, to knowledge?[3]

'Next I tried to investigate how things perish,[4] and what went on in the heavens and on the earth, until in the end I decided that I had c simply no gift whatever for this sort of investigation. To show how right I was about that, I may tell you that, whereas there were some things which up till then I had, as I thought myself and other people thought too, definitely understood, I was now smitten with such complete blindness as the result of my investigations that I unlearnt even what I previously thought I knew, including more particularly the cause of a human being's growth. I had supposed that to be obvious to anybody: he grew because he ate and drank; on taking food flesh was added to flesh, bone to bone, and similarly the appro- D priate matter was added to each part of a man, until in the end his small bulk had became a large one, and so the little child had become a big man. That was what I used to believe: reasonably enough, wouldn't you say?'

'I would', said Cebes.

'Now see what you think about this. I used to find it perfectly satisfactory when a tall man standing beside a short one appeared to be taller just by a head; similarly with two horses. And to take an even E plainer case, I thought that ten was more than eight because of the addition of two, and that an object two yards long was greater than one

---

[1] The reference is to a theory of Archelaus, that the first animals were produced from slime (ἰλύς) which resulted from putrefaction ensuing upon the meeting of hot substance and cold. This slime he seems to have regarded as both their source and their nutriment, and συντρέφεται here probably means both 'grow together' and 'are nourished'. See Burnet's notes for details of this theory and of those which follow in B 4–8.

[2] As suggested by Empedocles, Anaximenes followed by Diogenes, and Heraclitus respectively.

[3] This is probably a reference to Alcmaeon, a younger contemporary and associate of Pythagoras though not, it seems, actually a member of the Pythagorean order; it was he who pronounced the brain, rather than the heart, to be the focus of the senses; ἀπάσας τὰς αἰσθήσεις συνηρτῆσθαί πως πρὸς τὸν ἐγκέφαλον (DK 24 A 5). This purely empirical theory of knowledge is of course incompatible with Plato's ἀνάμνησις.

[4] I take τούτων to refer not to thought, knowledge, etc., but to things in general, like the ἑκάστου of A 9. This involves regarding the question-mark of B 8 as a strong stop. αὖ answers the πρῶτον of B 1.

only one yard long because the one extended by half its own length beyond the other.'[1]

'And what do you think about it all now?'

'I asure you I am very far from supposing that I know the cause of any of these things;[2] why, I am dubious even about saying that, when we add one to one, either the one to which the addition is made becomes two,[3] or that the one and the other together become two by reason of 97 the addition of this to that. What puzzles me is that when the units were apart from each other each was one, and there was as yet no two, whereas as soon as they had approached each other there was the cause of the coming into being of two, namely the union in which they were put next to each other. Nor again can I any longer persuade myself that if we divide one it is the division this time that causes two to come into B being; for then the cause of two would be the opposite of that just suggested: a moment ago it was because the units were brought into close proximity each to each, and now it is because they are kept away and separated each from each. And for that matter I no longer feel sure that by adhering to the old method I can understand how a unit comes into being or perishes or exists; that method has lost all attraction for me, and in its place I am gaily substituting a new sort of hotch-potch of my own.

' One day, however, I heard someone[4] reading an extract from what C he said was a book by Anaxagoras, to the effect that it is Mind that arranges all things in order and causes all things; now there was a cause that delighted me, for I felt that in a way it was good that Mind should be the cause of everything; and I decided that if this were true Mind

---

[1] This strange way of expressing double length is due to Socrates's wish to put this instance on all fours with the preceding ones. A (τὸ δίπηχυ) is bigger than B (τὸ πηχύαιον) because of something having happened to A, viz. its being given that extra half of itself without which it would be equal to B. This extra half corresponds to the tall man's head, and to the extra 2 by which 10 exceeds 8.

[2] As these puzzles are all going to be given their solution by reference to the theory of Forms (100D–101C), it is surprising (though it does not seem to trouble the commentators) that Socrates should reply thus to Cebes's question νῦν...τί σοι δοκεῖ περὶ αὐτῶν; Socrates must mean that the problems still appear to him insoluble with the old conception of cause: in other words, the limitation expressed by κατὰ τοῦτον τὸν τρόπον τῆς μεθόδου must be felt as applying to the whole of this speech.

[3] The insertion of ἢ τὸ προστεθέν strikes one at first as a neat detection of haplography, but I think Robin is right in rejecting it, since there was no need for all three possibilities to be mentioned.

[4] Whether or not we take this incident as historical, it is natural, as Burnet says, to think of the reader as Archelaus, the successor of Anaxagoras at Athens.

must do all its ordering and arranging in the fashion that is best for each individual thing. Hence if one wanted to discover the cause for anything coming into being or perishing or existing, the question to ask was how it was best for that thing to exist or to act or be acted upon. D On this principle then the only thing that a man had to think about, whether in regard to himself or anything else, was what is best, what is the highest good; though of course he would also have to know what is bad, since knowledge of good involves knowledge of bad. With these reflexions I was delighted to think I had found in Anaxagoras an instructor about the cause of things after my own heart;[1] I expected him to tell me in the first place whether the earth is flat or round,[2] and then go on to explain the cause why it must be the one or the other, E using the term "better", and showing how it was better for it to be as it is; and then if he said the earth is in the centre of the universe,[3] he would proceed to explain how it was better for it to be there. If he could make all these things plain to me, I was ready to abandon the 98 quest of any other sort of cause. Indeed I was ready to go further, applying the same principle of inquiry to sun, moon and stars, their relative velocities and turnings and so forth: I would ask which is the

---

[1] In his interpretation of Anaxagoras as a teleologist *manqué* Plato is closely echoed by Aristotle, *Met.* A, 985 A 18 ff. Nowadays this is generally doubted: see Burnet, EGP³, § 132, and Cornford in *Camb. Anc. Hist.* IV, p. 571: 'Mind is nowhere' (*sc.* in the fragments of Anaxagoras) 'described as aiming at goodness or perfection; it only sets things in order. If the notion of design is suggested by the name, it remains implicit; and Mind is called in only to impart a mechanical impulsion.' Yet, as Sir W. D. Ross reminds us in his note on the *Met.* passage, νοῦς is thought of in *frag.* 12 as knowing and foreseeing: 'Anaxagoras, in fact, is on the verge of discovering a genuinely spiritual and teleological principle of explanation.' This seems to me a just compromise.

[2] The Ionian and Pythagorean views respectively. The discovery that the earth is spherical is attributed to Pythagoras himself, or alternatively (by Theophrastus) to Parmenides, who was at one time a Pythagorean. Since Democritus still believed in a flat earth (according to the doxographer Aetius, quoted in EGP³, § 31) and Arist. *de caelo* 293 B 34 refers to it as a disputed question, I do not understand why Burnet should say that the question was 'still a living problem in the days when Socrates was young, but not later'. In the *Timaeus* of course a spherical earth is taken for granted.

[3] That the earth lies at the centre of the universe was a belief retained, in all probability, by Plato to the end of his life. That he ever came to regard it as a planet revolving round a Central Fire (the doctrine of some fourth-century Pythagoreans) is a supposition resting on a remark attributed by Plutarch (*Plat. Questions* 1006 C) to Theophrastus, that τῷ Πλάτωνι πρεσβυτέρῳ γενομένῳ μεταμέλειν ὡς οὐ προσήκουσαν ἀποδόντι τῇ γῇ τὴν μέσην χώραν τοῦ παντός. But Cornford (*Plato's Cosmology*, pp. 125 ff.) has argued, convincingly as I think, that this can be reconciled with our other evidence. Whether Plato believed in an axial rotation of the earth is another matter, which it would be irrelevant here to discuss.

better way for these bodies to act or be acted upon. For I never supposed that when Anaxagoras had said that they are ordered by Mind he would bring in some other cause for them, and not be content with showing that it is best for them to be as they are; I imagined that in B assigning the cause of particular things and of things in general he would proceed to explain what was the individual best and the general good; and I wouldn't have sold my hopes for a fortune. I made all haste to get hold of the books, and read them as soon as ever I could, in order to discover without delay what was best and what was worst.

'And then, my friend, from my marvellous height of hope I came hurtling down; for as I went on with my reading I found the man making no use of Mind, not crediting it with any causality for setting C things in order, but finding causes in things like air and aether and water and a host of other absurdities. It seemed to me that his position was like that of a man who said that all the actions of Socrates are due to his mind, and then attempted to give the causes of my several actions by saying that the reason why I am now sitting here is that my body is composed of bones and sinews, and the bones are hard and D separated by joints, while the sinews, which can be tightened or relaxed, envelop the bones along with the flesh and skin which hold them together; so that when the bones move about in their sockets, the sinews, by lessening or increasing the tension, make it possible for me at this moment to bend my limbs, and that is the cause of my sitting here in this bent position. Analogous causes might also be given of my conversing with you, sounds, air-currents, streams of hearing and so on E and so forth, to the neglect of the true causes, to wit that, inasmuch as the Athenians have thought it better to condemn me, I too in my turn think it better to sit here, and more right and proper to stay where I am and submit to such punishment as they enjoin.[1] For, by Jingo, I fancy these same sinews and bones would long since have been somewhere 99 in Megara or Boeotia, impelled by their notion of what was best, if I had not thought it right and proper to submit to the penalty appointed by the State rather than take to my heels and run away.

'No: to call things like that causes is quite absurd; it would be true to say that if I did not possess things like that—bones and sinews and

---

[1] In the *Crito* (51 D–E) the argument is put forward by the personified laws of Athens that anyone who continues to reside in a state has entered into an implicit contract to observe its judicial decisions. This may well be the reason, or a reason, for Socrates's refusal to attempt escape.

so on—I shouldn't be able to do what I had resolved upon; but to say
that I do what I do because of them—and that too when I am acting
with my mind—and not because of my choice of what is best, would be
to use extremely careless language. Fancy not being able to distin- B
guish between the cause of a thing and that without which the cause
would not be a cause![1] It is evidently this latter that most people,
groping in the dark, call by the name of cause, a name which doesn't
belong to it. Hence we find one man making the earth be kept in
position by the heavens, encompassing it with a rotatory movement;[2]
and another treating it as a flat lid supported on a base of air;[3] but the
power thanks to which heaven and earth are now in the position that C
was the best possible position for them to be set in, *that* they never look
for, and have no notion of its amazing strength; instead they expect to
discover one day a stronger and more immortal Atlas, better able to
hold things together; for they don't believe in any good, binding[4]
force which literally binds things together and holds them fast.

'Well, I for my part should be most happy to be instructed by anybody about a cause of this sort; but I was baulked of it: I failed to discover it for myself, and I couldn't learn of it from others: and so I have
had recourse to a second-best method[5] to help my quest of a cause;
would you like me to give a formal account of it, Cebes?'   D

'Yes, indeed: I should like that immensely.'

As might be expected, there has been much discussion in modern
times as to whether the experiences (πάθη) which Socrates here
describes as his own are to be taken at their face value as a historical

---

[1] In *Timaeus* 46c we again find the distinction between final or purposive
causes and physical causes, the latter being there called συναίτια. But Plato holds
there that they are deserving of study when recognised for what they are, and
even speaks of ἀμφότερα τὰ τῶν αἰτιῶν γένη.

[2] A theory of Empedocles mentioned by Arist. *de caelo* 295 A6 ff.

[3] A theory attributed by Aristotle (*de caelo* 294 B 14 ff.) to Anaximenes,
Anaxagoras and Democritus. I have adopted Burnet's suggestion to read
καρδοπίῳ πλατεῖ for the reasons given in his note.

[4] Socrates may well be right in suggesting a semantic coincidence between
τὸ δέον, that which is fitting, and τὸ δέον, that which binds, though what we call
the impersonal verb δεῖν was no doubt commonly thought of as distinct from
the δεῖν which means 'to bind'.

[5] The proverbial phrase δεύτερος πλοῦς is said to have originated in the practice of taking to the oars in the absence of a wind. We should not regard it as
ironical here: relatively to a discovery of the sort of cause which he had hoped
to find worked out by Anaxagoras that which he is about to describe is second-best;
if there were also a suggestion that it is second-best relatively to the method
of the physicists (which I do not believe), that no doubt would be ironical.

record or autobiography. In view of their general identification of the Platonic with the historical Socrates, it was only to be expected that John Burnet and A. E. Taylor should answer this question with a decided affirmative; but because their general view is nowadays almost universally rejected it does not necessarily follow that they are wrong on the narrower question; thus it might well be that what Socrates here says of his dissatisfaction with the Ionian physicists, of his disappointment with Anaxagoras, and even perhaps of his mathematical puzzles, is a true record of his own intellectual development, and yet that when we come to the δεύτερος πλοῦς, the *pis aller* in which he took refuge, we pass the boundary into a region which belongs to Plato, a region of logical and ontological doctrine centring on the Platonic theory of Forms.

Many readers will no doubt be reluctant to accept the existence of such a boundary, or dichotomy of an ostensibly unbroken narrative; and indeed I should not accept it myself without an important modification: namely, that while the πάθη are at least for the most part those which Plato thought it reasonable to ascribe to Socrates, yet he is at the same time giving us his own estimate of the inadequacy of Ionian science in so far as the question of causality is concerned; and because that is so, he allows himself to include some points such as the difficulties concerning quantity, addition and the unit, which Socrates was unlikely to have felt.

The strength of the Burnet-Taylor contention in regard to the πάθη (as distinct from their sequel, the δεύτερος πλοῦς) lies in the facts that (1) it is *a priori* likely that an inquiring mind like that of the young Socrates took some interest in physical speculation, (2) this is compatible with his denial in the *Apology* (19 C, 33 A) that he ever *taught* anybody natural science, or indeed anything else, (3) tradition recorded by Theophrastus and others (Diels-Kranz, *Vors.* II, p. 46) made him a disciple of Archelaus, the successor at Athens of Anaxagoras, (4) the scientific doctrines mentioned in Socrates's speech, or most of them, are those current in the mid-fifth century, when he was about twenty years of age.

On the other hand, the chief weakness of these scholars' contention is that Socrates's disillusion with the methods and results of the physicists is followed, in the narrative, not as we should expect by a decision to abandon the pursuit of science and devote himself to the spiritual welfare of his fellow-men—the divine mission which in the *Apology* appears as his life-work—but by the adoption of an original logical method and a novel conception of causality. The sequel to the πάθη cannot but cast doubt on the authenticity of the πάθη themselves.

There is then both strength and weakness in the theory which accepts all the experiences as veritably Socratic. That being so, we should not at once dismiss the opposite view (maintained by Stallbaum and tentatively by Archer-Hind [1]) that they are simply and solely Platonic. Two at least of the arguments which have been brought against this interpretation seem to me weak, namely (a) that it is inconsistent with Aristotle's account in *Metaphysics* A and M of the origin of Plato's metaphysical doctrine, and (b) that it is inconsistent with the Seventh Epistle, which mentions no interests felt by the youthful Plato other than political.

To take (b) first, it is surely not impossible for the same person at the same time to have interests both political and scientific, but it would have been quite irrelevant for Plato to say anything about the latter to the unhappy followers of Dion. As to (a) it is, I think, plain that Aristotle's account is incomplete, inasmuch as it mentions no influences save those of the Pythagoreans, Heracliteans and Socrates; does anyone suppose that Parmenides counted for nothing with Plato, or that Heraclitus was the only Ionian against whom he reacted? The truth is rather that, on the assumption that the πάθη are Plato's πάθη, the account in the *Phaedo* and that in the *Metaphysics* are not inconsistent but complementary: each leaves out what the other puts in; and the omissions in the *Phaedo* are, if anything, more understandable than those in the *Metaphysics*. For what need was there, in a passage which has the limited aim of contrasting two (or, if we count in Anaxagoras's νοῦς, three) conceptions of causality, to say anything about Heraclitus or the Pythagoreans? I will not contend that mention of them would have been wholly irrelevant, but I cannot see that their omission is a serious objection to the view under discussion.

But now, what positive reasons can be given for what I may call for convenience this anti-Burnet theory? I can see two: (a) it avoids the need to assume a dichotomy, by which I mean the assignment of the πάθη themselves and of their sequel to different people; (b) the probability that Plato would give his own grounds for discoveries or doctrines which seemed to him of the first importance, as the method of hypothesis and the causality of the Forms plainly did seem.

So far as I can find any valid objection to the anti-Burnet view other than the points already mentioned in favour of Burnet, it is in the carefulness with which the characterisation is kept up, particularly the irony of such touches as οὕτως ἐμαυτῷ ἔδοξα πρὸς ταύτην τὴν σκέψιν ἀφυὴς εἶναι ὡς οὐδὲν χρῆμα (96c), ἀλλά τιν' ἄλλον τρόπον αὐτὸς εἰκῇ φύρω (97β) and the typically Socratic blend of humour and

[1] In note on p. 86 of his edition: 'Such inquiries must have been always alien to the strongly practical genius of Sokrates. Plato may be merely describing in its supposed effect on an individual mind the development of philosophy to the theory of ideas; but it is not impossible that he is recounting his own experience.... But in the lack of direct evidence it would be rash to speak positively.'

seriousness at 98 E–99 A ἐπεὶ νὴ τὸν κύνα, ὡς ἐγῷμαι, πάλαι ἂν ταῦτα τὰ νεῦρα καὶ τὰ ὀστᾶ ἢ περὶ Μέγαρα ἢ Βοιωτοὺς ἦν, εἰ μὴ δικαιότερον ᾤμην καὶ κάλλιον εἶναι πρὸ τοῦ φεύγειν τε καὶ ἀποδιδράσκειν ὑπέχειν τῇ πόλει δίκην ἥντιν' ἂν τάττῃ. This sort of thing makes it impossible to forget that Socrates is ostensibly talking about himself all the time, and *pro tanto* increases the difficulty of believing that he is nothing but Plato's mouthpiece.

There remains, however, a further possibility, namely that the account is neither of Socrates's experiences nor of Plato's nor a mixture of both men's, but an impersonal sketch of philosophical development *in abstracto*, experienced by no actual man or group of men: the biographical dress is simply a disguise. This view was held by Zeller, and in a modified form by Bonitz. Zeller writes: 'Die Stelle des *Phädo* macht aber überhaupt nicht den Eindruck eines biographischen Rechenschaftsberichts, sondern in der Form einer persönlichen Bekenntnisses wird die allgemeine Notwendigkeit des Fortgangs von den materiellen zu den Endursachen und weiter zu den Ideen dargestellt.'[1] Bonitz's words are 'Platon, so scheint mir, gibt nicht eine historische Erzählung weder von seinem eignen noch von des Sokrates philosophischen Entwicklungsgange, sondern er legt in den Hauptumrissen die Gründe dar, welche von der Naturphilosophie zu der Begriffsphilosophie führen. Diese Gründe sind im wesentlichen dem Platon mit Sokrates gemeinsam, und es ist dadurch nach der Weise des Platons Darstellung vollkommen gerechtfertigt, dass Sok. sie als die seinigen darlegt. Indem aber als Ziel gerade derjenige Punkt erscheint, der die Platonische Lehre specifisch von der des Sokrates unterscheidet, nämlich die Realität der Ideen, so wird die Auffassung gerechtfertigt sein, dass in dem fraglichen Abschnitte eine subjektive Begründung der Plat. Ideenlehre enthalten sei.'[2]

Apart from Bonitz's first sentence, I should accept what he says, but the extract as a whole seems to me an attempt to 'have it both ways'; surely the passage cannot be intended as both personal and suprapersonal. Zeller's view is clear-cut: but I can only say that on me the passage does make that impression of a biographical account which he denies.

My conclusion then is that Plato, having reached a point in the dialogue at which it is recognised that the soul's immortality can only be proved by an investigation of the general cause or causes of coming-to-be and perishing, feels the need to explain how he has come to hold a novel conception of causality, resting on his theory of Forms. This explanation must of course be given through the mouth of Socrates; it could no doubt have been given in further conversation between Socrates and Cebes; but Plato, knowing that his master had

[1] *Gesch. der gr. phil.*[4] II, I, p. 398. [2] *Plat. Stud.*[3], p. 310.

as a young man acquainted himself with the material or mechanical causation of Ionian science, and had soon become dissatisfied with it and turned his interest elsewhere, and believing (as we too may believe) that his own source of dissatisfaction was essentially the same as that of his master, not unnaturally adopted the device of an ostensible autobiography of Socrates, the details of which should be, so far as possible, accommodated to a critic of the mid-fifth century, yet which should also, in sum and substance, express his own attitude some seventy years later.

It is important to notice that the reason given by Socrates for his becoming dissatisfied with the pursuit of natural science is not that he doubted the truth of this or that scientific pronouncement, nor yet that the scientists disagreed with one another, but that his study forced upon him the recognition of deeper problems concerning causation, which he had never suspected to be problems; and that not only within the sphere of φύσεως ἱστορία (such as the problem of nutrition, 96D) but outside it also (such as the logico-mathematical problems of relative size, of addition and division, and of the nature of the unit, 96E–97B).

Some of these deeper problems had their origin, no doubt, in pre-Socratic philosophy: that of nutrition was suggested by Anaxagoras, that of the nature of the unit probably by Zeno, who had shown that the unit as conceived by the Pythagoreans was a self-contradictory conception. Others are unreal problems: the question whether *A* is taller than *B* 'by a head' only appears a question of causality because of a confusion between two usages of the Greek dative case; the question whether the addition of 2 is the cause of 10 being greater than 8 is meaningless, because there is no more a cause of 10 being greater than 8 than there is of Thursday coming after Wednesday.

The question raised at 96E–97A about the 'cause of there being two' is, so far as I can see, not due, or at all events not directly due, to Zeno's arguments: and it is the kind of problem more likely to originate in a mathematical mind like Plato's than in that of an unmathematical thinker, even if he be a Socrates. The answer of common sense (though perhaps common sense should be mistrusted in mathematical matters) surely is that (*a*) two cannot come to be by the addition of one to one because there could be no such addition unless there were two already: in other words, there is no *cause* of the existence of numbers; and (*b*) division is no more than the separation of two (or more) parts which already exist, though not as separate parts.

I interpret Socrates's confession at 99C of his inability to discover the Final Cause, the 'good and binding force which literally binds things together and holds them fast', as reflecting Plato's own attitude when he wrote. In the *Republic* we shall find this τὸ ἀγαθὸν καὶ δέον reappearing in the guise of the ἰδέα τοῦ ἀγαθοῦ, the Form of Good, that unhypothetical first principle which he declares to be the ground of all knowledge and all being, and to be accessible to the philosopher by a dialectical method which seems to be a further development of that to be described in our next section. But it may be doubted whether this intellectual optimism, if I may so style it, was a permanent part of Plato's thought; in any case I should say that it is consonant with what we have been told in the earlier part of our dialogue about the incompleteness of the philosopher's grasp of truth during his earthly life to believe that the Plato of the *Phaedo* regarded the consummation of his 'marvellous hope' as something not merely beyond his own ability, but beyond the power of human reason. I do not say beyond the power of νοῦς, for νοῦς in Plato is an untranslatable word sometimes meaning the faculty of reasoning, or that by which we reason, sometimes a suprarational apprehension of truth; and I should say that Plato's normal belief, outside the *Republic*, is that it is only by means of this latter that the ultimate principle of the universe can be revealed to us in this life.

However this may be, we shall not find anything more said about a Final Cause in our dialogue; the method of hypothesis, to which we are now coming, does not seek to attain it, and the Forms will shortly appear as causes of a different sort.

XVI

THE NEW METHOD OF HYPOTHESIS

Socrates explains the nature of his 'second-best' course: it consists in approaching reality not by the 'direct' method of sense-perception and observation, but by the 'indirect' method of propositions (λόγοι): more specifically, it is a method of hypothesis, that is to say the establishment of some proposition through deduction from a hypothesis, or proposition assumed to be true, followed (if need be) by a defence of this hypothesis through deduction from some 'higher' one. The method is exemplified by a proposal to deduce the immortality of the soul from the hypothesis (which will need no defence, since all present accept it) of the existence of the Forms. The relevance of this to the inquiry, which in the preceding section Socrates had declared to be necessary, into the cause of coming-to-be and perishing, is now made clear: the Forms are the sole and sufficient causes, and are adequate to resolve all the doubts and problems which Socrates had encountered in his early scientific inquiries.

'Well, at that point, when I had wearied of my investigations, I felt 99D that I must be careful not to meet the fate which befalls those who observe and investigate an eclipse of the sun; sometimes, I believe, they ruin their eyesight, unless they look at its image in water or some other medium. I had the same sort of idea: I was afraid I might be completely E blinded in my mind if I looked at things with my eyes and attempted to apprehend them with one or other of my senses; so I decided I must take refuge in propositions, and study the truth of things in them. Perhaps, however, my comparison in one aspect does not hold good: for I don't altogether admit that studying things in propositions is 100 more of an image-study than studying them in external objects. Anyhow, it was on this path I set out: on each occasion I assume the proposition which I judge to be the soundest, and I put down as true whatever seems to me to be in agreement with this, whether the question is about causes or anything else; what does not seem to be in agreement I put down as false. But I should like to make my meaning clearer to you: I fancy you don't as yet understand.'

'Indeed no,' said Cebes, 'not very well.'

'Well, here is what I mean; it is nothing new, but what I have con- B stantly spoken of both in the talk we have been having and at other times too. I am going to attempt a formal account of the sort of cause that I have been concerned with, and I shall go back to my well-worn theme and make it my starting-point; that is, I shall assume the existence of a beautiful that is in and by itself, and a good, and a great, and so on with the rest of them; and if you grant me them and admit their existence, I hope they will make it possible for me to discover and expound to you the cause of the soul's immortality.'

c   'Why of course I grant you that', said Cebes: 'so pray lose no time in finishing your story.'

'Now consider whether you think as I do about the next point. It appears to me that if anything else is beautiful besides the beautiful itself the sole reason for its being so is that it participates in that beautiful; and I assert that the same principle applies in all cases. Do you assent to a cause of that sort?'

'Yes, I do.'

'It follows that I can no longer understand nor recognise those other learned causes which they speak of; if anyone tells me that the reason
D why such-and-such a thing is beautiful is that it has a bright colour or a certain shape or something of that kind, I take no notice of it all, for I find it all confusing, save for one fact, which in my simple, naïve and maybe foolish fashion I hug close: namely that what makes a thing beautiful is nothing other than the presence or communion of that beautiful itself—if indeed these are the right terms to express how it comes to be there:[1] for I won't go so far as to dogmatize about that, but merely affirm that all beautiful things are beautiful because of the beautiful itself. That seems to me the safest answer for me to give
E whether to myself or to another; if I hold fast to that I feel I am not likely to come to grief; yes, the safe course is to tell myself or anybody else that beautiful things are beautiful because of the beautiful itself. Do you not agree?'

'I do.'

'Similarly big things are big, and bigger things are bigger, because of bigness; while smaller things are smaller because of smallness.'

'Yes.'

'Then you would reject, as I do, the assertion that one man is bigger

---

[1] Reading προσγενομένου, as suggested by Ueberweg, and defended by Cornford, *Plato and Parmenides*, p. 77, who quotes *Hippias Major* 289 D and 292 D to show that it is the Form that προσγίγνεται. It should, however, be added that Oxyr. Papyri xviii, 2181 appears to support Wyttenbach's conjecture προσαγορευομένη.

than another by, or because of,[1] his head, and that the latter is smaller by, or because of, that same thing; you would protest that the only 101 thing you could say is that anything bigger than another thing is so solely because of bigness, that bigness is the reason for its being bigger; and again that a smaller thing is smaller because of smallness, and smallness is the reason for its being smaller. You would, I fancy, be afraid that if you said that someone was bigger or smaller 'by a head', you would be met with the objection that in the first place it would be by the same thing that the bigger is bigger and the smaller smaller, and in the second place that the head by which the bigger man is bigger is itself small; and that, it would be objected, is monstrous, for a big man to be big by, or because of, something small. Or wouldn't you be B afraid of that?'

'Yes, I should', replied Cebes with a laugh.

'Then would you be afraid to say that ten is more than eight by two, and that two is the cause of the excess, instead of saying by quantity and because of quantity? Or that a length of two yards is greater than a length of one yard by half its own length, rather than by greatness? Surely you should have the same qualms as before.'

'Quite so.'

'Or again, wouldn't you hesitate to say that when one is added to one the addition is the cause of there coming to be two, or that when C one is divided the division is the cause? Would you not loudly protest that the only way you know of, by which anything comes to be, is by its participating in the special being in which it does participate; and that in the case just mentioned you know of no other cause of there coming to be two save coming to participate in duality, in which everything that is to be two must participate, just as anything that is to be one must participate in unity; all these divisions and additions and suchlike subtleties you would have nothing to do with; you would leave questions about them to be answered by wiser folk; conscious of your inexperience you would shy, as the phrase goes, at your own D shadow, cling to the safety of your hypothesis, and answer accordingly. And if anyone were to fasten upon[2] the hypothesis itself, you would disregard him, and refuse to answer until you could consider the

---

[1] The dative, or rather instrumental case, τῇ κεφαλῇ, is thought of by Socrates as causal, though in fact it is not. The double translation attempts to indicate this.

[2] The verb ἔχεσθαι is used in two different senses in D 1 and D 3. It is better to accept this fact as a piece of rather careless writing than to attempt to emend; none of the suggested emendations (ἔφοιτο, ἅπτοιτο, etc.) is convincing.

consequences of it, and see whether they agreed or disagreed with each other. But when the time came for you to establish the hypothesis itself, you would pursue the same method: you would assume some more ultimate hypothesis, the best you could find, and continue until E you reached something satisfactory. But you wouldn't muddle matters as contentious people do, by simultaneously discussing premiss and consequences, that is if you wanted to discover a truth. Such discovery is perhaps a matter of complete unconcern to the contentious, whose wisdom enables them to jumble everything up together, and nevertheless to be well pleased with themselves. But you, I fancy, if you are 102 a philosopher, will do as I have said.'

'What you say', replied Simmias and Cebes together, 'is perfectly true.'

The content of this important section may best be discussed under three headings: (1) Socrates's decision to adopt a second-best course of inquiry; (2) the general account of this second-best course; (3) the illustrative example of it in which the Forms appear as causes of coming-to-be and perishing.

(1) We may begin by discarding certain misconceptions which have misled commentators, misconceptions some of which have indeed been removed already by Goodrich's papers in *C.R.* XVII–XVIII.

(*a*) τὰ ὄντα in 99D5 and τὰ πράγματα in E3 do not mean Platonic Forms: it is strange that this should ever have been supposed. But neither do they, I believe, mean physical objects as opposed to Forms. I would indeed admit that, if we had to choose between these two meanings, it would be right to choose the latter. But in fact we need not do this: both expressions are as vague and metaphysically non-committal as the word 'things'.

(*b*) The sun has no metaphysical symbolism. It is not intended as the counterpart in the physical world of the Form of Good in the intelligible world. In other words there is no allusion to or anticipation of the famous simile of the sun in *Republic* VI.

(*c*) Still less has the eclipsed state of the sun any metaphysical symbolism or significance. So far as his argument went, Plato might have omitted the word ἐκλείποντα: but people are in fact apt (unless forewarned) to gaze at the sun during an eclipse more than at other times.

(*d*) βλέπειν and σκοπεῖν (σκοπεῖσθαι) are not synonymous. What Socrates is talking about is not the *mere* looking at things, but the investigation of or inquiry into things by the method of looking at them. The error of the φυσικοί lay not in their observation of phenomena but in their assumption that sense-perception is the right basis for science. (Even in the illustration the observers are described as θεωροῦντες καὶ σκοπούμενοι.)

(e) There is no difficulty in Socrates saying that *after* he had grown weary of investigating things he was afraid that he *would* become completely blinded in soul (μὴ παντάπασι τὴν ψυχὴν τυφλωθείην). Though he has grown weary, he is still at a point of time in his account *before* that indicated by ἔδοξε in E4, i.e. before making his decision to cease 'looking at things'.

As to the phrase δεύτερος πλοῦς, whether we accept Menander's explanation (*frag.* 241) that it arose from the practice of taking to the oars in the absence of a wind, or the alternative suggestion of the paroemiographers that it expresses the idea of a *safer* second attempt, in any case usage shows that *inferiority* to a πρῶτος πλοῦς is involved: it is a next-best course; cf. *Statesman* 300C; *Philebus* 19C; Ar. *Pol.* 1284B19; *E.N.* 1109A35.

The phrase is not used by Socrates ironically: it comes in the immediate content not of his experiences with the φυσικοί in general, but of his particular disappointment in regard to Anaxagoras. The πρῶτος πλοῦς would have been a discovery of the detailed operations of Mind throughout the universe—a task which Plato was to attempt many years later in the *Timaeus*. The method of λόγοι *is* inferior to that.

The scientists whose methods Socrates has been employing imagined that our minds can apprehend reality by the simple direct method of sense-perception, so that scientific pronouncements derived therefrom are wholly true and capable of covering the whole field of inquiry; they can reveal, if not to-day at all events in due time, the truth, the whole truth, and nothing but the truth. Socrates, however, has found that, so far from this being so, they have merely landed him in confusion: to his puzzles about causation they can offer no satisfactory answers. If he goes on with the 'direct' method, he will merely make his mental blindness complete. His mental vision will be as irretrievably damaged as the physical vision of one who looks direct at an eclipse of the sun. (All this is of course consonant with what has been said earlier in the dialogue about the senses being a hindrance rather than a help to the mind that seeks truth and understanding.) He therefore decides to try an indirect method: he must copy the man who looks at the image of the sun in water, by directing his mental vision to λόγοι. Having said this, he hastens to add that the parallel is not exact: it is a good parallel in so far as the contrast of direct and indirect apprehension goes; but in so far as it might imply that λόγοι stand to physical objects (ἔργα) in the relation of images to real things, it is misleading. The sun which the eclipse-observer looks at directly is a sense-object, an αἰσθητόν not a νοητόν: both λόγοι and ἔργα are reality only as imperfectly apprehended by our minds and our senses respectively. The form of words at 100A οὐ γὰρ πάνυ συγχωρῶ τὸν ἐν λόγοις σκοπούμενον τὰ ὄντα ἐν εἰκόσι μᾶλλον σκοπεῖν ἢ τὸν ἐν ἔργοις is such as to suggest, though it does not actually say, that the mental images are a truer representation of reality than the sense-images.

But what are these λόγοι, and how can reality be studied in them? Or, to put the question in another form, in what sense are they 'images'?

To find an English word for λόγοι which will suit both 100A1 and A4 appears impossible, because there is (as I think) a shift of meaning—at least for us, though perhaps a Greek reader would not be conscious of any. In the latter λόγος evidently means a proposition which someone lays down or postulates as the foundation of an argument; but in the earlier place λόγοι seem to be arguments themselves, trains or processes of ratiocination; and the contrast there drawn is between observing physical objects (ἔργα) and constructing arguments, as alternative methods of studying reality.

In some sense the λόγοι are images of reality: they are like[1] real being, but in what sense? In attempting to answer this we may perhaps get some help from *Symposium* 211A, where the final revelation of Beauty will, we are told, not be οἷον πρόσωπόν τι οὐδὲ χεῖρες οὐδ' ἄλλο οὐδὲν ὧν σῶμα μετέχει, οὐδέ τις λόγος οὐδέ τις ἐπιστήμη. On this passage Bury has a helpful note: after hesitating between 'discourse', 'argument' and 'concept' as a rendering of λόγος he writes: 'But after all, the difference is not of vital importance. The essence of the statement, in either case, is that the Idea is not dependent upon either corporeal or mental realisation, i.e. that it is not subjective, as a quality or product of body or mind, but an objective, self-conditioned entity.'

It is, I suggest, this same notion that Plato seeks to express when he calls λόγοι images of reality. Not that each individual λόγος in the sense of proposition is such an image; but the world of discourse through which we move when σκοπούμενοι τὰ ὄντα ἐν λόγοις in the way that he proceeds to describe, viz. the method of hypotheses, is a faithful representation of true being, a body of true knowledge save for the inevitable element of subjectivity that must enter into it.

(2) Socrates's formal account of his second-best course, or hypothetical method, is given in two very brief passages at 100A and 101D;[2] all that lies between is an illustrative example, namely the deduction from the hypothesis of the existence of Forms of a general theory of

---

[1] I cannot understand how Mr Murphy in *C.Q.* xxx, p. 43, can believe that 'the λόγοι are in no sense *like* the things being studied'.

[2] Though I differ considerably from Mr Robinson's conclusions here, I owe much to his discussion (*op. cit.* ch. IX).

causality which is to be applied to establish the immortality of soul. This illustrative example is, however, so important in itself that Socrates seems temporarily to lose sight of the reason for which, formally speaking, it was introduced, and consequently fails to explain the precise relation of the two reasoning processes described respectively before and after it. The account of the method is only half given in the first passage which, taken by itself, can hardly be said to indicate a method at all. Our problem then is to relate the first passage to the second, to see how the two together do, for all their brevity, describe something intelligible, free from internal contradiction, and deserving to be called a method.

All that is said at 100 A is that Socrates takes the strongest hypothesis (which presumably means that one amongst those occurring to him as relevant which seems least likely to be challenged), accepts as true what seems to him to agree with it, and rejects as false what seems to him not to agree with it. This I take to mean that any proposition arrived at by what the inquirer deems a valid process of deduction is accepted, and the contradictory of any such proposition is rejected.

Here there seem to be two difficulties: (a) why should there be a plurality of propositions arrived at? Surely the purpose of the method is to establish the truth of a single proposition: in the example, the proposition that the soul is immortal. Possibly this might be got over by saying that the plural is simply due to Socrates thinking of a plurality of cases in which the method is employed; but that seems unlikely in view of the mention of τὰ ὁρμηθέντα, and the possibility of their disagreement with one another, in the second passage; there he must be speaking of a single instance of the method. (b) The other difficulty is the use of the word συμφωνεῖν, not, one would think, a natural substitute for συμβαίνειν, which is the ordinary word in Plato and elsewhere for resulting by inference. My attempted answer to both these difficulties can only be given through an examination of the second passage. Now I think it is commonly, and not unnaturally, assumed that the second passage describes something additional to that described in the first, some sort of check on the first process after that is completed. I would suggest that this is not so: what the second passage gives is the detail of the process described in the first. Thus— in order to establish a proposition A you assume a proposition H, and proceed by arguing that H implies G, G implies F, and so on down to 'B implies A'. But at each step you may have to rebut some objection which occurs either to yourself or your interlocutor. The propositions asserted at each of the steps from G to B are what Socrates calls τὰ ὁρμηθέντα, the things that 'proceed from' or 'are based on' the hypothesis. They are not results, but intermediate propositions; that is why they are not called τὰ συμβάντα: there is only one συμβάν, for there is only one proposition conceived as an ultimate result. That solves the difficulty about the plural in the first passage.

If an objection is raised, say, to *F*, and is successfully rebutted, the two ὁρμηθέντα, *G* and *F*, are 'in agreement with each other'; but if it cannot be rebutted, they are 'at variance': the one is not a valid inference from the other. I do not think these terms are unnatural, if we grant that Plato wants to avoid συμβαίνειν, a term to be reserved for the establishment of the final proposition, the *demonstrandum A*.

Of course it might be the first step, *G*, to which objection is taken; in that case the agreement or variance would be not between two ὁρμηθέντα, but between a ὁρμηθέν and the hypothesis *H*. But it is reasonable that Socrates should accommodate his language to the more numerous cases, as they would probably be, of objections later in the series of steps.

If an objection at any stage, say *D*, of the process cannot be rebutted, presumably there is the choice of substituting either a new *D*, or a whole new series *G* to *D*, or even a new hypothesis *H*. If all objections are rebutted, plainly there will be agreement the whole way from *H* to *A*: we shall put down as true whatever agrees with *H*, every intermediate proposition as well as the final proposition *A*. It is just because all these propositions are put down as true that Socrates uses συμφωνεῖν (not συμβαίνειν) in the first passage as well as in the second.

Of course this interpretation is conjectural, but so must any be in view of Plato's brevity and of the disjunction of the two passages giving his theory. But I find a certain amount of confirmation—not indeed complete confirmation—in the *Meno*. In that dialogue the proposition to be established at 86 D is that virtue is teachable, and Socrates decides to argue this ἐξ ὑποθέσεως. The hypothesis taken is that virtue is knowledge, and the inference from this, that virtue is teachable, is reached in a single step. ('We haven't taken long over that', as Socrates remarks at 87 C.)

But of course we have then to establish the hypothesis itself—a process mentioned, but not illustrated, in the *Phaedo*. To do this we take the higher hypothesis, virtue is good, this being treated as what the *Phaedo* calls ἱκανόν τι. The steps now are:

H　　Virtue is good.
G　　Virtue is beneficial.
F　　Nothing is beneficial save φρόνησις.
A　　Virtue is φρόνησις (or ἐπιστήμη).

But objection is raised to *F* on the ground that Right Opinion also is beneficial. Admittedly this objection comes not at the point where it ought to come, conformably to the *Phaedo* scheme (as I have interpreted it), but only considerably later (97 A), after practical objections to *A* itself have intervened. But it remains true that the attempt to prove the proposition 'virtue is φρόνησις' fails in the end (at least ostensibly) because of the impossibility of upholding *F* in face of an objection.

It must, however, also be admitted that the parallelism to the *Phaedo* scheme is vitiated by the fact that *F* is not a ὁρμηθέν of *H*, since it is not an inference from *G*, but a new agreed premiss. Nevertheless it is possible, and I should say reasonable, to regard the δεύτερος πλοῦς as an improved version of the logically very imperfect reasoning of the *Meno*.

We must now consider 101 D 5–E 1. Socrates has just said that no account is to be taken of any objection to the hypothesis itself until the deductive process is completed: 'But when the time came for you to establish the hypothesis itself, you would pursue the same method: you would assume some more ultimate hypothesis, the best you could find, until you reached something satisfactory.'

What precisely is meant by (*a*) 'pursuing the same method' (ὡσαύτως), (*b*) 'more ultimate' (τῶν ἄνωθεν) and (*c*) 'something satisfactory' (τι ἱκανόν)? I would reply that (*a*) means that the original hypothesis is to be deduced from the new one, which will be 'best' in the sense of most likely to lead to the required conclusion; that (*b*) means merely that the new hypothesis is logically prior to the old one, as it obviously must be, and that (*c*) means a hypothesis to which the interlocutor can find no ground for objection or doubt.

Nobody, I imagine, would have suggested any other meaning for τι ἱκανόν if he had not supposed Plato to have in mind the 'unhypothetical first principle' of *Republic* VI (511 B). Now the injunction which Socrates gives in a later passage (107 B), that our first hypotheses, even if we are convinced of them, ought to be further examined, does strongly suggest—inasmuch as the first hypotheses there in question are simply the existences of this or that Form—the doctrine of the unhypothetical first principle, identical with that Form of good which is the source of all Being, and itself 'beyond Being'. Nevertheless I do not believe that Plato is alluding to that doctrine here, in the words τι ἱκανόν: for surely the phrase could not easily be understood as carrying this vast implication; moreover Socrates is not envisaging a process of reasoning which will satisfy a philosopher's ultimate demand, but one which will serve the purpose of proving to the satisfaction of an interlocutor some particular theorem. The method of hypotheses is a practical method for everyday use, and Plato does not expect us to ascend to the αὐτὸ ἀγαθόν every time we seek to establish a contested point.

A question that we must attempt to answer at this point is how this method of Hypothesis is to be related to the doctrine of Anamnesis, the doctrine that all acquisition of knowledge is recollection of truth known to the soul before its birth in the body. The answer is not forthcoming in the *Phaedo* itself, but may be inferred from *Meno* 98 A, where it is declared that true opinions are of little value until they are converted into knowledge by being bound together by 'reflexion on the reason' (αἰτίας λογισμῷ). Taken together with an earlier passage (81 C) in which all reality is said to be akin, this may be interpreted as meaning that knowledge in the full sense is not an accumulation of isolated truths, but a coherent whole of which all the parts are seen in their interdependence; and that recollection includes or involves this advance from single truths to the whole truth[1]—an advance which in the *Republic* is taken a step further by the doctrine of the Form of the Good, on which all reality and all knowledge depend. Now the method of Hypothesis, so far as it goes, is the same process: it is the establishment of a proposition through its connexion with another proposition or propositions: it is an αἰτίας λογισμός, but not a complete αἰτίας λογισμός, if the meaning which I attach to the words τι ἱκανόν be correct.

(3) I come now to the longest and most important part of the present section, namely the illustrative example which Socrates offers of his new method.

The hypothesis in this example is of course the existence of those Forms which have already figured so largely in the dialogue, and which perhaps for that reason alone are called a 'well-worn theme' (πολυθρύλητα). What Forms precisely exist we are not told, any more than we were before; Socrates mentions 'a beautiful in and by itself, and a good, and a great, *and all the rest of them*' (καὶ τἆλλα πάντα), a vague phrase, which should surely be taken not as implying the definite doctrine of *Rep.* 596A—a Form for every group of things having a common name—but rather as an indication that the extent of the world of Forms is either as yet unconsidered by Plato, or not deemed necessary to specify in the present context.

We are then to assume the existence of certain Forms. And perhaps the question will at once present itself, does Plato mean that this is not, as he has previously in the dialogue represented it, a certain, incontrovertible fact, but a mere assumption?

It seems to me that Plato has no doubt whatever about the existence of the Forms: to assume this proposition as the basis of an argument does not in itself imply any doubt, any more than there is doubt about the proposition in the *Meno* (87D) that Virtue is good; of that proposition Socrates and Meno at once agree that it 'stands firm' (αὕτη ἡ ὑπόθεσις μένει ἡμῖν), and Socrates might well have said the same here. Yet the other Forms are, according to the *Republic* (509B), dependent

---

[1] Cf. Cornford, *Princ. Sap.* p. 59.

both for their existence and their being known upon the Form of
good: that is an unhypothetical, ultimate principle, relatively to which
all other Forms are hypothetical; and in view of Socrates's later
injunction (107B) that our first hypotheses should be more clearly
examined, even if we are convinced of their truth, it seems probable,
as I have suggested above, that Plato had this doctrine already in mind.
There is then a sense in which the Forms are hypothetically existent,
but it is not a sense which implies doubt on the part of one affirming
their existence. To speak *tout court*, as is sometimes done, of the
Forms in the *Phaedo* as 'mere hypotheses' is seriously misleading.

It is the existence of Forms that is assumed, but nothing beyond
that. That there is a relation between Forms and sensibles, a relation
which involves causality, is not part of the hypothesis, but rather
regarded as an immediate and inescapable consequence of their existence.
In affirming this consequence Plato is affirming something new, but
not entirely new. Hitherto the Forms have been sharply contrasted
with sensibles; their transcendence, their existence apart (χωριστά,
αὐτὰ καθ' αὐτά) has been emphasised; and yet sensibles, we have been
told, can remind us of them, and can be recognised as defective
representations of them, striving to be what they are, but failing;
hence they have not been conceived as an order of being totally apart
from the sensible order of 'things that become' (γιγνόμενα). Plato
now definitely affirms the relation of the two orders, but is deliberately
vague as to its nature, save that it is a causal relation. The 'beautiful itself' is declared to be that 'by which' all beautiful things are
beautiful.

It should not be supposed that this formula is no more than a declaration that all predication about particulars implies the logical relation
of particular to universal; it is indeed true that the Theory of Forms
is in one aspect a theory of predication: all predication, for Plato,
involves the assertion of a Form; but 'the beautiful', 'the great',
'the small', are not mere universals, not mere logical entities: they are
real existents, in such a sense that their 'presence' (παρουσία) in
sensibles, and the 'sharing' (κοινωνία) in them by sensibles, are at least
conceivable terms to express the relation in question. The word
μετέχειν (participate in) is also used (100C, 101C), but this is as non-
committal as the use of the dative in τῷ καλῷ τὰ καλὰ καλά.[1] Later,
however, we shall find Socrates distinguishing the Form from the
corresponding immanent character, αὐτὸ τὸ μέγεθος from τὸ ἐν ἡμῖν
μέγεθος (102D), which implies that in the *Phaedo* itself, whatever be

---

[1] Such expressions as μετέχειν τοῦ καλοῦ belong to ordinary language, and
per se imply nothing technical or metaphysical: see, for example, *Gorgias* 467E
τὰ δὲ μήτε ἀγαθὰ μήτε κακὰ ἆρα τοιάδε λέγεις, ἃ ἐνίοτε μὲν μετέχει τοῦ ἀγαθοῦ, ἐνίοτε δὲ τοῦ
κακοῦ, ἐνίοτε δ' οὐδετέρου, οἷον καθῆσθαι καὶ βαδίζειν καὶ τρέχειν καὶ πλεῖν;

the case in other dialogues,[1] the Forms are not themselves immanent; and that is at least a negative determination of the relation in question.

It is plain then that the Forms are here affirmed to be the causes of particulars: the causal dative, the preposition διά with accusative, and finally the noun αἰτία are all used in this section. But of what particulars precisely are they causes? Here it becomes important to observe that all Forms mentioned in the dialogue hitherto are non-substantial; we have not heard of 'the man himself', 'the rose itself' (let alone 'the bed itself'), but of 'the equal', 'the great', 'the beautiful', 'the just', etc. These are all qualitative Forms (or in the case of great, small, etc., relational Forms, which Plato does not, at all events in the *Phaedo*, distinguish from qualitative). Hence the particulars of which they are causes are qualities of concrete things, not concrete things themselves. Beauty itself is not the cause of a beautiful thing, but of a thing's being beautiful. Plato makes this quite clear, but it is important to emphasise it, not only in view of Aristotle's criticism but also because, when Socrates spoke of the need to examine the whole question of the cause of coming-to-be and perishing (95 E), it was natural to expect an account of the γένεσις and φθορά of animate and inanimate substances rather than of the origin and loss of their attributes. This restriction, or limited treatment, of the terms γένεσις and φθορά is dictated, or at least made intelligible, by Plato's ultimate purpose: the general form of the question before his mind is 'why does *A* become tall, beautiful, equal to *B*, etc.?' which will lead to the question 'are there certain attributes which certain things cannot have?' and to the answer 'yes: "dead" is an attribute which soul cannot have'.

Aristotle's criticism just referred to is as follows (*de gen. et corr.* 335 B 7 ff.):

But the third originative source must be present as well—the cause vaguely dreamed of by all our predecessors, definitely stated by none of them. On the contrary some amongst them thought the nature of the Forms was adequate to account for coming-to-be. Thus Sokrates in the *Phaedo* first blames everybody else for having given no explanation, and then lays it down that some things are Forms, others Participants in the Forms, and that while a thing is said to be in virtue of the Form, it is said to come-to-be *qua* sharing in, to pass away *qua* losing the Form. Hence he thinks that, assuming the truth of these theses, the Forms must be causes both of coming-to-be and of passing away. [After a sentence criticising other thinkers Aristotle proceeds.] Neither of these theories, however, is sound. For if the Forms are causes, why is their generating activity intermittent instead of perpetual and continuous—since there always are Participants as well as Forms? Besides, in some instances we see that the cause is other than the Form. For it is the doctor who implants health and the man of science

---

[1] The doctrine criticised in the *Parmenides* is in the main that of the *Phaedo*, but immanence is there a feature of it (131 A–E).

who implants science, although 'Health itself' and 'Science itself' are as well as the Participants; and the same principle applies to everything else that is produced in accordance with an art.

(Joachim's trans. with inverted commas mostly removed.)

It is not clear whether Aristotle is here imputing to 'Sokrates in the *Phaedo*' an explanation of what he himself calls γένεσις ἁπλῆ, i.e. the coming to be of a substance, or of what he calls τὶς γένεσις (*de gen. et corr.* 317B3), i.e. the coming to be of an attribute. It is only the latter that Socrates does in fact seek to account for by participation in Forms, e.g. the coming to be of beauty, tallness, duality, etc. Aristotle's instances, health and science, which are for him τινὲς γενέσεις κατὰ τέχνην, suggest that he is reporting correctly; on the other hand the sentence translated above 'while a thing is said to be in virtue of the Form, it is said to come-to-be *qua* sharing in, to pass away *qua* losing the Form', if taken in the most natural way, tells against this.[1] In any case, whatever sort or sorts of 'becoming' Aristotle finds in our present section, there is no dispute about what his criticism is: namely that the Forms cannot play the part of 'efficient' or 'moving' causes. It is indeed on the weakest point in the theory that he lays his finger, viz. on the *acquisition* of attributes rather than the *possession* of them, on μετάσχεσις (101C5) (his own word is μετάληψις), rather than μέθεξις. It is not easy to see how Plato could have answered the point about intermittent operation of the Forms in terms of the *Phaedo* doctrine.

In another passage (*Metaphysics* 988A8) Aristotle maintains that Plato recognises neither efficient nor final causes; but Sir David Ross, commenting on this, remarks (*op. cit.* p. 234):

Even in the *Phaedo* the efficient and the final cause are not ignored. The efficient cause is recognized in the passage in which Socrates criticizes Anaxagoras for not remaining true to his own maxim that reason is the cause of all things.... And with this conception of mind as the efficient cause of the world's being as it is there is associated the notion of the good as the final cause with a view to which mind acts.... It is indeed because Plato has failed to discover the nature of 'the best'—because he does not see his way, for the time being, to a teleological explanation—that he falls back on explaining by the presence of Ideas the fact that things are as they are—an explanation which clearly does not exclude a teleological explanation, but may be supplemented by one.

---

[1] The Greek is εἶναι μὲν ἕκαστον λέγεται κατὰ τὸ εἶδος, γίνεσθαι δὲ κατὰ τὴν μετάληψιν καὶ φθείρεσθαι κατὰ τὴν ἀποβολήν. Cornford (*Plato and Parmenides*, p. 79) takes εἶναι to mean 'to be (so and so)', and γίνεσθαι might be similarly taken as = γίνεσθαί τι: but there would remain the difficulty of φθείρεσθαι, which cannot mean 'to lose an attribute'. A possible solution would be to take ἕκαστον as meaning 'each attribute', but I do not much favour this.

It is well that we should be reminded that the doctrine of Forms as causes is put forward by Socrates as a second-best doctrine relatively to that which he had hoped to build on the principle suggested by Anaxagoras. Nevertheless Plato seems in our present section, and indeed throughout the rest of the argument which gives his final proof of immortality, to have forgotten this; for again and again Socrates asserts that γένεσις and φθορά, in the restricted sense in which he is using these terms, viz. the acquisition and loss of attributes by particular sensible things, are due *solely* to things coming, or ceasing, to participate in Forms. This makes it difficult immediately to agree that the doctrine 'does not exclude a teleological explanation'. Nevertheless I believe that Ross is at bottom right about this. These 'exclusive' statements, such as φαίνεται γάρ μοι...οὐδὲ δι' ἓν ἄλλο καλὸν εἶναι ἢ διότι μετέχει ἐκείνου τοῦ καλοῦ, should be interpreted in the light of all that Socrates has said about the explanations of the physicists, together with a new point somewhat cursorily made at 100D. To take the new point first, he is ruling out the notion that an attribute *A* of a concrete whole *x* can be accounted for by specifying a part or feature of *x* as that to which the attribute properly belongs; if I say a rose is beautiful because it has a bright colour, I merely provoke the question 'Do you mean that a bright colour is beautiful, and if so, why?' But far more important of course in these 'exclusive' statements is the implied ruling-out of mechanical explanations, explanations in terms of material 'forces', 'things like air and aether and water and a host of other absurdities'. It is not non-material, spiritual activity, it is not design and purpose that Plato wishes to deny, though we must perhaps admit that his restricted interpretation of γένεσις and φθορά has resulted in certain affirmations which, taken at their face value, justify Aristotle's criticism of 'Sokrates in the *Phaedo*'.

XVII

102A–105B   THE EXCLUSION OF OPPOSITES

This section, which does not readily admit of summary, is chiefly con-
cerned with showing that there are certain immanent characters ('forms')
which exclude, or will not admit into themselves, one or other of a pair of
opposites. The whole argument prepares us, by means of general principles
and analogies, for the next section, where it will be asserted that soul will
not admit the character 'dead'.

[*At this point Phaedo's narrative is once more interrupted by Echecrates,*
but only for a few lines.]

Ech.   Upon my word, Phaedo, they had good reason to say so. As I see   102 A
it, Socrates made matters wonderfully clear even to a feeble intelligence.

Phaedo.   Just so, Echecrates: that is what everyone there thought.

Ech.   As do we who were not there, your present audience. But how
did the conversation proceed?

Phaedo.   It was like this, I think. When Socrates had gained their
assent, and it was agreed that every Form was a real existent, and that   B
other things bore their names by virtue of participating in those Forms,
he then put this question:

'If', he said, 'that is your view, then when you say that Simmias is
taller than Socrates and shorter than Phaedo, are you not saying that
both tallness and shortness are in Simmias?'

'Yes, I am.'

'But of course you admit that the words "Simmias overtops Socrates"
do not express the truth of the matter. For surely it isn't part of the
nature of Simmias to overtop him: he doesn't do so by being Simmias,   C
but by tallness which he happens to possess. Again, you will admit that
he doesn't overtop Socrates because Socrates is Socrates, but because
Socrates possesses shortness over against Simmias's tallness.'

'True.'

'Once again, Simmias is not overtopped by Phaedo because Phaedo
is Phaedo, but because Phaedo has tallness over against Simmias's
shortness.'

'Yes.'

'So that is how Simmias comes to be spoken of as both short and tall,

being as he is between the two others: he offers his shortness to the
D tallness of Phaedo to be overtopped, and presents his tallness to
Socrates to overtop the shortness of Socrates.'

Socrates smiled as he said this, and added: 'That sounds as if I were
going to talk like a book; however, what I have said surely is true.'
Simmias agreed, and Socrates contined: 'My purpose in saying this
is to get you to share my view: which is this, that not only will tallness
itself never consent to be simultaneously tall and short, but the tallness
in us can never admit shortness, and never consent[1] to be overtopped;
instead, one of these two things must happen: it must either retreat
E and withdraw when its opposite, shortness, advances, or it must perish
at that advance; what it won't consent to is to endure[2] and admit shortness, and so to be something other than it was. For example, I have
admitted and endured shortness, and am short without ceasing to be
what I am; but the Form that is tall can never bring itself to be short:
and similarly shortness, even the shortness in us, can never consent to
be or become tall; nor can any other opposite, while still being what it
103 was, simultaneously become or be its own opposite; when that threatens,
it either takes its departure or perishes.'[3]

'I agree entirely', said Cebes.

On hearing this one of the company (I am not sure who it was)
intervened: 'Look here,' he said, 'did we not agree a while ago[4] to the
exact opposite of what is now asserted? Didn't we say that the greater
comes into being from the smaller, and the smaller from the greater?
Was not the coming-to-be of an opposite agreed to be just this coming
out of its opposite? Whereas now apparently it is maintained that that
can never happen.'

Socrates inclined his head towards the speaker, and having listened
B to him remarked: 'A courageous reminder; but you don't realise the
difference between what we said then and what we say now. Then we
said that of two opposite *things* the one comes into being from the
other; now we say that an opposite *itself* can never become its own

---

[1] The use of οὐκ ἐθέλειν, here and in E7, 103C1, involves a faint personification of the immanent characters, which is partly whimsical, partly a corollary
of the military metaphors φεύγειν, ὑπεκχωρεῖν, προσιέναι which immediately follow.

[2] In view of ὑπομείνας τὴν σμικρότητα just below, ὑπομένον cannot be in-
transitive, as Burnet supposes.

[3] These alternatives are repeated at D8–11, and 104C1; that of 'withdrawal'
is exemplified in the single case of soul (106E5–9), and is apparently brought in
solely to provide for that case. 'Perishing' occurs in all other cases, even in that
of an odd number threatened by 'evenness' (106B7–C3).   [4] 70Dff.

opposite, whether the opposite in question be in us or in the world of true being. Previously, my friend, we were speaking of things that *have* opposites, and calling them by the names of those opposites which they possessed; but now we are speaking of the opposites themselves from whose immanence the things called after them derive their names: c these opposites themselves, we maintain, could never consent to originate from one another.'[1]

With these words he glanced at Cebes, and added: 'Can it be, Cebes, that you too were disturbed by anything our friend here said?'

'No,' said Cebes, 'I don't feel like that on this occasion; yet I won't deny that many matters[2] do disturb me.'

'We agree then, without reserve, on this point, that no opposite will ever be its own opposite.'

'Absolutely.'

'Now please consider whether you will agree to my next point. Do you speak of "hot" and "cold"?'

'I do.'

'Meaning by them the same as "snow" and "fire"?'

'Why no, of course not.'   D

'That is to say, the hot is different from fire, and the cold from snow.'

'Yes.'

'But I think you would agree that what starts as snow cannot ever, as we were saying just now,[3] admit the hot[4] and still be what it was:

---

[1] The unnamed speaker has some excuse for his misunderstanding, for though in some places (e.g. 71 B 2 μείζονος μὲν πράγματος καὶ ἐλάττονος μεταξὺ αὔξησις καὶ φθίσις) Socrates did make clear that he was speaking of *things possessing attributes*, in others (e.g. 70 E 4 ἄρα ἀναγκαῖον ὅσοις ἔστι τι ἐναντίον μηδαμόθεν ἄλλοθεν αὐτὸ γίγνεσθαι ἢ ἐκ τοῦ αὐτῷ ἐναντίου) he did not.

[2] What are these? Nothing that Cebes says later supplies an answer; but maybe he was troubled by the apparent contradiction between the principle of mutual exclusion of opposites and the simultaneous presence in Simmias of shortness and tallness (see further in commentary below).

[3] Presumably the reference is to 102 D 5–E 3, but the difficulty is that there it was said that one opposite will withdraw or perish at the approach of another, whereas here it is snow, a concrete thing *containing* an opposite (cold), that will withdraw or perish at the approach of its opposite (hot). The difficulty, however, vanishes in the light of 103 E, where it becomes clear that Socrates is *extending* what was said above, rather than repeating it. Thus there is a formal inaccuracy in ὥσπερ. . .ἐλέγομεν, but nothing more.

[4] 'The hot' (τὸ θερμόν) is here not a substance nor yet an expression in which, as in Ionian science, substance and quality are not yet distinguished; it is a character immanent in a substance, a 'form', we might say, using the small initial letter (as I shall use it hereafter) to distinguish it from αὐτὸ τὸ θερμόν, the transcendent Form, hotness (heat).

still be snow and also hot; on the approach of the hot it will either withdraw or perish.'

'Quite so.'

'Again fire, when the cold approaches it, will either get out of its way or perish; it will never bring itself to admit coldness and still be what it was, still be fire and also cold.'

E   'That is true.'

'Then in some of these cases we find that it is not only the form itself that is entitled to its own name for all time, but something else too which, though not being that form, yet always bears that form's character,[1] whenever it exists. Here's an example which will perhaps make my meaning clearer: the odd, I presume, must always have this name which we now give it,[2] mustn't it?'

'Of course.'

'But will it be the only thing in the world to have it—that is what 104 I am asking—or is there something else which, though not identical with the odd, nevertheless must be called by the name "odd" as well as by its own name, owing to the fact that its nature is such that it can never be apart from the odd? What I mean may be illustrated by the case of the number three, to take one of many instances. Consider the number three: wouldn't you say that it must always be designated both by its own name and also by the name "odd", though it is not identical with the odd? Not identical: nevertheless such is the nature of three

---

[1] At first sight it might seem natural to take αὐτὸ τὸ εἶδος in E 3 and ἐκεῖνο in E 4 to mean the transcendent Form, and this would make the words ἔχει τὴν ἐκείνου μορφήν easier to understand. But it is immanent forms—characters like τὸ ψυχρόν which can *approach* and reside in concrete subjects that Socrates has been and still is concerned with; and although when he needs a noun (rather than the adjective ἐναντίον) to denote the immanent form he mostly uses ἰδέα (104B9, D2, 6, 9, E1), yet εἴδη is used at 104C7, where οὐχ ὑπομένει ἐπιόντα ἄλληλα rules out reference to transcendent Forms.

The 'something else' (ἄλλο τι) which 'always bears the form's character' is, in terms of the example just given, the concrete lump of snow which always has 'cold' immanent in it. The words ἔχει τὴν ἐκείνου μορφήν are, strictly speaking, illogical, since ἐκεῖνο (in the example, τὸ ψυχρόν) is itself a μορφή (character); they are loose for ἔχει ἐκεῖνο ἐνόν. That μορφή and ἰδέα are synonyms is evident from 104D9–10.

From the example of the snow which, though not the same as 'cold', yet always has the character 'cold' Socrates now (E5 ff.) passes to another example, viz. that of the number three which, though not the same as 'odd', yet always has the character 'odd'. On the difference in kind between these two examples, of which the former involves a concrete subject and a physical fact, while the latter does not, see the commentary below.

[2] I.e. 'odd'.

and five and half the entire number-series that every one of these numbers is odd. Correspondingly two and four and the whole of the B other column of numbers are not identical with the even, but nevertheless each of them is for ever even. Do you agree?'

'Certainly.'

'Then mark what I want to show; it is this, that not only do we find the opposites that we spoke of refusing to admit each other, but all things which,[1] while not being mutually opposed, always possess opposites, themselves likewise appear not to admit the character which is opposite to that contained in themselves; when that character advances upon them they either perish or withdraw. Thus shall we not C affirm that three[2] will sooner perish, sooner allow anything to happen to it, than endure, while still being three, to become even?'

'Indeed we shall', said Cebes.

⟨'And similarly shall we not affirm that two will sooner perish, sooner allow anything to happen to it than endure, while still being two, to become odd?'

'Indeed we shall.'⟩

'Nevertheless two is not the opposite of three.'[3]

'No, it is not.'

'Hence it is not only two opposite forms[4] that won't endure an onset by one on the other: there are others also[5] that won't endure the onset of opposites.'

'Very true.'

'Then would you like us, if we can, to specify what sort of forms these are?'

'Certainly.'

'Must they not be those which compel the object which they come D to occupy to have not only its own character, but also the character of a certain opposite, which it will never lose?'

'How do you mean?'

---

[1] ὅσα, as is plain from the instances which follow, means 'all forms which' (e.g. δυάς and τριάς); but so to translate it would be improper.

[2] τὰ τρία is not of course three *things*, but (as is evident from the immediate substitution of τριάς in c5) immanent 'threeness'.

[3] The remark in 104c5 οὐδὲ μὴν ἐναντίον γέ ἐστι δυὰς τριάδι seems to have no relevance. Logic would be restored by inserting immediately before it ⟨καὶ τὰ δύο ὡσαύτως καὶ ἀπολεῖσθαι πρότερον καὶ ἄλλο ὁτιοῦν πείσεσθαι πρὶν ὑπομεῖναι ἔτι δύο ὄντα περιττὰ γίγνεσθαι; | πάνυ μὲν οὖν⟩ or words to that effect. I have translated accordingly.

[4] See p. 150 n. 1 above. [5] ἀλλ' ἄττα (*sc.* εἴδη).

'Remember what we said just now. You know presumably that anything occupied by the character of three must be not only three but also odd.'

'Certainly.'

'Well, what we maintain is that such a thing can never be visited by the character that is opposite to the form which brings that about.'

'No.'

'And what brought it about was the form of odd?'

'Yes.'

'Whose opposite is the form of even?'

'Yes.'

E   'Then the character of even will never visit three.'[1]

'No, it will not.'

'That is to say, three has nothing to do with even.'

'Nothing.'

'In fact three is non-even.'

'Yes.'

'Now I was saying that we must specify[2] what sort of things they are which, while not the opposite of a given thing, nevertheless will not admit that thing;[3] our example just now was the refusal of the number three to admit the even, despite its not being the opposite of even; the reason being that three always brings up[4] the opposite of even, just as two brings up the opposite of odd, fire the opposite of cold, and so on 105 and so forth. Well, I wonder if you would specify them in this way:[5] it is not only two opposites that refuse to admit each other, but if any

[1] See p. 151 n. 2 above; here again the meaning of τὰ τρία is determined by the substitution of ἡ τριάς in E5.

[2] ἔλεγον = ἐκέλευον (I bade), and the construction begun by the relative clause is dropped owing to the illustrations of lines 8–11. A new construction is substituted at 105 A1 with ἀλλ' ὅρα δή.

[3] I follow Wyttenbach's suggestion of bracketing τὸ ἐναντίον, which I take to be a misguided gloss on αὐτό. αὐτό has of course the same reference as the preceding τινί.

[4] ἐπιφέρει, as Burnet remarks, is another military metaphor: the object of attack 'brings up', so to say, its reserves.

[5] Socrates now amplifies the specification given at 104D1–3 by explaining the nature of the compulsion (ἀναγκάζει) there mentioned: that compulsion is due to the fact that the form which is not an opposite carries with it (in the metaphor, 'brings up') one which is an opposite. Thus 'threeness', which is not an opposite of anything, brings up the form of 'oddness', and so (a) refuses itself to admit the form of 'evenness', and (b) compels any set of three objects which it 'occupies' (κατέχει) to have, in addition to its own form (threeness), the form 'oddness' also, and prevents the set from 'admitting' the form 'evenness'.

form brings up one of two opposites into that which it itself enters, that form itself will never admit the character opposite to the one brought up. Let me refresh your memory; it does no harm to hear a thing more than once; five will not admit the character of even, nor ten, its double, the character of odd. Of course the double is also in itself opposite to something else: nevertheless ten will not admit the character of odd.[1] B Again the fraction ⅔ and all the other members of the series of halves will not admit the character of wholeness, and the same is true of ⅓ and all the terms of that series.[2] I hope you go along with me here and share my view.'

'I do so most emphatically.'

This section may be divided for the purpose of comment into two parts: (*a*) 102 A 3–103 C 9; (*b*) 103 C 10–105 B 4.

(*a*) This consists of an argument the conclusion of which is, in Socrates's words, that 'an opposite will never be its own opposite': that is to say, neither a transcendent Form nor an immanent character can take on the Form or the character contrary to itself: e.g. 'tallness' cannot take on 'shortness', nor *vice versa* (the only instance given in this part of our section).

It is important to note (i) that here, as in other places,[3] Plato thinks that the adjective expressing the quality of a particular thing can properly be applied to the transcendent Form or to the immanent character in virtue of which the particular is so qualified: e.g. 'Tallness itself' and 'the tallness in us' are both tall; this is evident from 102 D 6–8; and (ii) that what is declared impossible is not that a character X should change into its contrary Y in the sense that X is wholly replaced by Y;

---

[1] I have in part borrowed Cornford's translation in his article in *C.Q.* III (1909), p. 189, though I do not agree with all his comment. Burnet in his edition (1911) abandons the insertion of οὐκ before ἐναντίον which he accepted in his Oxford text, and I have no doubt that his second thought is right. The real difficulty seems to me to lie in ὅμως. Why should the fact that τὸ διπλάσιον has an opposite, viz. τὸ ἁπλοῦν or perhaps τὸ ἥμισυ, be a reason for not expecting ten to exclude oddness, as ὅμως implies? Because (I would reply) we might expect any double, anything which, like ten, brings up doubleness, to exclude nothing else but singleness (or perhaps halfness). Oddness is not a character which τὸ διπλάσιον *qua* τὸ διπλάσιον would exclude: nevertheless ten, the double of five, does exclude oddness: the fact that it happens to be a double is irrelevant to the truth of this exclusion.

[2] i.e. any fraction with denominator 3. I agree with the last paragraph of Cornford's article, in which he suggests that the passage 105 A 8–B 3 'was inserted by the author (if by him at all) as an afterthought.... It is just the sort of addition which a modern author might make in a footnote, when some more complicated instance, which interested him but was not very relevant, occurred to his mind.'

[3] E.g. *Protag.* 330 C–D, *Parm.* 132 A.

in point of fact such replacement is precisely what happens when an 'advance' of *Y* upon *X* occurs; what is impossible is that *X*, while still *X*, should also be its opposite *Y* (τὸ σμικρὸν τὸ ἐν ἡμῖν οὐκ ἐθέλει ποτὲ μέγα γίγνεσθαι οὐδὲ εἶναι, οὐδ' ἄλλο οὐδὲν τῶν ἐναντίων, ἔτι ὂν ὅπερ ἦν, ἅμα τοὐναντίον γίγνεσθαί τε καὶ εἶναι, ἀλλ' ἤτοι ἀπέρχεται ἢ ἀπόλλυται ἐν τούτῳ τῷ παθήματι, 102 E–103 A).

It will probably surprise the reader that Socrates should make so much of what appears to us, so far as we can attach any meaning to it, a mere truism. No doubt, if we go beyond our present section and take account of the application which is to be made of this apparent truism, we shall be inclined to see more in it. What is that application? It is, of course, that the form[1] 'aliveness' (if the word be permitted) cannot while remaining itself take on the form 'deadness': which fact, taken along with another to be established, namely that *soul* always brings into the field, and keeps there, the form 'aliveness', yields the conclusion that soul cannot have the form 'deadness'—in short ψυχή is ἀθάνατον.

But perhaps it is hardly legitimate to remove, or seek to remove, our difficulty by this application of *respice finem*. To attach any meaning to the proposition 'shortness cannot be at once both short and tall' we have first to put ourselves in Plato's position, according to which 'shortness' is not a mere universal, but a really existent Form, of which it seemed to him obvious that 'short' could be predicated; yet, when we have done that, we shall probably still say that to deny that shortness can be tall as well as short is to deny something that no one in his senses could ever think of affirming; and I think we should be right in saying that. Nevertheless we can see why Plato deemed it necessary to make the denial; it was because he had reflected upon what he makes Socrates point out at 102 B–C, namely that a man—a concrete subject— can be short and tall simultaneously, or (as we might put it) a short man can be also, and simultaneously, tall. If this can be true of a concrete subject, why should it not be true of ἡ ἐν ἡμῖν σμικρότης? It looks perhaps, at first sight, as if no answer were forthcoming to this question: it looks as if Plato were content with simply registering a difference between concrete subjects on the one hand and Forms (and forms) on the other. But I believe that an answer is in fact given, or at least implied, in the speech which begins at 102 B 8 (ἀλλὰ γάρ . . .) together with Socrates's next two speeches. Simmias, we are told, overtops Socrates not in virtue of being Simmias, but because of the tallness which is in him; that is to say, Simmias is conceived as no more than a container of forms, a container which always remains what it is, but in which various forms, amongst which are two opposites, reside. There is no difficulty, Plato feels, about that: once we realise that tallness and shortness, and every other possible attribute which we

[1] By 'form' without an initial capital I mean an immanent character.

can attach to Simmias, belong to him not intrinsically, not 'in virtue of his being Simmias', but because he is a possessor or container of certain forms, we shall see why what is impossible in the case of Forms themselves, and of forms, is perfectly possible for him. It is, I fancy, usually supposed that in these speeches Plato means to distinguish between essential and accidental predicates: and certainly the language of 102C1–2 (πεφυκέναι and τῷ μεγέθει ὃ τυγχάνει ἔχων) does suggest this; yet such a distinction would, in my opinion, be irrelevant both to his immediate purpose and to the whole final argument for immortality, of which this section forms a part. The distinction is not that, but one between subjects conceived strictly as subjects, devoid of all attributes—what I have called 'containers'—and predicates conceived as forms or immanent characters.

I have argued that the reason why Plato has laboured the point about opposites excluding opposites is that he thought it was *prima facie* incompatible with the phenomena of the short man who is also tall, and the tall man who is also short. Probably his readers, or most of them, would have felt this incompatibility to be real, and for that reason he was right in attempting to explain it away. But in point of fact it is illusory, since 'tall' and 'short' are not qualities, but relations; or to put it in other words, Simmias does not in fact contain two forms which he presents to Socrates and Phaedo respectively, but only one (relevant) form, namely *stature*, which remains unchanged whatever bystanders there may be. The curious thing is that Plato appears to be at least on the verge of realising this when he makes Socrates say that he possesses smallness 'towards' or 'relatively to' (πρός) the tallness of Simmias, and that Phaedo possesses tallness 'towards' his shortness. Yet this semi-awareness of the distinction between qualities and relations is, it seems, only momentary; from 102D5 onwards it disappears.

Burnet points out that the argument about opposites excluding one another is formulated in the language of a military metaphor: one is spoken of as advancing upon, or withdrawing from another, of enduring its onset, and so forth; and the metaphor will be kept up in the next section. It cannot fail to strike us as unnatural, but I have little doubt that it first came into Plato's mind in connexion with the *physical* event to be mentioned at 103D—the melting of snow at the approach of 'the hot': for it is natural enough to think of the heat of a fire attacking and annihilating the cold in a lump of snow, or at any rate far more natural than to think of tallness attacking shortness. Plato then extends his metaphor both backwards into the first part of the present section, and (as we shall see) forwards also into the next section: soul, with its form 'aliveness' will be conceived as attacked by the opposite form 'deadness', and as thereupon 'withdrawing'. It may fairly be said that without this elaborate and sustained metaphor the final proof of immortality would lose much of such plausibility as it has.

(*b*) The difficulties of the second part of this section are difficulties of detail, and indeed mainly lie in grasping the exact meaning of the Greek text. I do not think that when this has been done anything remains obscure—indeed I think Plato has expressed his meaning with perfect clarity except for certain ambiguous pronouns (e.g. at 104D1–3 and 105A3–4), and for the fact that expressions like τὰ δύο and τὰ τρία are used in the sense of the characters 'twoness' and 'threeness' immanent in sets of two or three things, i.e. as equivalent to δυάς and τριάς, instead of the more ordinary sense of those sets themselves. I must rely on the translation and footnotes to guide the reader through a few passages which certainly require him to keep a clear head, but should cause no trouble if he does.

The general purpose of this second part is to extend the principle established in the first. Not only do opposite forms exclude each other, as we have already learnt, but certain forms which are not opposites (or, as perhaps it might be more clearly expressed, which *have* no opposites) exclude certain other forms which are (or again, which *have*) opposites. Thus 'twoness' excludes 'oddness', and 'fieriness' excludes 'coldness'. These two examples are given at 104E10–105A1 in the words καὶ ἡ δυὰς τῷ περιττῷ καὶ τὸ πῦρ τῷ ψυχρῷ, which as the context shows, mean καὶ ἡ δυάς, οὐκ ἐναντία οὖσα τῷ περιττῷ, οὐ δέχεται τὸ περιττόν, καὶ τὸ πῦρ, οὐκ ἐναντίον ὂν τῷ ψυχρῷ, οὐ δέχεται τὸ ψυχρόν. It seems to me beyond doubt that here at least, whatever be the case elsewhere (see p. 162 *infra*), τὸ πῦρ is conceived as a form, fieriness, not as a particular fire; not merely because it is mentioned in the same breath with ἡ δυάς, but also because the whole paragraph in which it occurs is concerned not with things but with forms, not with κατεχόμενα but with κατέχοντα. But what sort of forms possess this characteristic of excluding one of a pair of opposites? Plato defines them by reference to the things which they come to 'occupy' (104D1, D6): and that he should do so is quite natural, since the form which he has in mind—the form to which all the illustrations of his principle point—is *soul*, which occupies a body, and 'brings up' into that body the form of an opposite, viz. the form 'aliveness' (life).[1] But, simply for the purpose of specifying what sort of forms possess the characteristic in question, there was no need to bring in this reference to a κατέχον and a κατεχόμενον: it would have been enough to say that they are any such forms as entail, or are inseparable from, one of a pair of opposites.

Hence the whole principle for which this section argues is that

---

[1] I shall argue, in commenting on the next section (pp. 162 f. *infra*) that Plato conceives souls as immanent forms down to 105 E9, but not thereafter.

opposites exclude each other, and that any form entailing one of a pair of opposites excludes the other member of that pair.

I have already suggested that the military metaphor of attack and retreat probably occurred to Plato in connexion with fire and snow, hot and cold, of which we hear first at 103 C–D. But it should be realised that one effect of extending the metaphor to cover cases like odd and even numbers is to obscure an important difference. The refusal of a cold lump of snow to admit heat, while yet remaining snow, is a physical fact known through sense-perception; whereas the refusal of 'twoness' to admit 'threeness' and 'oddness', and that of soul to accept 'deadness', are statements about the implications of terms: they are in fact somewhat unnatural expressions of analytical propositions, and the final 'proof' of immortality is a disguised assertion that the term 'soul' implies, as part of its meaning, the term 'alive'.[1] But by putting all these instances of exclusion on all fours with one another, as the military metaphor helps him to do, Plato disguises—from himself, as I believe, as well as from us—the fundamental weakness of his argument. The fact that snow melts away when you empty a brazier on to it does nothing whatever to make it more probable that the soul withdraws intact when a man dies.

[1] A friendly critic suggests that the instance of twoness excluding oddness (*et similia*) is not precisely on a level with soul excluding death, inasmuch as it rests on what might be called 'observation of mathematical phenomena': hence it is, so to say, half-way between the record of a physical event and the assertion of a *purely* analytical proposition. I think this is true; but I keep it for a footnote as it serves rather to complicate than to clarify the point I have sought to make.

XVIII

105B–107B   THE ARGUMENT CONCLUDED. SOUL IS BOTH
DEATHLESS AND INDESTRUCTIBLE

*Applying the principle just established, Socrates argues that soul always
'brings up' life into that which it 'occupies' (as an immanent form), and
excludes death. Hence we have proved that 'soul is deathless'. But this is
not, in his view, the same as proving that it is indestructible or imperishable;
hence the rest of the section consists mainly in an attempt to establish this
further proposition, and the imperishability of each individual soul is
proclaimed at the end of* 106E.

*Some doubt still lingers in the mind of Simmias, despite his assent to the
foregoing argument; whereupon Socrates recommends a further examination of 'the original assumptions'.*

105B   'Well now, go back to the beginning, will you? And please don't
meet my questions with that safe answer we spoke of, but copy my
example. I say that because the course of our argument has led me to
discern a different kind of safety from that which I mentioned originally.[1]
Thus, if you were to ask me what must come to be present in a thing's
C body to make it hot, I should not give you that safe, stupid answer
"heat", but a cleverer one now at my disposal, namely "fire". Again,
if you ask what must come to be present in a body to make it sick,
I shall not say "sickness" but "fever". Similarly, what must be present
in a number for it to be odd? Not oddness, but a unit;[2] and so on.
I wonder if you see clearly by now what I want?'

'Oh yes, quite clearly.'

'Then tell me, what must come to be present in a body for it to be
alive?'

'Soul.'

D   'Does that hold good always?'

---

[1] The text of 105 B 6–7 seems to me meaningless, and the attempts of editors
to translate it unsuccessful. I suggest that ἀπόκρισιν τὴν ἀσφαλῆ ἐκείνην should
be transposed to follow ἀποκρίνου, and that παρ' ἣν should be understood as
παρ' ἣν ἀσφάλειαν.

[2] μονάς is surely to be explained not by supposing that Plato is thinking of one
odd number only, viz. the number one itself, but as meaning the 'one left over
in the middle' the μονὰς ἐν μέσῳ περιοῦσα of Stobaeus, *Ecl.* I, p. 22, 19 (quoted in
E.G.P.[3], p. 288): εἰς δύο διαιρουμένων ἴσα τοῦ μὲν περιττοῦ μονὰς ἐν μέσῳ περίεστι, τοῦ
δὲ ἀρτίου κενὴ λείπεται χώρα καὶ ἀδέσποτος καὶ ἀνάριθμος.

'Certainly.'

'Then soul always brings life along with it to anything that it occupies?'

'Yes indeed.'

'And is there an opposite to life, or is there none?'

'There is.'

'What?'

'Death.'

'Now soul will assuredly never admit the opposite of what it introduces: that has been agreed already, hasn't it?'

'Emphatically so.'

'Well now: what name did we give just now to the thing that won't admit the character of even?'

'Non-even.'

'And to that which won't admit "just" or "musical"?'

'"Unjust" and "unmusical".'   E

'All right: then what name shall we give to that which won't admit death?'

'Deathless.'

'And isn't it soul that won't admit death?'

'Yes.'

'Then soul is deathless.'

'It is deathless.'

'Very well; may we say that that has been proved? Or how do you feel about it?'

'Yes, and very adequately proved, Socrates.'

'Now a further point, Cebes: if the non-even were necessarily 106 imperishable, presumably three would be imperishable.'

'Undoubtedly.'

'Or again, if the non-hot were necessarily imperishable, then when you confront snow with something hot, the snow would retreat out of its way, intact and unmelted; for it couldn't perish, nor could it endure to admit heat.'

'That is true.'

'Similarly, I suppose, if the non-coolable were imperishable, then when a cold object approached fire, the fire could never be extinguished, or perish, but would take itself off intact.'

'It would have to do so.'   B

'Then must we not apply the same principle in the case of what is deathless? That is to say, if the deathless is also imperishable, it is impossible for a soul to perish when death approaches it, for it follows from what we have said that the soul will not admit death, will never be dead, any more than three, and of course oddness, will ever be even, or fire, and of course the heat in fire, ever be cold. But it may be objected,

c "Granting that the odd cannot become even when the even approaches, what is to prevent it perishing, and an even taking its place?" In reply, we could not contend that the odd cannot perish, for the non-even is not imperishable. Of course, if that had been admitted to be so, we could easily now contend that on the approach of the even oddness and three take their departure; and we could have maintained the same thing about fire and the hot, and the rest of them, couldn't we?'

'Yes indeed.'

'Then similarly in our present instance of the deathless, if that is

D admitted to be also imperishable, soul would be imperishable in addition to being deathless; but if that is not admitted, we shall need a further argument.'

'Oh but, so far as that goes, we need nothing further: for if the deathless, which lasts for ever, is to admit destruction, it is hardly likely that anything else will escape destruction.'

'Yes, and I suppose it would be agreed by everyone that God, and the Form of life itself,[1] and any other deathless entity there may be, can never perish.'

'Why yes, to be sure: agreed by every human being: and the gods, I expect, would be even more inclined to agree.'[2]

E 'Then inasmuch as the deathless is also indestructible, I presume that soul, if it really is deathless, must be indestructible too.'

'There can be no question of that.'

'So when death approaches a man his mortal part, it seems, dies, but his immortal part gets out of the way of death and takes its departure intact and indestructible.'

'Evidently.'

107 'Beyond all doubt then, Cebes, soul is deathless and imperishable, and our souls will in truth exist in Hades.'

'I for my part, Socrates,' replied Cebes, 'cannot dispute that, nor

---

[1] αὐτὸ τὸ τῆς ζωῆς εἶδος probably means the transcendent Form ('aliveness'): but it might mean that immanent ζωή which soul was said to bring to anything that it occupied (105 D 3).

[2] Cebes speaks humorously: the gods, for whom ἀθάνατοι is virtually a second name, are the last people in the world to doubt their own immortality.

can I feel any doubt about our arguments. But if Simmias here or any-one else has anything to say, it is desirable that he should not suppress it; any further discussion of these matters that may be desired can hardly, I think, be put off for a later occasion.'

'I can assure you', said Simmias, 'that I find it as impossible as you do to feel any doubt arising from our arguments; nevertheless the B great importance of the matter under discussion, together with a poor opinion of human fallibility, forces me still to remain doubtful about our assertions.'

'You are quite right there, Simmias,' replied Socrates: and I would add this: our original assumptions, acceptable as they are to you both, ought nevertheless to be more precisely examined. If you have a thoroughgoing inquiry into them, you will be following up the argument to the furthest point accessible to man; and if that inquiry itself ends in certainty, you will be at the end of your quest.'

'What you say', replied Simmias, 'is true.'

The purpose of Socrates's first speech (105 B 5–C 7) is to show how the original conception of the Forms as causes can be carried a stage further as the result of the principle of exclusion of opposites reached in the last section. Instead of saying that the cause of a subject *x* having an attribute *A* is the existence of the Form *A* and the immanence of the corresponding form *a*, we can now say that the cause is a form which is always associated with ('brings up') *a*, and which therefore refuses to admit into itself—and incidentally excludes from the subject which it 'occupies'—the opposite of *a*.

The use which will be made of this emended, or rather extended, account of causation becomes apparent immediately. But before dis-cussing this it should be remarked that as a general account of causation it has a weakness noted by Sir David Ross: namely that 'it loses the universality of the old answer' (*op. cit.* p. 33). If I may amplify this point in a slightly different form from that of Ross, the weakness lies in the fact that it will seldom be the case that there is *one* and only one form which 'brings up' one of a pair of opposites and refuses to admit the other. Fever is not the only thing which brings up sickness, nor fire the only thing which brings up heat; though indeed Socrates's third instance, that of the unit bringing up oddness is, if I have rightly understood it (see p. 158 n. 2 above), free from this objection: the μονὰς ἐν μέσῳ περιοῦσα is the one and only cause (in Socrates's sense) of any set of 3, 5, 7, etc., things having the attribute 'odd'.

But we should not attach too much importance to the weakness of the general principle: what Plato cares about is its application to the matter in hand, its application to that which has evoked the whole examination of the cause of γένεσις and φθορά, the whole argument in response to the doubts of Cebes: and that is, of course, the human soul. How then is this application made?

Perhaps the simplest answer is to say that ψυχή is taken to be an ἰδέα ἐπιφέρουσα ἐναντίον τι—an immanent form of the sort which we have been considering, one which, because it 'brings up' another form, cannot admit the opposite of that other form. Just as μονάς brings up περιττότης and excludes ἀρτιότης, so ψυχή brings up ζωή and excludes θάνατος. All these are forms—a fact which may seem strange in the case of θάνατος: but for the purpose of this argument we should think, as Plato is thinking, not of the *states* of life and death, nor yet of death as extinction, but of the attributes 'aliveness' and 'deadness'.

Taking into account the examples in 105 C, we get the following scheme:

Importing form[1]	*Imported form*[2]	*Excluded form*
Fever	Sickness	Health
Unit	Oddness	Evenness
Soul	Aliveness	Deadness
[Fire][3]	[Heat]	[Cold]

It seems to me beyond question that ψυχή is *at present* (i.e. down to 105 E 9) regarded as an immanent character or form. For only so can what is now asserted of soul be a corollary, or deduction, or application—whatever one chooses to call it—of the elaborate argument about exclusion of opposite forms: provided, that is, that I have been right in regarding that argument as concerned with forms; only so (to put it the other way round) could that argument have any point, any bearing on the matter for the sake of which it was introduced. And if any doubt still lingers in the reader's mind, surely the use of the word κατάσχῃ in 105 D 3 is, despite Burnet's note, conclusive; to my mind, at all events, it is inconceivable that it could mean there anything other than what it meant at 104 D 1, namely the occupation of a subject by an immanent form. But it must be emphasised that this conception of soul as form is confined to our present argument; apart from the final proof of immortality soul is tacitly assumed to be a substance, and indeed Plato, as I shall shortly point out, reverts to that view even in the present argument before its conclusion.

It is well known that Aristotle in his dialogue *Eudemus*, written about 354–3 B.C., argued for the soul's immortality on the lines of the

---

[1] ἰδέα ἐπιφέρουσα.   [2] ἰδέα ἐπιφερομένη.

[3] I put Fire in brackets because Plato appears to fluctuate between conceiving πῦρ as a form ('fieriness') as at 105 A 1, C 2, and as a concrete substance co-ordinate with snow, as at 103 D 10, 106 A 9. As we shall see immediately, there is a similar fluctuation in the case of soul itself.

Phaedo, and it seems possible to detect in the extant fragments or testimonia a trace of these two alternative views, though we cannot say how Aristotle reconciled them. At the end of *frag.* 45 (Rose) Olympiodorus (or Proclus) quotes his argument against the ψυχή ἁρμονία doctrine thus: τῇ ἁρμονίᾳ ἐναντίον ἐστὶν ἀναρμοστία, τῇ δὲ ψυχῇ οὐδὲν ἐναντίον· οὐσία γάρ. On the other hand in *frag.* 46 Simplicius says ἐν τῷ Εὐδήμῳ εἶδός τι ἀποφαίνεται τὴν ψυχὴν εἶναι. The latter statement cannot of course refer to Aristotle's later doctrine of the soul as the 'actuality' (ἐντελέχεια) of the body; as Jaeger remarks (*Aristotle*, E.T. p. 45), 'what distinguishes Aristotle's early view of the soul is in fact that the soul is not yet the form *of something*, but a form in itself, not yet εἶδός τινος but εἶδός τι, an Idea [i.e. a Platonic Form] or something of the nature of an Idea'. May it not be that this something was in fact a 'form', as distinct from a Form?

At 105 E we reach the conclusion expressed in Greek by the words ἀθάνατον ἄρα ψυχή. Although the further question whether ψυχή is also ἀνώλεθρον has still to be discussed, this seems the most convenient point to ask what validity this long argument which started at 100 C possesses. I have observed already that its conclusion is really nothing more than an analytical proposition in disguise: that is to say, what has been shown is that the predicate 'deathless' is contained in the meaning of the subject, soul; whenever, therefore, this subject exists it has this predicate: but to show that the subject always does exist is quite another matter. The point cannot perhaps be better expressed than it was some half-century after Plato's death by Strato of Lampsacus: μή ποτε ὡς τὸ πῦρ, ἔστ᾽ ἂν ᾖ, ἄψυκτον, οὕτω καὶ ἡ ψυχή, ἔστ᾽ ἂν ᾖ, ἀθάνατος· καὶ γὰρ ἐπιφέρει ζωήν, ἔστ᾽ ἂν ᾖ.[1] It should be added that, like all the arguments except possibly that from Recollection, this plainly does nothing to prove *individual* immortality.

I have translated ἀθάνατον ἄρα ψυχή by 'soul is deathless' rather than by 'the soul is immortal' for two reasons: (*a*) the absence of the definite article is conformable to my conviction that down to the end of 105 E ψυχή is thought of not as a substance, but as a form,[2] and (*b*) the associations of 'immortal' are such as to suggest that the whole great question is now finally settled, whereas it immediately becomes apparent that it is not—another whole page is deemed necessary; 'deathless', a word somewhat less fraught with associations, may suggest to the reader (it is at least intended to do so) that the adjective ἀθάνατον signifies no more than soul's immunity from that particular kind of extinction which might be supposed to befall it when it parts company with the body. The succeeding page (106 A–C),

---

[1] *Frag.* 123 (m) Wehrli. See below, p. 196.
[2] Nothing, however, can safely be inferred from the absence of the article in the Greek, since MSS. vary on this point in 105 E 4, 6 and 106 E 2.

in which it is argued that soul is ἀνώλεθρον (ἀδιάφθορον) as well as ἀθάνατον, starts from the implied assumption that there are other possible kinds of extinction. Nor is this an unreal assumption: it might well be that soul survives θάνατος and yet perishes later. Does the argument then prove that this cannot happen? I cannot see that it does; I agree with Strato (see p. 196 below) that Plato has 'too readily assumed' this final point. Reverting to the assault metaphor, he argues that, in cases other than that of soul, the exclusion of an attacking opposite may result in the annihilation of that which refuses to admit the attacker: we could not (so he puts it) argue that in these other cases perishing is impossible; but soul is in a special position: because that which it excludes is θάνατος, in other words because it is ἀθάνατον, it is therefore ἀνώλεθρον. But despite this show of proof nothing has in fact been said in 106B–C to advance the argument; the most that has been shown is something too obvious to need any argument, namely that anything which is ἀθάνατον is more likely to be ἀνώλεθρον than anything which is not.

What follows at 106D is, on the surface, no more than a rhetorical flourish, which dismisses the question at issue as if it should never have been raised;[1] but it may be that beneath the surface there is an appeal to religious faith: if the soul is deathless it is divine, and therefore ἀΐδιον, everlasting (though not, like the Forms eternal, in the sense of being outside the order of temporal things). 'In the end', says A. E. Taylor,[2] 'the imperishability of the soul is accepted as a consequence of the standing conviction of all Greek religion that τὸ ἀθάνατον = τὸ θεῖον = τὸ ἄφθαρτον.'

However that may be, it is only if we allow that the appeal is to faith that we can avoid a feeling of deep disappointment in this matter, inasmuch as from the standpoint of logic the argument has petered out into futility. What remains unsatisfactory is that the transition from reasoning to religious appeal is disguised from the reader, or hidden by a screen of unreal argument.

The conclusion of the whole matter is stated in terms of the assault metaphor: the soul, the immortal part of a man, gets out of the way of death, and takes its departure intact and indestructible. This alternative to annihilation, this 'withdrawal' was, as we have seen, long since provided for (103A): it is now asserted to be applicable in this special

---

[1] In ordinary parlance no doubt ἀθάνατος and ἀνώλεθρος as applied to ψυχή would be used synonymously; and probably no distinction was intended (as I have remarked above) when the two words were used together earlier, at 88B and 95C. It is quite intelligible that, having now made the distinction which he felt to be necessary for the reason I have explained, Plato should be content to use ἀθάνατος by itself at 107C2 and 8 instead of the more precise ἀθάνατος καὶ ἀνώλεθρος of 106E9.

[2] *P.M.W.* p. 206.

case. But since soul is not conceived as an extended object which can move in space, this is no more than a picturesque way of repeating the assertion that it continues to exist after parting from the body.

There is, however, another feature of this section which calls for comment, a change in what may be called Plato's conception of the logical status of soul. For the purpose of differentiating soul from the ἰδέαι ἐναντίον τι ἐπιφέρουσαι amongst which he has hitherto included it, he treats it no longer as a form or immanent character, but as a subject which contains or possesses a form, an immaterial subject on a level, save for its immateriality, with snow which contains the form 'cold' and excludes the form 'hot'. That this is so is most clearly apparent from 106 E 5–7, where τὸ θνητόν and τὸ ἀθάνατον are obviously body and soul respectively: the body, we are there told, dies when death 'comes against' a man, but the soul 'gets out of the way of death and takes its departure intact and indestructible'; just as snow, if its excluded form had necessarily involved indestructibility, would, instead of perishing, have withdrawn before the onset of heat (106 A). The parallel of ὑπεξήει ἂν ἡ χιὼν οὖσα σῶς καὶ ἄτηκτος with τὸ δ' ἀθάνατον σῶν καὶ ἀδιάφθορον οἴχεται ἀπιόν (106 E) emphasises the identical *logical* status which Plato now assigns to snow and to soul.

This transition—a reversion, as I have said, to the view of soul as a substance taken in the earlier parts of the dialogue—from soul as form to soul as possessor of form is disguised and facilitated by the military metaphor which, though never lost sight of, comes to the front again just at the point where the transition occurs;[1] for the notion of assault not only makes the alternatives of perishing and withdrawal far more vivid than they would have been if the reader had no more before his mind than a purely logical admission or exclusion of attributes, but almost compels him to substitute in his mind a quasi-concrete *thing* for an immanent character.

Despite Socrates's triumphant proclamation at the end of 106 E, and its endorsement by Cebes, that 'most obstinate sceptic in the world' (77 A), the section ends on a note of scepticism. But it is scepticism of a special sort: neither Simmias himself nor Socrates in supporting him feels any doubt about the cogency of the argument that has just been concluded: what they doubt is whether we ought in the last resort to accept even the most irrefutable reasoning as infallible 'beyond a peradventure'. A note is struck here, in the words τὴν ἀνθρωπίνην ἀσθένειαν ἀτιμάζων, which re-echoes the cautious rationalism of Simmias earlier in the dialogue (85 C–D); divine revela-

---

[1] The precise point is perhaps doubtful; I think it may be at 105 E 10 rather than at 106 A 3: the question is whether the ambiguous τῷ ἀναρτίῳ and τὰ τρία mean respectively 'that which is uneven' and 'three things' or the forms 'unevenness' and 'threeness'.

tion (θεῖος λόγος) was there mentioned, but only as something that we must do without; similarly here his allusion to the feebleness of human reason implies the same wistful longing for something stronger. Yet Socrates and Plato would certainly not wish us to depreciate reason overmuch; we ought still to bear in mind the warning against that 'misology' in which undue scepticism is likely to end.

Socrates's final exhortation to examine our original assumptions more precisely I have already anticipated in commenting (p. 141 *supra*) on the method of hypothesis. There must, I suggested, be an allusion to that doctrine known to us only from Books VI–VII of the later *Republic*, but perhaps already formed or forming in Plato's mind, of the unhypothetical first principle (ἀνυπόθετος ἀρχή), the source of all being and all knowledge, which is the Form of good. Only when this first principle is reached, and the Forms are seen in their dependence on it, will the goal of all inquiry be reached and οὐδὲν ζητήσομεν περαιτέρω. I think that Plato wavers on the question whether that goal can ever in fact be reached by any man in this life: the earlier part of our dialogue seems to suggest that it cannot, the present passage and the *Republic* that it can. If he does waver, who will blame him for it? In any case Socrates's suggestion of further examination is not intended to cast doubt upon the existence of the Forms nor upon the arguments that have been based upon their existence. If a paradox may be permitted, he is already certain, though he could become more certain still.

XIX

After remarking that the establishment of the soul's immortality is of immense practical significance in its bearing on our moral life, Socrates begins a long 'myth'—an imaginative picture of the destiny of souls, good and evil, after the life on earth. The picture is based on an ostensibly scientific account of the earth: the earth is spherical, but we live not on its circumference but in certain hollows which we mistake for the true earth above. The brightness and splendour of the true earth are contrasted with the gloom and murkiness of our dwelling-place, and the section ends with Socrates's promise to describe the former in more detail.

'But now, good sirs,' Socrates continued, 'there is a further point 107C on which we should do well to reflect: if the soul is immortal, it certainly calls for our attention not only in respect of this present period which we call our lifetime, but in respect of all time; and now, if not before, the danger of neglecting it may well seem terrible. For if death were the end of all things, it would be a heaven-sent boon for the wicked, when they die, to be at one stroke released both from the body and, with the death of the soul, from their own wickedness; but now that we have found the soul to be immortal, there can be no other escape from evil, no other salvation for it save by becoming as good D and intelligent as possible; seeing that the soul brings nothing with it to Hades except what nurture and upbringing have made of it: and that, we are told, avails much for weal or for woe from the very first moment of its departure to that other world.

'Now this is the story: when a man has breathed his last, the spirit[1] to whom each was allotted in life proceeds to conduct him to a certain place, and all they that are there gathered must abide their

---

[1] The notion of a guardian spirit attendant on each individual, not yet depersonalised into his 'fate', seems to have been familiar in the classical age; Burnet *ad loc.* quotes examples from Pindar and Lysias, and in the generation following Plato from Menander. In *Rep.* 620D he is described as φύλαξ τοῦ βίου καὶ ἀποπληρωτὴς τῶν αἱρεθέντων. The common belief, which Plato follows in the present passage, was that our δαίμων is allotted to us, but in the *Republic* myth we ourselves choose him: οὐχ ὑμᾶς δαίμων λήξεται, ἀλλ' ὑμεῖς δαίμονα αἱρήσεσθε. Heraclitus's famous saying ἦθος ἀνθρώπῳ δαίμων implies the same idea of a self-chosen or self-shaped destiny.

judgement,[1] and thereafter journey to Hades in company with that
E guide whose office it is to bring them from this world unto that other.
There that befalls them which must befall; and having there abided
for the due span of time they are brought back hither by another guide;
and so they continue for many long circuits of time. But in truth their
journeying is not such as is told by Telephus in the play of Aeschylus:[2]
108 he says that a clear path leads to Hades, but it seems to me to be neither
a clear nor a single path; for then there had been no need of guides, since
surely none could go astray where there is but one road. Rather is
it likely that there are many branchings and forkings of the way, to
judge by the sacrificial observances[3] here on earth.

'Now the soul which is well-ordered and intelligent follows its guide
and finds no strangeness in the scene;[4] but one that longs for the body
hovers distracted, as I said before,[5] for a long time in the neighbourhood
B of that body and of the visible region, with much struggling and much
vexation, until at last it is dragged forcibly away by its appointed spirit.
Now if amongst the company brought thither there be a soul which is
unpurified, and has done some impure deed, has taken part, maybe, in
some unrighteous bloodshed, or wrought some other evil akin thereto,
such as souls of that kindred do indeed commit, all flee from it and turn
aside from it; none will journey beside it nor consent to be its guide;
C alone it wanders, beset with all manner of distress until the time is
fulfilled, whereupon it is borne by constraint to the dwelling-place meet
for it. But every soul which has spent its lifetime in purity and sober-
ness finds gods to journey beside it and be its guides, and each goes to
dwell in its proper region.

[1] In the *Gorgias* myth the judgement of souls after death is prominent, the
judges being named as Minos, Rhadamanthys and Aeacus (523 E). In *Rep.* 614 C
they are unnamed. Rohde (*Psyche*, E.T., 239) holds, I think rightly, that it was
not a popular belief; it is probably not too hazardous to reckon it as Orphic.
A form of it is known to Pindar, who in *Olympian* 11, 58—an ode coloured by
Orphic allusions—says τὰ δ' ἐν τᾷδε Διὸς ἀρχᾷ ἀλιτρὰ κατὰ γᾶς δικάζει τις, and also
to Aeschylus, who makes Hades himself the judge (*Eum.* 273: μέγας γὰρ Ἅιδης
ἐστὶν εὔθυνος βροτῶν ἔνερθε χθονός).
[2] *Frag.* 239 (Nauck). Little is known about this lost play.
[3] Robin adopts the variant reading ὁσίων for θυσιῶν, but a corruption of θυσιῶν
into ὁσίων is much more probable than the reverse. Burnet (after Olympiodorus)
comments: 'The sacrifices to Hecate (Trivia) at the meeting of three ways are
well attested, and Socrates means that these shadow forth the τρίοδος in the
other world.'
[4] The μελέτη θανάτου has taught it what to expect, whereas to the unpurified
soul everything is strange and terrible.
[5] 81 C 10.

'Now the earth has many marvellous regions, and neither its nature nor its size is such as is supposed in the customary accounts: someone[1] has persuaded me of that.'

Here Simmias interrupted, 'What makes you say that, Socrates? D I also have heard many accounts of the earth, but not this one which has prevailed with you; so I should like to hear about it.'

'Well, you know, Simmias, I don't think it needs a scientific genius[2] to explain merely what the account is: but to show that it is true seems to me too difficult even for a great scientist; and not only is the task probably beyond my powers, but even if I had the knowledge, the span of life left to me seems insufficient for the lengthy argument required. However, there is nothing to prevent me from telling you what I believe about the nature of the earth and its regions.'   E

'Well,' said Simmias, 'I will be content with that.'

'In the first place then,' he resumed, 'I believe that if the earth is a spherical body at the centre of the heavens, it has no need of air to prevent its falling, nor yet of any other such forcible constraint: the 109 mere fact that the heavens are equiform in every direction, together with the earth's own equilibrium, is sufficient to keep it in position: for a body in equilibrium situated at the centre of an equiform container can have no possibility of inclining more or less in one direction than in another: it will be in a state of "indifference" and keep in position without any inclination.[3] So that is my first article of belief.'

'And a correct one', said Simmias.

'Secondly, I believe that it is of vast size, and that it is only a small part of it that we occupy who live between the Phasis and the Pillars of B Heracles; living round our sea we are like ants or frogs round a pool, and there are many other people dwelling in many other regions like ours. For all round the earth there are numerous hollows, varying in appearance and size, in which water and mist and air have collected; but

---

[1] It is not necessary to suppose that the τις is any real person: the form of words may well be no more than Plato's reminder that Socrates was not a scientist (*Apol.* 19 B–C). The clause seems to me distinctly unfavourable to Burnet's suggestion that 'the theory is that of Socrates himself'.

[2] Γλαύκου τέχνη was a proverbial phrase, the origin of which was variously explained by the paroemiographers. Their views are recorded by a scholiast quoted in Burnet's Appendix II, but I think it unnecessary to give them.

[3] This theory is mentioned by Aristotle *de caelo* 295 B 10 ff. and is there ascribed to Anaximander. As J. L. Stocks points out in his translation of the treatise, 'Plato makes ὁμοιότης an attribute of the whole heaven or universe, not of the earth', as Aristotle's report appears to say.

the earth itself is as untainted as the heaven in which it is set, the heaven which contains the stars, and which in most[1] of the ordinary accounts

C is called "aither"; it is the sediment of this aither that is always collecting as water, mist and air in the hollows of the earth.

'Now we ourselves do not realise that we live in these hollows: we imagine we live up on the earth's surface; it is as if someone living half-way down towards the bottom of the ocean were to suppose himself to live on the surface of the sea; he would see the sun and the stars through the water, and believe the sea to be the sky; slow of

D movement and feeble, he would never have reached the top of the sea, never have emerged with his head above the water to get a sight of this our earthly region, and to behold how much purer and fairer it is than the world where he and his fellows dwell, a region of which he had never even heard from any that had seen it.

'That, as I said, is a precise analogy to our own case. We live in one of the earth's hollows, and imagine ourselves to be living on its surface; and we call the air the heaven, taking it to be the heaven through which the stars move. But in fact it is the same thing as before:[2] we are so

E feeble and slow of movement that we cannot get out of our hollow and reach the confines of the air; of course if one of us could get to the top of it, or acquire wings and fly aloft, then just as a fish which gets its head above water in this everyday world can see its sights, he would behold the sights of the world above; and if he were one who could endure to contemplate them, he would realise that *there* was the real heaven, the genuine daylight, the actual earth. The earth that we know, the

110 stones that it contains, all this region of our earthly dwelling is spoilt and eaten away, as are rocks in the sea by salt water; nothing of any value can grow in the sea, little or nothing can fully develop in it; where there is anything solid, it is all eroded rocks and sand and a vast extent of slime and mud; it is utterly unworthy to be compared with the beauty to be found in our hollow. But far and away more

B excellent still than that is the beauty of that world above. Indeed, if it is a good thing to end with a story, it will not be out of place,

---

[1] What exceptions Plato had in mind it is difficult to guess; hardly Empedocles: for though, as Burnet points out, he often uses αἰθήρ for atmospheric air, yet in *frag.* 38 he clearly distinguishes ὑγρὸς ἀήρ from Τίταν ἠδ' αἰθὴρ σφίγγων περὶ κύκλον ἅπαντα.

[2] The phrase is a mere variant for ταὐτὸν δὴ τοῦτο καὶ ἡμᾶς πεπονθέναι: we are in the same case as the imaginary person ἐν μέσῳ τῷ πυθμένι τοῦ πελάγους οἰκῶν.

Simmias, to hear what things are like on that upper earth beneath the heavens.'

'Why of course, Socrates,' said Simmias, 'we at all events should be delighted to hear that story.'

The first sentences of this section serve to remind us that the establishment of the soul's immortality is for Socrates and Plato not merely an explanation of the philosopher's serenity in face of death, nor merely the settling of an interesting and important philosophical question, but a matter of the utmost practical significance, inasmuch as it reinforces to an incalculable extent the fundamental demand of Socratic and Platonic moral philosophy, the 'tendance of the soul' (ἐπιμέλεια ψυχῆς): ὁ κίνδυνος νῦν δὴ καὶ δόξειεν ἂν δεινὸς εἶναι, εἴ τις αὐτῆς ἀμελήσει. The coincidence of goodness and happiness, which is the goal of all human endeavour, can be attained, as we learnt earlier in the dialogue, only by a purging of our souls from the taint of the body—a process at once moral and intellectual; and this is now recalled in simple words which contrive to gather up the whole complex of ideas, ethical, psychological and religious, pervading the dialogue; νῦν δ' ἐπειδὴ ἀθάνατος φαίνεται οὖσα, οὐδεμία ἂν εἴη αὐτῇ ἄλλη ἀποφυγὴ κακῶν οὐδὲ σωτηρία πλὴν τοῦ ὡς βελτίστην τε καὶ φρονιμωτάτην γενέσθαι. And then, in the next sentence, with the mention of what 'is said' (λέγεται) about the effect, for weal or woe, upon our future destiny of what we have made of our souls in this life, we pass into a myth: that is to say, Plato invites us to follow his story of that journey (πορεία) which we all must one day make.

Except for the last scene of all—the narrative of the actual passing of Socrates—this myth occupies the remainder of the dialogue, corresponding in position, and partly in substance, to the myth of the judgement of souls in the *Gorgias* and to that of the choice of lives in *Republic* x. The fourth of Plato's great eschatological myths, that of the *Phaedrus*, is placed exceptionally in the middle of the dialogue; but there is good reason for that, namely that over and above the aim which it shares with the other three, of reinforcing or supplementing philosophical argument by an appeal to the imagination, it is also a 'palinode', a correction of the unworthy conception of Eros which has preceded it.

The purpose common to all these four myths is to supplement the bare doctrine of immortality,[1] which is all that Plato conceives susceptible of proof,[2] by such an imaginative picture of the after-life of

---

[1] The *Gorgias* myth, however, does not assert immortality in the strict sense, but only some after-life of the soul apart from the body.

[2] Note the clearly implied distinction between the dialectical argument of *Phaedrus* 245 C–E and the myth which follows, introduced by comparison of the soul to a pair of winged horses and their driver.

souls as will satisfy the ethical demand for discrimination between the righteous and the wicked.[1] We need not doubt that Plato is also responding to a demand from within himself, and that he enjoyed the opportunity of exercising his literary powers with a greater freedom than was elsewhere possible.

The first page of the present myth (107 D 5–108 C 5) is an impressive sketch, to be supplemented later (113 D ff.), drawn mostly from Orphic or Pythagorean doctrine,[2] of the judgement of souls, their punishments and rewards. But the most striking and original part is that which begins with a reference to the 'many wonderful regions of the earth' at 108 C 5, and for this most of my comment must be reserved.

One of the effects of myths such as these is to extend our mental horizon both in time, beyond this brief life, and more especially in space, beyond this little corner (or 'hollow') of the earth which is all that we know by sensible experience.

The *Phaedrus* takes us beyond the heavens themselves to the 'supracelestial region' which all souls visit before their incarnation; in the *Republic* Er tells how he journeyed with other souls to a 'marvellous place',[3] the meadow of judgement, and afterwards to a place where the whole structure of the universe was visibly revealed to them. In the present section of the *Phaedo* myth we are taken up to a 'real earth', the circumference of the sphere; later we shall be taken down into its interior, and to Tartarus, the chasm which extends right through the sphere.

Such accounts of places which the eye of man has never seen, nor will see, must of course, if they are to win a reader's interest and carry him along in imagination with the writer, be presented, so far as possible, as an extension of beliefs and ideas already familiar to him. Some of these will be what we call 'scientific', that is to say they will represent what we think we know to be facts about the physical universe; others will be what we call 'mythological', that is to say ideas which were once perhaps taken for facts, but which have long since ceased to be so taken, yet remain vivid and precious to us, whether it be for some symbolic significance which has come to be attached to them, or for their sheer literary beauty and power.

After the introductory page of which I have spoken, the main part of our myth opens with a scientific 'fact', one indeed which is still, in part, a fact to-day: namely the sphericity of the earth, motion-

---

[1] Such discrimination was part of the 'hope' of Socrates early in the dialogue (εὔελπίς εἰμι εἶναί τι τοῖς τετελευτηκόσι καὶ . . . πολὺ ἄμεινον τοῖς ἀγαθοῖς ἢ τοῖς κακοῖς, 63 C).

[2] But I would repeat the caution given by Frutiger (*op. cit.* p. 260) that the eschatological myths are not to be regarded as sheer transcriptions of some Orphic 'Book of the Dead'—'car Platon ne s'est sûrement pas fait faute d'utiliser d'autres sources, et surtout de modifier ou d'enrichir la tradition dont nous parlons'.

[3] τόπον τινὰ δαιμόνιον, 614 C. Compare the θαυμαστοὶ γῆς τόποι of *Phaedo* 108 C.

less[1] at the centre of the universe, and kept in position without any support. But that, I believe, is the whole of the 'fact'; what follows in the present section is *extension* of fact, and *mythical* extension; by which I mean that it is not offered as 'science', although it makes use of existing scientific theories. In its later sections the myth will become an extension of the other sort of beliefs, those which are already mythical themselves.[2]

In taking this view of Plato's purpose and method I am differing from those scholars[3] who find an important element of genuine scientific theory in the story of the 'hollows'. Plato, they believe, is concerned to conflate or reconcile Pythagorean and Ionian doctrines about the earth; and ostensibly indeed he does so. The hollows or depressions belong to the flat-earth theory of the Ionians, in the form in which it was maintained by the Athenian Archelaus: 'the earth', he is quoted[4] as saying, 'was originally a lake, high at its circumference and κοίλη in the centre' (i.e. concave); while the doctrine of a spherical earth was Pythagorean.[5]

It seems to me probable that Plato's 'hollows' were indeed partly suggested by Archelaus's concave earth, but partly also by Anaxagoras. The latter is reported (DK 59 A 42, § 5) as saying that the earth is κοίλη and has water in its κοιλώματα: this seems to be a different (and no doubt earlier) theory from that of Archelaus; κοίλη for Anaxagoras probably meant not 'concave' but 'hollow' in the sense implied by the mention of κοιλώματα: the earth's interior was not solid throughout, but contained masses of water. In our next section we shall see that Plato postulates a great mass of water as a kind of reservoir in one 'hollow', that called Tartarus, which is pierced right through the earth.[6]

[1] Though in the *Timaeus* Plato in all probability maintains the rotation of the earth (see Cornford, *Plato's Cosmology*, pp. 120ff.), there is no sign of this here, and indeed κεῖσθαι in 109 B 7 seems to rule it out.

[2] In *Rep.* x scientific (astronomical) 'fact' bulks much larger; in the *Timaeus* there is so much science (astronomy, physics, physiology, etc.) that we become almost unconscious of the mythical framework. But the *Timaeus* is far removed in structure and purpose from the eschatological myths.

[3] See Taylor, *P.M.W.* p. 208; Friedländer, *Platon* I, Exkurs I (Platon als Geograph); Robin, pp. lxvff. and, for criticism of these views, Frutiger, p. 66.

[4] DK 60A 4, § 4. Cf. Democritus in DK 68A94.

[5] It is attributed either to Pythagoras himself (which is unlikely) or (by Theophrastus *apud* DK 28A 44) to Parmenides, who was at one time a Pythagorean. E. Frank attributes it to Archytas or some other Pythagorean of his date (i.e. about 400 B.C.).

[6] I have followed Burnet in assigning to Anaxagoras as well as to Archelaus an influence on Plato's account. Friedländer, however (*Platon* I, p. 250), denies the influence of Anaxagoras, saying that his κοιλώματα 'resemble neither the Platonic κοῖλα of the earth's surface nor his Tartarus pierced right through the earth'. But it is difficult to maintain this denial, especially in view of the mention of water in the κοιλώματα.

Now it is undeniable that Plato has added to the Pythagorean spherical earth a feature suggested by these Ionian assertions of a concave surface of the earth, or of hollow places in its interior; nevertheless his hollows are not the same thing as the concavity of Archelaus and Democritus, nor do they seem to be the same as Anaxagoras's watery hollows in the earth's interior. Rather are they Plato's own adaptation of these theories, an adaptation springing not from any desire to reconcile rival theories of the earth's shape, but from his recognition of its convenience as a symbol of his own philosophic doctrine. In other words the *raison d'être* (in all literalness) of the hollows is that they enable Plato graphically to contrast the world of ordinary experience with another, a better world which is literally nowhere, but which we can only conceive as a 'place' (τόπος), the abode of such discarnate souls as have deserved, by a good life on earth, to reach this abode of bliss. Tradition gave this abode the name of Elysium, or the Isles of the Blest, and in the *Gorgias* myth (524A) the traditional contrast between the Isles of the Blest and Tartarus, the place of punishment, is preserved. In our present myth Tartarus is still the place of punishment, but the μακάρων νῆσοι are replaced by the 'true earth' whose splendour and loveliness are to be described in the next section; but it is obvious that the true earth is essentially the same as Elysium or the μακάρων νῆσοι, although it is not until later (114B–C) that we are explicitly told that it is the abode of those who have 'made notable progress on the road to righteous living'.

Yet though it is this, it is also something more. The contrast in Plato's mind is not only between a better world (on the surface) and a worse (in the hollows), but also between a world of reality and a world of appearance; to express this in another way, Plato has given his myth a metaphysical symbolism as well as an eschatological. The essential point to notice, in this connexion, is that the dwellers in the hollow suppose themselves to be dwelling on the surface, and take the impure 'air' in which they live to be the heaven in which the stars move (109D). Now for the purpose of eschatology, of contrasting earthly misery with heavenly bliss, this ignorance, this mistaking of one world for another, is irrelevant; and it is plain that, as Frutiger has seen, our 'hollow' is, in one aspect, another version of the famous cave of *Republic* VII, and the 'true earth' another version of the world outside the cave,[1] which, as Plato himself tells us (517B), symbolises the νοητὸς τόπος, the intelligible world; the prisoners in the cave, like the men in the hollow, believe what they see (in their case shadows on a wall) to be fully real, and the only reality there is; the existence

---

[1] The similarities in *language*, however, between the two relevant passages are perhaps less striking than Frutiger, who prints a French translation in parallel columns (pp. 64–5), seems to think.

of a world outside the cave, a world above the hollow, is unsuspected by either.

The metaphysical symbolism is, however, secondary in the *Phaedo*; and the incorporation of it in a myth which is primarily eschatological, though happy in a way, involves Plato in a difficulty. The 'true earth', as we shall find, is not the abode of souls which have attained lasting separation from bodies: it is a temporary abode of discarnate souls which have lived one or more righteous lives on earth, but are still subject to reincarnation.[1] For those which are 'fully purified through philosophy' there are reserved 'even fairer habitations' (114c); and it must be these latter, and not habitations on the true earth, that may properly be identified with the νοητὸς τόπος of the cave allegory, in spite of what was said or implied earlier.

This confusion, such as it is, is the price which Plato has to pay for his attempt to run together the 'two-world' metaphysical antithesis (ὁρατὸς τόπος and νοητὸς τόπος) with the 'four-world' scheme of eschatology (earthly existence, Elysian, Tartarean, and celestial, if we may use this adjective for the 'still fairer habitations').

There is, however, one further difficulty to be considered, namely that, on the face of it, the myth only begins *after* our present section, being introduced by Socrates in its closing words εἰ γὰρ δὴ καὶ μῦθον λέγειν καλόν, ἄξιον ἀκοῦσαι (110B). Does it not follow that all that has preceded is not μῦθος but λόγος, serious science? I would reply that what has preceded (109B–110A)—the page which I have described as extension of scientific fact—was probably conceived by Plato as something between λόγος and μῦθος: the term μῦθος he reserves for the detailed description of the beauties of the 'real' earth, in which he feels himself completely free to exercise his imaginative faculty in the elaboration of what has gone before. This reservation, however, is not absolute: in the end (114D7) he uses the word in a wider sense, corresponding to our own usage, to cover apparently everything from the λέγεται δὲ οὕτως of 107D to the end of 114C.

---

[1] In this respect it is equivalent to the 'heaven' (οὐρανός) of *Rep.* x, 614D, 615A).

XX

The true earth (Socrates continues) is like a ball of divers colours, all purer and more brilliant than those we know in our murky dwelling-place. The flowers and trees are more beautiful, and there is abundance of precious stones whose lustre is never impaired. The climate banishes sickness; men there behold the gods face to face, and know the sun, moon and stars as they truly are.

There follows a contrasted picture of the hollows, especially of Tartarus, the great watery hollow which pierces through the whole of the earth's sphere; from Tartarus all rivers flow, and into it all return; the point of re-entry is always lower (that is, nearer the earth's centre) than the point of issue, and no river can flow beyond the centre.

IIOB   'Well then, my friend, in the first place it is said that the earth, viewed from above, looks like one of those balls made of twelve pieces of leather,[1] painted in various colours, of which the colours familiar to us through their use by painters are, so to say, samples. Up there the c whole earth displays such colours, and indeed far brighter and purer ones than these. One part is a marvellously beautiful purple, another golden; the white is whiter than chalk or snow, and so it is with all the colours in the earth's composition, which are more in number and more beautiful than any we have beheld. Even these hollows of the earth, brimful as they are of water and air, give an appearance of colour as they glisten amongst the various colours of the surface, with the result D that to the observer's eye the earth has a single unbroken but multi-coloured aspect.

'Moreover this difference in colour is matched by a like difference in the trees and flowers and fruits that grow in that upper earth; and again its mountains contain stones which are correspondingly smoother,

---

[1] The dodecahedron is the nearest of the five regular solids to a sphere, so that balls could be made of twelve pieces of *flexible* leather, each having the shape of a regular pentagon. Here it is the spherical earth that is imagined as thus constructed; in the *Timaeus* (55 c) it is the spherical universe, the other regular solids being there the constituent particles of the 'four elements': see F. M. Cornford, *Plato's Cosmology*, pp. 218 f.

more transparent, and more beautiful in hue; it is fragments of them that constitute the bits of stone which we cherish, cornelians, jaspers, emeralds and so forth; there every single stone is a jewel, and a fairer E jewel than those we know. And the reason for that is that the stones there are pure, not eaten away nor ruined, as ours are, by the mildew and brine produced by[1] the sediment which has collected in our hollow, and is the source of ugliness in stones and soil, and of sickness in animals and plants.

'With all these precious stones is the real earth adorned, and with gold also and silver and all other precious metals; for they are plainly visible, abundant, massive, and spread all over the earth; happy therefore are 111 they whose eyes dwell upon that spectacle.

'Now besides many other creatures that live there there are men, of whom some dwell inland and others at the edge of the air, just as we dwell at the edge of the sea, others again in islands near the mainland which are surrounded by air. In short, the needs which for us are met by the waters of the sea are there met by the air, while in place of our air they have the aither. The climate they enjoy keeps them free from B sickness and allows them to live much longer than we do, while their superiority in vision, hearing, intelligence and other faculties is proportionate to the greater purity of air as compared with water, and of aither as compared with air. Moreover they have sacred groves and temples for the gods, which the gods do verily inhabit; by omen and oracle and vision and suchlike they have direct communion with the C divine beings; sun and moon and stars they behold as they really are, and with all other such bliss are they blessed.

'Such then is the nature of all that earth and its surroundings. But all round about it there are many places where it is hollowed out; some of these are deeper and have broader openings than that in which we dwell, while others though deeper are not so broad as ours, and yet others are shallower and broader. All are pierced with numerous subterranean D passages, sometimes narrow sometimes wide, leading through from one to another; this results in a quantity of water flowing into and out

---

[1] The explanation of this sentence given by Burnet, viz. that it is equivalent to οὐ κατεδηδεσμένοι οὐδὲ διεφθαρμένοι ὑπὸ σηπεδόνος καὶ ἅλμης ὥσπερ οἱ ἐνθάδε ὑπὸ τῶν δεῦρο συνερρυηκότων, seems to me quite impossible. Archer-Hind prints commas after διεφθαρμένοι and ἅλμης, and this is more possible, but leaves a clumsy and illogical sentence. I prefer to follow Stallbaum's suggestion of reading ἀπό for the second ὑπό. (Robin prints the sentence without commas, but his translation seems to imply ἀπό.)

of them as if they were mixing-bowls, and forming subterranean rivers of vast extent whose waters, whether hot or cold, flow on unceasingly; fire too is there in abundance, mighty rivers of fire, and again many streams of liquid mud of varying density, like those which precede the E lava-flow in the volcano of Sicily,[1] or like the lava itself.

'With such rivers are all the hollow places filled, as each in turn is reached by the circling stream of fire or water. The whole mass has an up and down movement due to a kind of oscillation in the earth, the cause of which is something such as I will now describe. One of the 112 openings in the earth is bigger than the rest, and pierces right through it from one side to the other: it is mentioned by Homer in the line[2]

Down, far down to the pit, to the depths of the earth will I hurl him—

the pit which the same poet elsewhere and many other poets too call Tartarus. Into that abyss all the rivers flow together, and from it they issue again, having divers characters according as they flow through divers lands.

B 'The reason why all the streams flow out of and into Tartarus is that the liquid mass can find no bottom on which to rest, and so swings and seethes up and down, as does the air or wind surrounding it also; for this latter follows the course of the waters when it inclines now to the far side of the earth and now to the near side;[3] and just as in our breathing the air is constantly flowing in and flowing out, so in the interior of the earth the wind swaying about with the waters, and entering or leaving a given place, causes gusts of appalling violence.

C 'Now when the water retreats to what we call[4] the lower hemisphere, it flows through the earth following the course of the rivers of those regions,[5] and fills them as in the process of irrigation; conversely, when it quits that hemisphere and rushes to our own, it fills the rivers of our

---

[1] If, as is probable, our dialogue was written after Plato's first visit to Sicily (388–387 B.C.) he may have seen Etna in eruption. Burnet's supposed allusion to Empedocles seems to me doubtful.   [2] *Iliad* VIII, 14.

[3] I have followed Burnet's explanation of τὸ ἐπ' ἐκεῖνα and τὸ ἐπὶ τάδε. The words seem to me to rule out Robin's assertion (p. lxxiv) that 'l'exposition de Platon ne concerne pas du tout un mouvement des courants d'un hémisphère à l'autre...mais la relation de ce mouvement entre les parties *invisibles* et les parties *visibles* d'une terre sphérique'.

[4] In a spherical earth, as Plato recognises, there is no absolute 'up' and 'down'. Cf. *Timaeus* 62 C.

[5] I retain διά before τῆς γῆς, and take the literal meaning to be 'it flows through the earth into the beds of the rivers of that region (hemisphere)'. Plato writes τοῖς κατ' ἐκεῖνα τὰ ῥεύματα rather than ἐκείνοις τοῖς ῥεύμασι simply because the

regions, which thereupon flow through their channels underground until each of them reaches the spot to which it has been channelled; and there they form seas and lakes and rivers and springs. Subsequently they vanish again below ground,[1] and discharge themselves back into Tartarus, some with long winding courses through many lands, others **D** more direct. All the streams re-enter at a lower point than that where they are drawn off, some much lower, others only a little, some on the opposite side, others on the same side as they issued;[2] some complete a full circle, winding round the earth once or more than once, like snakes, descending as low as they can before once again plunging into Tartarus. The limit of descent in either direction is the earth's centre, **E** for from whichever side a river flows the region on the other side[3] could only be reached by flowing uphill.'

This section falls into two parts, the first of which describes the splendours of the 'true earth'. As we have seen, this has been offered by Socrates as a μῦθος, and Plato has accordingly lavished his powers of verbal imagery on this Earthly Paradise of purity, colour and brilliance. It will be remembered that the 'true earth' stands primarily for the habitation of righteous souls not yet exempt from reincarnation, but secondarily symbolises that 'intelligible region' (νοητὸς τόπος) which is their final home. But in the present section this secondary symbolism drops, we may believe, out of sight: it is the temporary home of righteous souls that Socrates now describes, seeking, like all

ῥεύματα do not exist until the water fills (or refills) their beds. Burnet's suggestion of taking τὰ ῥεύματα as nominative, and τῆς γῆς as governed by κατ' ἐκεῖνα (excising διά) is surely impossible.

[1] The words πάλιν δυόμενα κατὰ τῆς γῆς do not imply that the seas, lakes, etc., just mentioned are above ground in the sense of being on the 'true earth'; they are, however, higher up (i.e. further from the earth's centre) than Tartarus, and a river can be said δύεσθαι κατὰ γῆς when it descends from a shallower hollow to a deeper (111C).

[2] i.e. the opposite, or the same, side of the earth's centre (not of Tartarus), as Burnet explains, rightly interpreting Aristotle's words πολλὰ μὲν καὶ κατὰ τὸν αὐτὸν τόπον, τὰ δὲ καὶ καταντικρὺ τῇ θέσει τῆς ἐκροῆς, οἷον εἰ ῥεῖν ἤρξαντο κάτωθεν, ἄνωθεν εἰσβάλλειν (Meteor. 356A9).

[3] If the text is right, we must translate, as Burnet does, 'for the part (of Tartarus) on either side (of the centre) is uphill to both sets of streams'. But surely this is not true: it is only if the river got *beyond* the centre that it would be flowing 'uphill'. πέρα τοῦ μέσου gives us the clue for emending ἑκατέρωθεν to ἑτέρωθεν and I translate accordingly; the corruption is easy in view of ἑκατέρωσε above. Incidentally, I am inclined to accept Robin's reading, ⟨πρὸς⟩ ἄναντες, conformably to Aristotle's words following those quoted in the previous note: εἶναι δὲ μέχρι τοῦ μέσου τὴν κάθεσιν· τὸ γὰρ λοιπὸν πρὸς ἄναντες ἤδη πᾶσιν εἶναι τὴν φοράν, where τὸ λοιπόν confirms the reading ἑτέρωθεν.

writers of apocalyptic, to picture the spiritual and invisible in terms of the material and visible. In particular we cannot fail to be reminded by the precious stones here mentioned—'cornelians, jaspers, emeralds and so forth'—of the New Jerusalem, the foundations of whose wall were 'garnished with all manner of precious stones: the first foundation was jasper, the second sapphire' and the rest.

That men should walk with gods there, and see them face to face, is consonant with the *Phaedrus*, where the souls of the gods, when they are carried upon the circumference of the revolving heaven, are accompanied by souls destined to inhabit human bodies. Both dialogues imply that all souls are originally and essentially divine; yet each in its own way also implies some distinction between the souls of gods and those that have been, or are to be, incarnate in a mortal frame.

It is curious, and perhaps significant, that the last feature to be mentioned in this picture of general happiness (εὐδαιμονία) is the vision of sun, moon and stars as they truly are. Coming as this does immediately after the mention of men consorting with gods, it can hardly fail to suggest to a reader familiar with the *Timaeus* those 'visible created gods', the stars and planets whose divinity, it seems (40D–E), is more assured than that of the anthropomorphic gods of the traditional religion. It is at least possible that by mentioning the heavenly bodies just where he does Plato is here hinting at the same thing.

The account of the rivers of the underworld in the second part of this section is bound up with, and indeed starts from, the notion of 'hollows', which has been used for a symbolic purpose earlier in the myth. Hence we shall, I think, be justified in regarding its 'science' as, in part at least, apparent rather than real.[1] In particular the notion of Tartarus as an opening pierced right through the spherical earth is not likely to be intended as sober fact; it proceeds rather, as the name itself implies, from Homeric or pre-Homeric mythology. And if Tartarus is not real, then neither are the rivers all flowing out of and into it; the picture is principally designed to prepare us for the introduction of the *named* rivers of the following section, Oceanus, Acheron, Cocytus, Pyriphlegethon and Styx; in other words the infernal geography and 'hydrography' is an extension of mythological belief parallel to the extension of scientific belief in the previous section. Indeed the whole complex of science, pseudo-science and mythology of which the myth (in the wide sense) consists, is designed with marvellous skill to support the eschatological doctrine of rewards and punishments hereafter by fitting it into a plausible framework, based upon the doctrine of a spherical earth—the one doctrine which we may assuredly reckon to have been accepted by Plato as solid scientific truth.

[1] Aristotle, however (*Meteorologica* 355 B 33 ff.), treats the account as purely scientific.

This general interpretation of the myth is, however, not incompatible with a recognition that in his extensions of science and mythology Plato is making use of earlier scientific pronouncements. Just as Anaxagoras and Archelaus probably suggested the 'hollows', so the notion of Tartarus as the great reservoir of rivers (which are, of course, on the general hypothesis all underground) doubtless owes something to those unnamed thinkers, some at least of whom may be probably reckoned as pre-Platonic, mentioned by Aristotle in the *Meteorologica* (349 B 3): 'Some think that water is drawn up by the sun and descends in rain, and gathers below the earth and so flows *from a great reservoir* (ἐκ κοιλίας μεγάλης), either *all the rivers from one* or each from a different one.'

XXI

112E–115A THE MYTH CONCLUDED. ITS TRUTH AND VALUE

The closing passages of the myth tell first of the four great rivers of the underworld, and of their courses; after which Socrates returns to the judgement of souls. According to the merit or demerit of a man's earthly life the souls fall into one or other of five classes: the worst are incurable sinners, and suffer eternal punishment in Tartarus; the best are of course those purified by philosophy, who live for evermore wholly discarnate, in glorious habitations. Those belonging to the three intermediate classes are assigned to their several dwelling-places, where they abide until the time comes for them to re-enter human or animal bodies.

112E   'Now in truth many are these rivers and great, and of divers natures; but four[1] there are amongst their number of especial note; and the greatest of these, whose course is circular and outermost, is that named Oceanus. Opposite it,[2] flowing in the contrary direction, is Acheron,

113   whose course is through many a waste place beneath the earth, until at last it reaches the Acherusian Lake; thither come the souls of most[3] of the dead, and after abiding there for their fated span, be it longer or shorter, they are sent forth to be born again as living creatures.[4]

'The third river issues midway between these two, and soon falls into a vast region of blazing fire,[5] so as to form a lake larger than our sea, seething with water and mud. Thereafter it continues its circular course,

B   turbid and muddy, and coiling itself round within the earth it reaches after a while the edge of the Acherusian Lake, but does not unite its waters therewith; then after many more coilings underground it discharges itself into Tartarus at a lower point. Now the name of this river is Pyriphlegethon, and its lava streams belch out fragments at divers points of the earth above.[6]

---

[1] Oceanus, Acheron, Pyriphlegethon, Cocytus. Homer's list (*Odyssey* x, 513–14) is Acheron, Pyriphlegethon, Cocytus, Styx (Cocytus being a branch of Styx. Plato makes Styx not a river, but a lake, and adds Oceanus which in Homer is not an infernal river, but one encircling the earth's surface.

[2] I.e. on the opposite side of the earth's centre.

[3] I.e. those who have lived 'indifferently well' (113D).

[4] ζῷων include both men and lower animals; cf. 81E–82B.

[5] As is implied in its name, Pyriphlegethon.

[6] Not, of course, on the true earth, but in our relatively shallow 'hollow'.

'Then opposite this again the fourth river issues, first into a region described as fearsome and wild, overspread with a sort of blue-grey colour; this is known as the Stygian region, and the lake formed by this c river is Styx. By falling into that lake its waters gain strange powers; then continuing its winding course beneath the earth it flows in the opposite direction to Pyriphlegethon, and reaches the Acherusian Lake from the opposite side. Like Pyriphlegethon, its waters are not mingled with any other, and it too winds round and discharges itself into Tartarus opposite the third river; and the name that poets give it is Cocytus.

'Such then is the nature of the earth's interior. Now when the dead D are come to that place whither their several guardian spirits bring them, they that have lived well and righteously submit themselves to judgement, and likewise they that have not so lived. And such as are deemed to have lived indifferently well set off for Acheron, embarking on certain vessels appointed for them, which bring them to the lake; and while they dwell there they are purged and absolved from their evil deeds by making atonement therefor, and are rewarded for their good deeds, each according to his desert.

'But some there be who because of the enormity of their sins are E deemed incurable: such as have stolen much and often from the temples, or wrought wicked murder time and again, or committed other such crimes; these their due portion befalls, to be hurled into Tartarus, never to escape.

'Others there be whose sins are accounted curable, yet heinous: such as have been moved by anger to lay violent hands upon father or mother, 114 yet have lived thereafter a life of repentance; or such as have slaughtered a man in some similar condition;[1] all these must be cast into Tartarus, but after abiding there for the space of a year the surging waters throw the parricides and matricides out by way of Pyriphlegethon, and the others by way of Cocytus. And when they have been swept along to a point near the Acherusian Lake, then do they cry aloud and call to those whom they have slain or despitefully used, begging and beseeching them that they would suffer them to come forth into the lake and give B them hearing. If they can prevail, they do come forth, and find an end to their trouble; but if not, they are swept back into Tartarus, and

---

[1] The vague expression τοιούτῳ τινὶ ἄλλῳ τρόπῳ seems to mean (in plain English) 'in other such extenuating circumstances as make the killing manslaughter rather than murder'. In spite of the order of clauses, we should probably regard the proviso of repentance as applying to these ἀνδροφόνοι as well as to the parricides.

thence into the rivers again; nor can they ever have respite from their woes until they prevail upon those whom they have injured; for such is the penalty appointed by their judges.

'But lastly there are those that are deemed to have made notable progress on the road to righteous living; and these are they that are c freed and delivered from the prison-houses of this interior of the earth, and come to make their habitation in the pure region above ground. And those of their number who have attained full purity through philosophy live for evermore without any bodies at all,[1] and attain to habitations even fairer than those others; but the nature of these it would not be easy to reveal, even were time enough now left me.

'But now, Simmias, having regard to all these matters of our tale, we must endeavour ourselves to have part in goodness and intelligence while this life is ours; for the prize is glorious, and great is our hope thereof.

D   'Now to affirm confidently that these things are as I have told them would not befit a man of good sense; yet seeing that the soul is found to be immortal, I think it is befitting to affirm that this or something like it is the truth about our souls and their habitations. I think too that we should do well in venturing—and a glorious venture it is—to believe it to be so. And we should treat such tales as spells to pronounce over ourselves, as in fact has been my own purpose all this while in telling my long story.

'And now surely, by reason of all this, no anxiety ought to be felt E about his own soul by a man who all his lifetime has renounced the pleasures of the body and its adornments as alien to him, and likely to do him more harm than good, and has pursued the pleasures of learning; who has adorned his soul with no alien adornment, but with its own, 115 even with temperance and justice and courage and freedom and truth, and thus adorned awaits that journey to Hades which he is ready to make whensoever destiny calls him.[2]

'Well, Simmias, you and Cebes and the others will make the journey some day later on; but now "'tis I am called", as a tragic hero might

---

[1] Although what we call 'death' is, broadly speaking, ψυχῆς ἀπὸ τοῦ σώματος ἀπαλλαγή (64c), yet all souls save those purified by philosophy 'drag something of the body with them' after death (80Eff., 82B–C); but we should think of this rather as a quality or taint of the soul than as actual bodily substance.

[2] I can see no reason for excising ὡς...καλῇ. The words do not, to my mind, spoil the effect of line 5 in which ἐμέ is of course emphatic. The words ἐμὲ δὲ νῦν ἤδη καλεῖ are no doubt the end of an iambic senarius.

say, by destiny; and it is just about time[1] I made my way to the bath;
I really think it is better to have a bath before drinking the poison
rather than give the women the trouble of washing a dead body.'

The four great rivers of the underworld are of course (with the
modification already noted) Homeric (*Odyssey* x, 513 f.), and Plato
has no doubt made use of popular legend lying behind or built upon
Homer's lines, as well as of later poets, especially such as concerned
themselves with Orphic beliefs. In the latter part of the section
especially we meet once more with the Orphic-Pythagorean beliefs in
purification, transmigration, and the final deliverance of the soul from
further incarnations.

How much precisely is original to Plato it is of course impossible
to say; it may be that the non-mingling of Pyriphlegethon and Cocytus
with the Acherusian Lake was invented by him for the purpose which
it serves in 114A–B, namely to exclude 'curable' sinners from the abode
of their innocent victims until their supplication for forgiveness has
been favourably received; more important, however, is the actual
introduction of the notion of forgiveness by the injured in the after-life
implied in the words ἐὰν μὲν πείσωσιν (114B2): this does not recur
in Plato's myths, nor, I believe, is it to be found anywhere else in the
literature of the classical and pre-classical ages.[2]

In the myths of the *Gorgias*[3] and *Republic*[4] only three classes of
souls are distinguished, the incurable sinners, the curable, and the
righteous; but here two more are recognised, one at the beginning
and one at the end, namely the 'indifferently good' and those purified
by philosophy, who are introduced as an *élite* of those who are 'deemed
to have made notable progress on the road to righteous living'. I do
not, however, think that any special significance should be attached
to these additions: the scheme of the *Republic* myth did not (as Rohde
points out) admit of a mention of those purified by philosophy, since
not being destined to further incarnations they could not be present
in the place of judgement where new lives are chosen.

As the whole mythical passage was introduced by a solemn warning
of the need, brought home to us by the establishment of immortality,
for a man's soul to be made 'as good and intelligent as possible' (107D),
so now at its end the same note is struck in a sentence of earnest appeal,

---

[1] The abrupt way in which Socrates 'comes down to earth' is perhaps intended
to suggest his characteristic avoidance of pomposity and staginess.
[2] Archer-Hind's reference to the Attic law concerning appeasement of the kin
in cases of *involuntary* homicide is hardly relevant.
[3] 525 B–C, 526 C.
[4] 615 B–C. I disregard the 'short-lived' souls of this passage as *extra classem*
for comparative purposes.

of simple, direct sincerity: ἀλλὰ τούτων δὴ ἕνεκα χρὴ ὧν διεληλύθαμεν, ὦ Σιμμία, πᾶν ποιεῖν ὥστε ἀρετῆς καὶ φρονήσεως ἐν τῷ βίῳ μετασχεῖν· καλὸν γὰρ τὸ ἆθλον καὶ ἡ ἐλπὶς μεγάλη. This is really the motto of the whole dialogue.

There follows at 114D a pronouncement by Socrates on the character and value of the myth, which is commonly and rightly taken as applicable to all Plato's myths of the after-life. What needs pointing out is that the pronouncement itself is, in a sense, mythical, and that in two respects: first, there are not and cannot be any οἰκήσεις for discarnate souls, since an immaterial being cannot occupy space: and secondly, there is no question of *inaccuracy*, of mistaken detail, in the myth; what the myth has done, as we have said before, is to present the immaterial in a material form, to suggest the invisible 'world' through the medium of language literally applicable only to the visible. This, the task of all the greatest and most serious art, can of course be done with greater or less success; and what Socrates says about 'approximate accuracy' is Plato's recognition that all such efforts must fail of complete success: it is always possible that the artist's aim, primarily to give expression to what he feels, and secondarily to make others feel with him, might have been more fully realised.

XXII

This final section needs neither summary nor comment.

To this Crito replied, 'Very well, Socrates; but what instructions 115 B
have you for our friends here or for me about the children, or about any
other matter? We want to do just what would be of most service[1] to you.'

'Only what I am always telling you, Crito, nothing very new. Look
after yourselves: then anything you do will be of service to me and
mine, and to yourselves too, even if at this moment you make no
promises to that effect;[2] but if you neglect yourselves, and refuse to
follow that path of life which has been traced out in this present conversation and in others that we have had before, then, plentiful and
vehement though your present promises may be, all you do will be c
fruitless.'

'Then,' said Crito, 'we shall strive to do as you bid us. But how are
we to bury you?'

'However you like,' said Socrates, 'provided you can catch me and
prevent my escaping you.' Then with a quiet laugh and a look in our
direction he remarked, 'You know, I can't persuade Crito that I am the
Socrates here present, the person who is now talking to you and
arranging the topics of our conversation; he imagines that I am the
dead body which he will shortly be looking at, and so he asks how he is D
to bury me. As for all I have been maintaining this long while, to wit
that when I have drunk the poison I shall no longer be with you, but
shall have taken my departure to some happy land of the blest, that,
I suppose, he regards as idle talk, intended to console you all and myself
as well. That being so, I want you to stand surety for me with Crito,
but for the precise opposite of that for which he sought to stand[3] surety

---

[1] ἐν χάριτι, here and in B 7 is difficult to render, because for Socrates it means
something different from what it means for Crito. The disciple is anxious to do
the master some more or less trivial 'kindness': but Socrates catches up his word
χάρις and gives it a deeper meaning.

[2] With κἂν μὴ νῦν ὁμολογήσητε I take ἐν χάριτι ἐμοί τι ποιήσειν to be understood.

[3] As Burnet, following Cook Wilson, explains in the Introductory Note to
his edition of the *Crito*, Crito's offer was 'intended to spare Socrates the indignity
of imprisonment during the time between the sentence and the return of the
sacred boat from Delos. This offer was not accepted, and that seems to be implied
by the imperfect ἠγγυᾶτο' of the present passage.

with the court. His pledge then, offered under oath, was that I would
stay where I was; but I want you to pledge yourselves under oath that
I will not stay where I am after I have died, but will take my departure;
E that will make it easier for Crito: when he sees my body being burnt or
put under ground he won't have to distress himself on my behalf, as
though I were being outraged, and won't have to say at the funeral that
it is Socrates whom he is laying out or carrying to the grave or burying.'

Then turning to Crito, 'My best of friends,' he continued, 'I would
assure you that misuse of language is not only distasteful in itself, but
actually harmful to the soul. So you must be of good cheer, and say
that you are burying my body; and do that in whatever fashion you
116 please and deem to be most conformable to custom.'

With these words he rose and went into another room to take his
bath. Crito went with him, and told us to stay where we were. This we
did, discussing amongst ourselves and meditating upon all that had
been said, or sometimes talking of the great sorrow that had come upon
us; for truly we felt like children who had lost a father, condemned to
live henceforth as orphans. However, when Socrates had had his bath
B his children—two little boys and one bigger—were brought in to him,
and those women relatives of his appeared; to these he addressed some
words in the presence of Crito, with certain directions as to his wishes.
He then told the women and children to withdraw, and himself came
over to us.

By this time it was near to sunset, for he had spent a long time in the
inner room. So he came and sat with us after his bath, and did not talk
much more. And now the agent of the prison authorities had arrived,
C and stepping up to him said, 'Socrates, I shan't have my usual ground
for complaint in your case; many people get angry and abusive when
I instruct them, at the behest of the authorities, to drink the poison; but
I have always known you, while you have been here, for the most
generous, the best tempered and the finest man of any that have entered
this place; and in particular I feel sure now that you are not angry with
me, but with those whom you know to be responsible for this. Well,
you know what I have come to tell you: so now good-bye, and try to
D bear as best you may what must be borne.' As he said this, he burst into
tears, and turned to leave us. Socrates looked up at him and said,
'Good-bye to you: I will do as you say'; and then to us, 'What
a delightful person! All these weeks he has been coming to see me, and
talking with me now and then, like the excellent fellow he is; and now

see how generously he weeps for me! Well, come now, Crito, let us do his bidding. If the draught has been prepared, will someone please bring it me; if not, tell the man to prepare it.'

'Oh, but I think, Socrates,' said Crito, 'that the sun is still upon the E mountains; it has not set yet. Besides, I know of people who have taken the draught long after they were told to do so, and had plenty to eat and drink, and even in some cases had intercourse with those whom they desired. Don't hurry: there is still plenty of time.'

'It is quite natural, Crito,' he replied, 'that the people you speak of should do that: they think it brings them some advantage; and it is equally natural that I should not do so: I don't think I should get any advantage out of taking the poison a little later on; I should merely 117 make myself ridiculous in my own eyes by clinging to life and eking out its last dregs. No, no: don't hamper me: do as I say.'

At this Crito nodded to his slave who stood close by; whereupon the latter went out, and after a considerable time came back with the man who was to administer the poison, which he was carrying in a cup ready to drink. On seeing him Socrates exclaimed, 'All right, good sir: you know about this business: what must I do?'

'Simply drink it,' he replied, 'and then walk about until you have a feeling of heaviness in your legs; then lie down, and it will act of B itself.' And as he spoke he offered Socrates the cup. And I tell you, Echecrates, he took it quite calmly, without a tremor or any change of complexion or expression. He just fixed the man with his well-known glare[1] and asked, 'What do you say to using the drink for a libation? Or is that not allowed?' The man replied, 'We only mix what we judge to be the right dose, Socrates.'

'I see', he rejoined. 'Well, at all events it is allowed to pray to the C gods, as indeed we must, for a happy journey to our new dwelling-place; and that is my prayer: so may it be.' With these words he put the cup to his lips[2] and drained it with no difficulty or distaste whatever.

So far most of us had more or less contrived to hold back our tears, but now, when we saw him drinking, and the cup emptied, it became impossible; for myself, despite my efforts the tears were pouring down

---

[1] ταυρηδόν probably is no more than a stronger word to describe the fixed gaze (διαβλέψας) of 86 D 5.

[2] Burnet, following K. F. Hermann, takes ἐπισχόμενος to mean 'holding his breath'. But there seems to be no evidence for this meaning, and in Apoll. Rhod. I, 472 ἦ καὶ ἐπισχόμενος πλεῖον δέπας ἀμφοτέρῃσιν | πῖνε κ.τ.λ. it is impossible because of ἀμφοτέρῃσιν.

my cheeks, so that I had to cover my face; but I was weeping not for him, no, but for myself and my own misfortune in losing such a friend.

D Crito had got up and withdrawn already, finding that he could not restrain his tears; as for Apollodorus, he had even before this been weeping continuously, and at this last moment he burst into sobs, and his tears of distress were heart-breaking to all of us, except to Socrates himself, who exclaimed, 'My dear good people, what a way to behave! Why, it was chiefly to avoid such a lapse that I sent the women away;

E for I was always told that a man ought to die in peace and quiet. Come, calm yourselves and do not give way.'

At that we felt ashamed, and ceased to weep. He walked round the room until, as he told us, his legs came to feel heavy, and then lay on his back, as he had been bidden. Thereupon the man who had brought the poison felt his body, and after a while examined his feet and legs, and then squeezed his foot tightly, asking if he felt anything. Socrates

118 said no; next he felt his legs again, and moving his hand gradually up he showed us that he was becoming cold and rigid. Touching him once more,[1] he told us that when the cold reached the heart all would be over.

By this time it had reached somewhere about the pit of the stomach, when he removed the covering which he had put over his face, and uttered his final words: 'Crito, we owe a cock to Asklepios;[2] pray do not forget to pay the debt.' 'It shall be done', said Crito. 'Is there anything else you can think of?' There was no reply to this question; a moment afterwards he shuddered; the attendant uncovered his face again, and his gaze had become rigid; seeing which Crito closed his mouth and his eyes.

And that, Echecrates, was the end of our friend, the finest man—so we should say—of all whom we came to know in his generation; the wisest too, and the most righteous.'

[1] I accept Forster's αὖθις for αὐτός. Burnet says that αὐτός means not Socrates, but the executioner, and adds 'it is implied that the others had touched Socrates by the executioner's directions'. But there is no such implication in the text, and the subject of the last main verb ἐπεδείκνυτο, is of course the executioner. Nor could αὐτός mean Socrates, for then we should have had αὐτὸς αὐτοῦ. Robin keeps αὐτός, but appears to translate αὖθις.

[2] Wilamowitz (*Platon* II, pp. 57f.) rightly rejects the idea that the offering to Asklepios is for his healing Socrates of the sickness of human life: 'das Leben ist keine Krankheit, und Asklepios heilt kein Übel der Seele.' I have little doubt that these were in fact the last words of Socrates, and that they mean just what they say; but it is of course idle to speculate about the occasion for the vow.

ADDITIONAL NOTES

62 A. ἴσως μέντοι...εὐεργέτην. The chief difficulty in this passage is that whereas ἴσως μέντοι θαυμαστόν σοι φανεῖται in A 2 introduces a hypothesis which Socrates regards, and expects Cebes to regard, as false, θαυμαστὸν ἴσως σοι φαίνεται in A 6 introduces what he regards as true, though doubtless paradoxical. In my translation I have attempted to suggest this by giving 'if' for the first εἰ and 'that' for the second (so Burnet), though I do not mean to imply that a Greek writer would be conscious of two possible meanings of θαυμαστὸν εἰ. But the difficulty itself arises from the failure of Socrates to make grammatical structure completely conform to logic. What he expects Cebes to be surprised at is not two things, but one thing: namely that, despite the extreme improbability of death *never* being preferable to life, suicide should *always* be sinful.

In Burnet's translation the word 'further' suggests that he fails to see this. Archer-Hind perhaps does see it, but certainly does not make it clear that he does so; and his note is wrong about the meaning of τοῦτο, as to which Burnet is right. The other suggestions referred to in Archer-Hind's note do not merit discussion.

Logically expressed, the passage would run in English something like this:

'But I daresay you find it surprising that, whereas in this matter (*sc.* of life and death) the same principle holds good as in other human affairs (it would be astonishing if it did not), namely that life is not invariably preferable, but for some people and on some occasions death is so, nevertheless it should be accounted sinful for those for whom death is preferable to be their own benefactors, etc.'

This paraphrase shows that, while grammatically ἴσως μέντοι θαυμαστόν...ἢ ζῆν is co-ordinate with οἶς δὲ...εὐεργέτην, in logic the former is subordinate to the latter.

The shift from φανεῖται in A 2 to φαίνεται in A 6 may well be insignificant: but possibly the future is due to the speaker having originally intended to use 'modal' futures (ἔσται, τεύξεται) in the first εἰ clause, with the force of 'if it is to be made out that...', and then shifting to presents as being a more vivid, and perhaps more natural, way of expressing a hypothesis which he regards as certainly false.

I do not claim that my translation makes the logic clear: no translation, but only a paraphrase, could. But the rendering of δέ in A 5 by 'so' (which it does not mean) is a liberty taken with the purpose of suggesting that, as I have said, Cebes is not being credited with surprise at two things.

69 A–C. My translation involves certain alterations of Burnet's text.

In A8 I read καταλλάττεσθαι, ⟨ἐλάττω πρὸς μεῖζω⟩ καὶ μεῖζω πρὸς ἐλάττω. In B1–2 I remove both sets of brackets. In B3 I insert a comma after δικαιοσύνη, and continue καὶ συλλήβδην ἀληθὴς ἀρετὴ ⟨ἢ⟩ μετὰ φρονήσεως. In B6 I retain καί.

Mr J. V. Luce has discussed this difficult passage in *C.Q.* (April–June 1944), pp. 60 ff. Although I cannot accept his general interpretation, I agree with his defence of ὠνούμενα and πιπρασκόμενα, and with his contention that in the phrase ἡ ὀρθὴ πρὸς ἀρετὴν ἀλλαγή the πρός must have the same meaning as in the next two lines, viz. exchange *for*. His article is criticised by Dr R. S. Bluck in *C.R.* (March 1952), pp. 4 ff., with whose objections I agree. Bluck's own translation and interpretation seem to me in the main correct; but I disagree with his notion that there is some question of 'buying with wisdom', i.e. of *paying out* φρόνησις to get something else, involved in the words τούτου ὠνούμενα in B1. That is indeed at first sight their inescapable meaning; but I have suggested below a way out of this particular difficulty.

Burnet, translating πρὸς ἀρετήν in A6–7 by 'judged by the standard of goodness', maintains that 'there is no question of exchanging pleasures and pains for goodness'. But that is just what Plato conceives the people he has been speaking of as supposing themselves to be doing: by exchanging, say, pleasure *A* for pleasure *B* (i.e. by rejecting *A* in favour of *B*) they imagine they are acting virtuously, getting ἀρετή (as well as *B*) by giving up *A*.

These people, says Socrates, behave as if the acceptance or rejection of this or that pleasure, pain or fear possessed some moral value, as if they (the pleasures, etc.) were moral currency, coins that could buy moral goodness. (The words ὥσπερ νομίσματα involve a difficulty which is apparent rather than real. One does not exchange one coin for another or others except in the obviously irrelevant sense of exchanging a shilling for two sixpences; but the words must be taken to refer not to the actual exchange of pleasure for pleasure, etc., but to the *implication* of that exchange, viz. that these experiences can be compared in point of moral value, one pleasure (etc.) being morally preferable to another. That, says Socrates, is not so: these πάθη are *per se* morally worthless, and all equally so: they must be exchanged not for one another, but for φρόνησις). The only moral currency is φρόνησις: we ought therefore, when faced with a choice between two courses of action, to ask ourselves not which contains the greater pleasure or the lesser pain or the smaller threat to our tranquillity, but only which is demanded by that ideal of detachment of soul from body in which true philosophy has been declared, in the preceding pages, to consist.

In saying this I am, of course, going beyond the immediate text, and endeavouring to interpret what Socrates calls 'exchanging all these things for φρόνησις'. Now it is no doubt confusing that in A6 he should speak of an exchange for ἀρετή, but in A10 of an exchange for φρόνησις. This must imply an identification, Socratic rather than Platonic, of intelligence and virtue; but in the lines that follow he seems to waver between this and the conception of φρόνησις as a *means* or *aid* to virtue. This latter conception prevails in the end, but both are present in the difficult words at B1–2 καὶ τούτου μὲν πάντα καὶ μετὰ τούτου ὠνούμενά τε καὶ πιπρασκόμενα, τούτου implying the former and μετὰ τούτου the latter. This running together of the two ideas is, it seems to me, the chief source of difficulty both in this particular sentence and in the passage as a whole.

The words τούτου πάντα ὠνούμενα, taken by themselves, could only mean 'bought by the payment of φρόνησις', and this would have no sense. But we should, I suggest, not attempt to find a sense for τούτου ὠνούμενα and τούτου πιπρασκόμενα *taken each by itself*, but think of them together as equivalent to τούτου καταλλαττόμενα. It may be objected that the notion of paying out intelligence is already involved in calling it νόμισμα ὀρθόν: but in that phrase Socrates is thinking of the value of what one *gets* in a transaction, not of what one gives; unless we get φρόνησις we get what is worthless.

Socrates does not deny that we have to traffic in pleasures, pains and fears. That we have to accept some and reject others is implied in B5–6, as also in B1–2 if we do not tamper with the text; but he insists that in doing so we ought to be guided by φρόνησις. Inasmuch, however, as the aim of φρόνησις is 'detachment', we shall endeavour to ignore the hedonic content of what we accept and reject; in his own words, we shall 'purge ourselves of all these things'. The moral virtues are states in which we thus purge (or have purged) ourselves, and φρόνησις is the purgative (καθαρμός).

74C. I accept Heindorf's emendation ὡς ἐάν for ἕως ἄν in c 13. As H. Richards, *Platonica*, p. 77, points out, ἕως ἄν ἐννοήσῃς could only mean 'until you have conceived'. To substitute the present subjunctive would be useless, for ἕως cannot lose its temporal sense, as Burnet seems to imply by his *dummodo*. ἕως ἄν ἐννοῇς could only mean 'while you are conceiving'. ὡς ἐάν has the additional advantage of avoiding an unlikely (though not impossible) asyndeton.

74D9. In the use of βούλεται here, of ὀρέγεται in 75A2, B1 and of προθυμεῖται in 75B7, it is possible that there is a notion of the Form being the Final Cause of its particulars, as Prof. Tate suggests in *C.R.* (1953), p. 157. This would fit in with the desire for a teleological account of everything in the universe which, as we learn later (97C ff.), Socrates hoped to find in Anaxagoras. But I am inclined to think that the words are no more than vivid ways of expressing the defectiveness of visible equals.

92Aff. Philoponus in his commentary (142, 4ff. Hayduck) on Aristotle, *de anima* 407B27ff., where the ψυχή ἁρμονία theory is discussed, takes the opportunity to expound or paraphrase the whole section 92A6–94B3. He finds five arguments in all, viz. (1) 92A6–E3; (2) 92E4–93A10, with 94B4–95A3; (3) 93A11–B7; (4) 93B8–E10; (5) 94A1–B3. His exposition of the first two is good, and he has the merit (against Olympiodorus and Burnet) of recognising that 93A14–B3 does not deny, but admits degrees of attunement. But he fails to see that 93A11–94B3 is all one argument, and is certainly wrong in saying that the notion of one ἁρμονία within another is treated as ridiculous (καταγέλαστον, 142, 31).

Miss W. F. Hicken's article in *C.Q.* (April 1954), with much of which I agree, appeared when my commentary was already in type.

104D3. I bracket αὐτῷ with Stallbaum and Ross (*PTI*, p. 132).

107E2. I retain the δεῖ of the MSS. as more probable than δή. Robin prints δή, but appears to translate δεῖ.

108A. Prof. Guthrie (*Orpheus and Greek Religion*, p. 176) suggests a possible connexion between these 'branchings and forkings' and the directions to the soul of the departed to go to the right or the left, which are found on some of the famous gold plates buried in graves in S. Italy and Crete: these are generally believed to be extracts from an Orphic poem or poems.

That there were two ways at the entrance to the underworld is a belief often mentioned; one led to the abode of the righteous, the other to that of the wicked (cf. *Gorgias* 524A, and see Rohde, *Psyche* (E.T.), p. 449 n. 62): the most familiar allusion is in Virgil, *Aen.* VI, 540ff., Hic locus est partes ubi se via findit in ambas, etc. In Plutarch, *de. lat viv.* 1130C there is a mention of *three* ways, ἡ δὲ τρίτη τῶν ἀνοσίως βεβιωκότων καὶ παρανόμων ὁδός ἐστιν, and Rohde suggests that his authority for this is Pindar, whom he has been quoting in the context. Plato's *many* forkings here probably correspond to the five categories of souls to be distinguished at 113D–114C.

112A. Prof. Guthrie (*Orpheus and Greek Religion*, p. 168) calls attention to the similarity between this description of Tartarus and that found in an Orphic fragment (Kern 66) quoted by Proclus:

μέγα χάσμα πελώριον ἔνθα καὶ ἔνθα·
οὐδέ τι πεῖραρ ὑπῆν, οὐ πυθμήν, οὐδέ τις ἕδρα.

If these lines are pre-Platonic it is highly probable that Plato had them in mind.

117B. We are nowhere in the *Phaedo* told that the poison was hemlock, but Burnet in Appendix 1 convincingly defends the traditional view.

THE CRITICISMS OF STRATO

Olympiodorus, the sixth-century Neoplatonist, has preserved in his commentary on the *Phaedo* some criticisms made by Strato, known as ὁ φυσικός, the third head of the Peripatetic school, who succeeded Theophrastus about 287 B.C. These may most conveniently be found in Fritz Wehrli, *Die Schule des Aristoteles*, Heft V, *Strato von Lampsakos* (1950). I have attempted a translation, following Wehrli's numbering of the fragments, and giving the pages of Norvin's edition of Olympiodorus. The meaning is usually clear enough; but two, viz. 123 (i) and (l), are unintelligible to me. I leave readers to decide for themselves on their cogency, but it may be remarked that W. Capelle, who gives a good account of their general purport in Pauly-Wissowa, *RE* IV, i (1931), s.v. Strato 13, speaks of them as 'bündig'.

A. OBJECTIONS TO
γένεσις ἐξ ἐναντίων OR ἀνταπόδοσις

122 (D 63, p. 221 N.):

(*a*) What has perished arises from what existed; yet inasmuch as the reverse is not true, what reason is there to believe in the cogency of an argument of this type?

(*b*) If a dead part of a body, e.g. a finger or a gouged-out eye, does not come back to life, then neither, plainly, can the whole ⟨creature⟩.

(*c*) It may be suggested that the identity between things that arise out of one another is not numerical, but only specific.

(*d*) Flesh may come from food, but food does not come from flesh; rust may come from bronze, and charcoal from wood, but not *vice versa*.

(*e*) The old come from the young; but the reverse does not happen.

(*f*) Opposites may come from opposites if a substratum persists, but not if it is destroyed.

(*g*) It may be suggested that the continuance of coming-to-be is no more than the constant renewal of a species or type, as we find even in man-made objects.

B. OBJECTIONS TO THE PRINCIPLE OF
EXCLUSION OF OPPOSITES

123 (C II 178–90, p. 183 N.):

(*a*) On this showing, is not every living creature deathless? For it cannot 'admit' death: that is to say, there could never be a dead living creature, any more than a dead soul.

(*b*) On this showing, are not even the souls of irrational creatures deathless, inasmuch as they 'bring up' life and cannot 'admit' the opposite of that which they bring up?

(*c*) And presumably, on this showing, the souls of plants too, for they too make their bodies into living bodies.

(*d*) Is not everything that comes-to-be imperishable? For they are all, equally with souls, incapable of admitting their opposites: a thing that comes-to-be could never be a thing that has perished.

(*e*) Would not this apply to every natural object? Any such object exhibits a development according to its nature, and therefore cannot admit of development contrary thereto; and *qua* incapable of admitting that, it can never perish.

(*f*) On this showing it will be equally true that a composite object will never be broken up: for it cannot admit its opposite: that is to say, while remaining a composite it can never be a broken-up object.

(*g*) If we grant that a negation can have more senses than one, the soul may be 'undying' (ἀθάνατος) not in the sense that it is, or possesses, inextinguishable life, but in the sense that it can only admit one of a pair of opposites, and must either exist together with that opposite or not exist at all.

(*h*) Is it not too readily assumed that, if the soul is incapable of admitting death, and in that sense deathless, it is therefore indestructible? A stone is deathless in the sense of this argument, but a stone is not indestructible.

(*i*) What is the ground for saying that the soul 'brings up' life as a concomitant, with the purpose of arguing that it cannot admit the opposite of what is brought up? In some cases the soul is brought up ⟨itself⟩.

(*k*) May it not be that a thing is alive, yet the life it has is imported from without, so that it can one day lose it?

(*l*) May it not be that the soul, while not admitting the death that is the opposite of that life which soul brings up, nevertheless does admit another death, that namely which is opposite to the life which brings up soul?

(*m*) May it not be that just as fire, so long as it exists, cannot be cold, so soul, so long as it exists, cannot be dead? For it brings up life so long ⟨only⟩ as it exists.

(*n*) May it not be that, even if we escape all the rest, we cannot rebut the objection that soul is limited and has ⟨only⟩ a limited power? Let us grant that it brings up life, that it can exist as a separate substance, that it cannot admit the death that is opposite to the life which it brings up: nevertheless it will wear itself out one day, will be extinguished and perish of its own accord, without any attack from outside.

124 (D 78, p. 226 N.):

But on this showing even life in a substrate cannot admit its opposite; for it cannot admit death and yet continue to exist, any more than cold can admit heat and yet continue to exist. Hence life in a substrate is incapable of being dead in the same sense as cold is incapable of being hot; nevertheless life does come to an end.

Secondly, the perishing of a thing is not the reception by it of death; if it were, a living creature would never perish; the fact is that a creature does not persist, having admitted death; rather it is dead because it has lost life; for death is loss of life.

[*The second part of this may be condensed as follows: to be dead is not to possess a positive attribute which the soul cannot in fact possess: it is the body's having lost an attribute, viz. life, which it previously possessed.*]

(*Note by Olympiodorus.*) To this argument of Strato's Proclus adds that the extinction of a soul is its dying, and dying, in Strato's own words, is the losing by the substrate ⟨or body⟩ of life.

C. OBJECTIONS TO THE THEORY OF RECOLLECTION

125 (D 25, p. 211 N.). Why can one not 'recollect' without demonstration?

126 (II 41, p. 158 N.). If there is such a thing as 'recollection', how is it that we do not attain scientific knowledge without demonstration? Or how is it that no one has ever become a wind-player or string-player without practice?

127 (D 65, p. 223 N.). The mind's possession of scientific knowledge is either (*a*) antecedent to time, in which case it has no need of time and is unaffected by time, so that men are eternally possessed of it; or (*b*) subsequent to time, in which case either the mind possesses it without 'recollection', learning ⟨what it learns in this life⟩ for the first time, or else what it recollects is knowledge immanent in it before its incarnation; ⟨I say knowledge⟩ for its maker presumably makes it a perfect, and therefore a *knowing* mind; yet on entering into this world minds need to learn, that is to 'recollect'.

[*This seems tantamount to complaining that Plato's assumption of a loss of knowledge at birth is arbitrary.*]

(*Note by Olympiodorus.*) Furthermore Strato in his division eliminates 'everlasting time'; the thing which ⟨supposedly⟩ has everlasting existence in time is, he argues, something that falls between that which exists before time was and that which exists at some point in time.

[*The argument seems to be that all existence must be either timeless (outside time) and eternal or temporal (in time) and impermanent.*]

And why, he asks, cannot we *readily* employ 'recollection'? Or is it the fact that some of us can, but most need training for it?

D. OBJECTION TO THE REFUTATION OF THE ψυχὴ ἁρμονία THEORY

118 (II 134, p. 174 N.). As one attunement is sharper (ὀξυτέρα) or flatter than another, so one soul is sharper or more sluggish than another.

[*This bears particularly on* 93 B 4–7.]

INDEX OF NAMES

(excluding speakers in the dialogue)